Better Homes and Gardens®

Romantic Crochet

© Copyright 1991 by Meredith Corporation, Des Moines, Iowa.
All Rights Reserved. Printed in the United States of America.
First Edition. First Printing.
Library of Congress Catalog Card Number: 90-63293
ISBN: 0-696-01845-4

BETTER HOMES AND GARDENS® BOOKS

Editor: Gerald M. Knox
Art Director: Ernest Shelton
Managing Editor: David A. Kirchner
Project Editors: James D. Blume, Marsha Jahns
Project Managers: Liz Anderson,
Jennifer Speer Ramundt, Angela K. Renkoski

Crafts Editor: Sara Jane Treinen
Senior Crafts Editors: Beverly Rivers,
Patricia Wilens
Associate Crafts Editor: Nancy Reames

Associate Art Directors: Neoma Thomas,
Linda Ford Vermie, Randall Yontz
Assistant Art Directors: Lynda Haupert,
Harijs Priekulis, Tom Wegner
Graphic Designers: Mary Schlueter Bendgen,
Michael Burns, Mick Schnepf
Art Production: Director, John Berg;
Associate, Joe Heuer;
Office Manager, Michaela Lester

President, Book Group: Jeramy Landauer
Vice President, Retail Marketing: Jamie L. Martin
Vice President, Administrative Services: Rick Rundall

BETTER HOMES AND GARDENS® MAGAZINE
President, Magazine Group: James A. Autry
Editorial Director: Doris Eby

MEREDITH CORPORATION OFFICERS
Chairman of the Executive Committee: E. T. Meredith III
Chairman of the Board: Robert A. Burnett
President and Chief Executive Officer: Jack D. Rehm

ROMANTIC CROCHET
Editor: Sara Jane Treinen
Contributing Writer: Ciba Vaughan
Project Manager: Angela K. Renkoski
Graphic Designer: Harijs Priekulis
Contributing Photo Stylist: Patricia Konecny
Contributing Photographer: Hopkins Associates
Contributing Illustrators: Mary Schlueter Bendgen;
Chris Neubauer
Electronic Text Processor: Paula Forest

Cover projects: See page 35.

The elegance of pattern laces and the artistry of stitches wrought by patient hands captivate today's needlecrafters and collectors. It is in these laces that admirers discover the splendor of a past era when life was lived more graciously. Through its exquisite examples of crochet projects, **Romantic Crochet** *allows the needle artist not only to reflect on this history and explore the joys of this craft but also to create beautiful and cherished items. This collection of more than 80 projects includes bedspreads, tablecloths, edgings, doilies, and afghans. Plus, special chapters offer children's items and trims for an old-fashioned Christmas. Turn the page to begin your journey into the romantic world of crochet.*

Contents

UPSTAIRS, DOWNSTAIRS ————————— 6

*The look of Victorian romance and formality distinguishes the pillows,
tablecloth, bedspread, afghans, and other projects in this chapter.*

PERENNIAL BORDERS ——————————— 30

*All white and wonderful, the lacy edgings found here can be used to turn
ordinary items into pretty accents that display your crafting skills.*

BEDROOM COMFORTS ——————————— 46

*Add handmade splendor to your own boudoir with any of our five bed-
covers, then complement them with crocheted trims on sheets, pillowcases,
or dust ruffles.*

TABLETOP TREASURES ———————————— 62

*Suitable for every occasion, these lacy table toppers are designed for
gracious living and stitching pleasures.*

LACY MEADOWS ——————————————— 80

*Flowers, birds, butterflies—wonderful images of nature—are featured
motifs in this collection of filet crochet projects that trim elegant linens.*

JUST FOR WEE FOLKS ——————————————— 104

Here's a collection of great gifts for little ones. Soft toys, sweaters, caps, and blankets are among the captivating projects.

NOSTALGIC CHARM ————————————————— 124

Add one or more of the crochet touches in this chapter to your home's decor to revive the spirit of cozy, old-fashioned comfort.

A SHOWCASE OF AFGHANS ——————————— 146

For those crocheters who love stitching with yarns, here are 10 spectacular afghan designs from which to choose.

AN OLD-FASHIONED CHRISTMAS ————————— 168

Stitch up these splendid designs—tree trims, matching stocking and afghan, and an angel decoration—for happy holiday celebrations year after year.

STITCHING PRIMER ————————————————— 186

ACKNOWLEDGMENTS ——————————————— 190

INDEX ———————————————————————— 191

Upstairs, Downstairs

LASTING
CROCHET ELEGANCE

"As home is the place where our best and happiest hours are passed, nothing which will beautify it or adorn it can be of trifling importance." So counseled a popular book of manners in 1868; by the turn of the century, many a Victorian reader had taken that precept to heart, eagerly stitching up cloths and coverlets, tidies, and pillow tops for every room in the house.

A pair of traditional pineapple patterns was used for these elegant pillow tops. Either the popcorn design, *opposite, far left,* or the star pattern, *opposite, near left,* also would be suitable for a doily. Instructions begin on page 14.

By the end of the 19th century, the possession of a "separate and proper" dining room had become a source of great pride to many Victorians, and dinner parties were becoming a popular and lavish form of entertainment.

Then, as now, the look of snowy linens layered over the gleam of polished wood was the setting of choice for an elegant repast. The handsome arrow-pattern 15x35-inch runner, *above,* is an understated accent for a buffet or sideboard, and the magnificent heirloom cloth, *opposite,* with its intricate pattern of clustered grapes and its graceful scalloped border (see inset, *opposite, top left*), turns even the simplest meal into a sumptuous feast. Instructions for the tablecloth begin on page 19; the runner instructions begin on page 22.

The drawing room or parlor was the most lavishly appointed room in the Victorian home. In this room, the mistress of the house strove to create an imaginative and inspirational environment for her family. Here she displayed her most treasured possessions and her finest bits of needlework. Crocheted lace and embroidered doilies, luxurious throws, and soft, inviting cushions were artfully placed about the room, adding a charming note of domestic intimacy to even the most formal of settings.

Lacy white antimacassars, also called "chair tidies," were the Victorians' pretty but practical solution to the problem of protecting upholstered furniture from the damaging stains of Macassar oil, which was the preferred men's hair tonic of the day. The tidy, *opposite,* works up quickly in a treble crochet variation of the filet crochet technique, using Size 10 thread. It measures approximately 25½x23 inches.

A cascade of ruffled rosettes and a fine scalloped border add to the ornamental appeal of the cozy 47x57-inch fireside throw, *right.* Worked using worsted-weight jewel-tone yarns, it becomes any Victorian parlor with its richly textured pattern. Instructions for the antimacassar and afghan begin on page 24.

In contrast to the deep, rich hues that prevailed in the more public rooms of the Victorian home—the parlor and dining room in particular—milady's bedchamber was generally done with a lighter palette. Pastel shades, lace-covered pillows, and floral patterns were everywhere. Here, as in every other room, madam was encouraged to enhance the room's comfort and appeal with some token of her domestic creativity. The crocheted spread and dainty throw pictured here would have served such a purpose—and were considered much more fashionable in many circles than the more homely calico quilts and woven coverlets of an earlier day.

Both the Water Lily spread and Lily Pond afghan at the foot of the bed, *right,* are based on hexagonal motifs. The airy, pastel 53x81-inch afghan is worked in a brushed acrylic mohair yarn, and the spread is stitched in traditional white cotton thread. Instructions are included for both a single- and a double-size bed. Instructions for the spread begin on page 26; instructions for the afghan begin on page 28.

STAR PINEAPPLE PILLOW

Shown on pages 6 and 7.

Finished pillow measures 16 inches in diameter.

MATERIALS

DMC Cebelia crochet cotton, Size 20 (50-gram ball): 2 balls of ecru
Size 11 steel crochet hook
16-inch pillow form
½ yard of 44-inch-wide fabric to cover pillow form

Abbreviations: See page 186.
Gauge: First 10 rounds = diameter of 3⅝ inches.

INSTRUCTIONS

Beg in center, ch 6; join with sl st to form ring.

Rnd 1: Ch 1, work 18 sc in ring; join with sl st to first sc.

Rnd 2: Ch 1, sc in same st as join; * ch 7, sc in next 3 sc; rep from * around; end sc in last 2 sc, join with sl st to beg sc—6 ch-7 lps around.

Rnd 3: Sl st in first 3 ch of ch-7 lp; ch 3, in same lp work dc, ch 3, and 2 dc; * ch 3, in next ch-7 lp work 2 dc, ch 3, and 2 dc; rep from * around; end ch 3, join with sl st to top of beg ch-3.

Rnd 4: Ch 3, dc in next dc, * ch 3, dc in center ch of next ch-3 lp, ch 3, dc in next 2 dc; ch 3, ** dc in next 2 dc; rep from * around, end last rep at **; join last ch-3 to top of beg ch-3.

Note: In the instructions that follow, the ** indicates the point where the last rep ends in the rnd. Then complete the rnd by joining the last ch-lp to the beg ch.

Rnd 5: Ch 3, * 2 dc in next dc; ch 4, dc in next dc, ch 4, 2 dc in next dc, dc in next dc; ch 3, ** dc in next dc; rep from * around; join last ch-3 to top of beg ch-3.

Rnd 6: Ch 3, dc in next 2 dc; * ch 4, in next dc work dc, ch 3, and dc; ch 4, dc in 3 dc; ch 3, ** dc in 3 dc; rep from * around; join last ch-3 to top of beg ch-3.

Rnd 7: Ch 3, dc in next dc; * 2 dc in next dc, ch 3, **holding back last lp of each dc on hook, work 3 dc in next dc, yo, draw through all lps on hook—cluster (cl) made;** ch 3, dc in center ch of ch-3 lp, ch 3, cl in next dc, ch 3, 2 dc in next dc, dc in next 2 dc; ch 3, ** dc in next 2 dc; rep from * around; join last ch-3 to top of beg ch-3.

Rnd 8: Ch 3, dc in next 3 dc; * ch 5, sk cl, in next dc work dc, ch 3, and dc; ch 5, sk cl, dc in next 4 dc; ch 3, ** dc in next 4 dc; rep from * around; join last ch-3 to top of beg ch-3.

Rnd 9: Ch 3, dc in next 2 dc, 2 dc in next dc; * ch 3, 3 dc in next dc, ch 2, dc in center ch of ch-3 lp; ch 2, 3 dc in next dc; ch 3, 2 dc in next dc, dc in next 3 dc; ch 3, ** dc in next 3 dc, 2 dc in next dc; rep from * around; join last ch-3 to top of beg ch-3.

Rnd 10: Ch 3, dc in next 3 dc, 2 dc in next dc; * ch 3, **holding back last lp of each dc on hook, work dc in each of next 3 dc, yo, draw through all lps on hook—cluster (cl) over 3 dc made;** ch 3, in next dc work dc, ch 4, and dc; ch 3, work cl over next 3 dc; ch 3, 2 dc in next dc, dc in next 4 dc; ch 3, ** dc in next 4 dc, 2 dc in next dc; rep from * around; join last ch-3 to top of beg ch-3.

Rnd 11: Ch 3, dc in next 4 dc, 2 dc in next dc; * ch 4, sk cl, 3 dc in next dc, ch 3, dc in ch-4 lp, ch 3, 3 dc in next dc, ch 4, sk cl, 2 dc in next dc, dc in next 5 dc; ch 3, ** dc in next 5 dc; 2 dc in next dc; rep from * around; join last ch-3 to top of beg ch-3.

Rnd 12: Ch 3, dc in next 5 dc, 2 dc in next dc; * ch 4, work cl over next 3 dc, ch 3, in next dc work dc, ch 5, and dc; ch 3, work cl over next 3 dc; ch 4, 2 dc in next dc, dc in next 6 dc; ch 3, ** dc in next 6 dc, 2 dc in next dc; rep from * around; join last ch-3 to top of beg ch-3.

Rnd 13: Ch 3, dc in next 6 dc, 2 dc in next dc; * ch 5, sk cl, in ch-5 lp work 9 dc; ch 5, sk cl, 2 dc in next dc, dc in next 7 dc; ch 3, ** dc in next 7 dc, 2 dc in next dc; rep from * around; join last ch-3 to top of beg ch-3.

Rnd 14: Ch 3, dc in next 7 dc, 2 dc in next dc; * ch 3, dc in next dc, (ch 1, dc in next dc) 8 times; ch 3, 2 dc in next dc, dc in next 8 dc; ch 3, ** dc in next 8 dc, 2 dc in next dc; rep from * around; join last ch-3 to top of beg ch-3.

Rnd 15: Sl st into next 2 dc; ch 3, dc in next 6 dc, 2 dc in next dc; * ch 4, sk ch-3 lp, sc in ch-1 lp; (ch 3, sc in next ch-1 lp) 7 times; ch 4, sk ch-3 lp, 2 dc in next dc, dc in next 7 dc; ch 3, in center ch of ch-3 lp work dc, ch 3, and dc; ch 3, ** sk 2 dc, dc in next 7 dc, 2 dc in next dc; rep from * around; join last ch-3 to top of beg ch-3.

Rnd 16: Sl st into next 2 dc; ch 3, dc in next 5 dc, 2 dc in next dc; * ch 4, sc in ch-3 lp; (ch 3, sc in next ch-3 lp) 6 times, ch 4, 2 dc in next dc, dc in next 6 dc; ch 3, sk ch-3 lp; in next ch-3 lp work (2 dc, ch 3) 3 times, work 2 dc in same lp—four 2-dc grp with three ch-3 lps in same lp; ch 3, ** sk 2 dc, dc in next 6 dc, 2 dc in next dc; rep from * around; join last ch-3 to top of beg ch-3.

Rnd 17: Sl st into next 2 dc, ch 3, dc in next 4 dc, 2 dc in next dc; * ch 4, sc in ch-3 lp; (ch 3, sc in next ch-3 lp) 5 times, ch 4, 2 dc in next dc, dc in next 5 dc; ch 3, sk next ch-3 lp; **(in next ch-3 lp work 2 dc, ch 3, and 2 dc—shell made; ch 1)** 2 times; in next ch-3 lp work 2 dc, ch 3, and 2 dc, ch 3; ** sk next 2 dc of 8-dc grp, dc in next 5 dc, 2 dc in next dc; rep from * around; join last ch-3 to top of beg ch-3.

Rnd 18: Sl st into next 2 dc, ch 3, dc in next 3 dc, 2 dc in next dc; * ch 4, sc in ch-3 lp; (ch 3, sc in next ch-3 lp) 4 times; ch 4, 2 dc in next dc, dc in next 4 dc, ch 4, sk next ch-3 lp, (shell in ch-3 lp of next shell; ch 3) 2 times, shell in ch-3 lp of next shell, ch 4; ** sk first 2 dc of next 7-dc grp; dc in next 4 dc, 2 dc in next dc; rep from * around; join last ch-4 to top of beg ch-3.

Rnd 19: Sl st into next 2 dc, ch 3, dc in next 2 dc, 2 dc in next dc, * ch 5, sc in ch-3 lp; (ch 3, sc in next ch-3 lp) 3 times; ch 5, 2 dc in next dc, dc in next 3 dc; ch 5, sk ch-4 lp; (shell in ch-3 lp of next shell; ch 5) 3 times; ** sk first 2 dc of 6-dc grp; dc in next 3 dc, 2 dc in next dc; rep from * around; join last ch-5 to top of beg ch-3.

Rnd 20: Sl st into next 2 dc, ch 3, dc in next dc, 2 dc in next dc; * ch 5, sc in ch-3 lp; (ch 3, sc in next ch-3 lp) twice; ch 5, 2 dc in next dc, dc in next 2 dc; ch 7, (shell in ch-3 lp of next shell, ch 7) 3 times; ** sk first 2 dc of 5-dc grp, dc in next 2 dc, 2 dc in next dc; rep from * around; join last ch-7 to top of beg ch-3.

Rnd 21: Sl st into next 2 dc, ch 3, 2 dc in next dc; * ch 5, sc in ch-3 lp, ch 3, sc in next ch-3 lp, ch 5, 2 dc in next dc, dc in next dc, ch 3, (shell in fourth ch of ch-7 lp; ch 1, shell in ch-3 lp of next shell, ch 1) 3 times; shell in fourth ch of ch-7 lp; ch 3, ** sk 2 dc, dc in next dc, 2 dc in next dc; rep from * around; join last ch-3 to top of beg ch-3.

Rnd 22: Sl st in next dc, ch 3, dc in next dc; * ch 7, sc in ch-3 lp, ch 7, dc in next 2 dc, ch 5, shell in ch-3 lp of next shell, ch 3; (sk ch-1 lp, dc in next 2 dc, 3 dc in ch-3 lp, dc in next 2 dc) 5 times; ch 3, shell in ch-3 lp of next shell; ch 5, ** sk first dc of next 3-dc grp, dc in next 2 dc; rep from * around; join last ch-5 to top of beg ch-3.

Rnd 23: Ch 3, dc in next dc; * ch 3, dc in next 2 dc, ch 7, shell in ch-3 lp of next shell; ch 5, sc in first dc of 35-dc grp; (ch 3, sk dc, sc in next dc) 17 times; ch 5, shell in ch-3 lp of next shell; ch 7, ** sk ch-5 lp, dc in next 2 dc; rep from * around; join last ch-7 to top of beg ch-3.

Note: Hereafter the instructions for working a shell in ch-3 lp of next shell will read "shell over shell."

Rnd 24: Ch 3, dc in next 3 dc; * ch 9, shell over shell; ch 3, sc in ch-5 lp; (in next ch-3 lp work dc, ch 3, and dc; sc in next ch-3 lp) 8 times; in next ch-3 lp work dc, ch 3, and dc; sc in ch-5 lp, ch 3; shell over shell, ch 9, ** sk ch-7 lp, dc in next 4 dc; rep from * around; join last ch-9 to top of beg ch-3.

Rnd 25: Ch 3, work cl over next 3 dc; * ch 13, shell over shell; ch 5, sk ch-3 lp, (sc in next ch-3 lp; in next sc work dc, ch 3, and dc) 8 times; sc in next ch-3 lp, ch 5, shell in ch-3 lp of shell, ch 13, ** cl over next 4 dc; rep from * around; join last ch-13 to top of beg cl.

Rnd 26: Sl st in next 7 ch, ch 3, in same ch work dc, ch 3, and 2 dc; * ch 5, shell over shell; ch 6, (sc in next ch-3 lp; in next sc work dc, ch 3, and dc) 7 times; sc in next ch-3 lp; ch 6, shell over shell; (ch 5, ** shell in seventh ch of next ch-13 lp) twice; rep from * around; join last ch-5 to top of beg ch-3.

Rnd 27: Sl st in next dc and into next ch, ch 3, in same lp work dc, ch 3, and 2 dc; * ch 5, in ch-3 lp of next shell work (2 dc, ch 3) twice; work 2 dc in same lp; ch 6, (sc in next ch-3 lp; in next sc work dc, ch 3, and dc) 6 times; sc in next ch-3 lp, ch 6, in ch-3 lp of next shell work (2 dc, ch 3) twice; work 2 dc in same lp; ch 5, shell in ch-3 lp of next shell, ch 5, sc in third ch of next ch-5 lp, ch 5, ** shell over shell; rep from * around; join last ch-5 to top of beg ch-3.

Rnd 28: Sl st in next dc and into next ch, ch 3, in same lp work dc, ch 3, and 2 dc; * work shell in center ch of ch-5 lp, work shell in next ch-3 lp, ch 5, shell in next ch-3 lp, ch 6, (sc in next ch-3 lp; in next sc work dc, ch 3, and dc) 5 times; sc in next ch-3 lp, ch 6, shell in next ch-3 lp, ch 5, shell in next ch-3 lp, shell in third ch of next ch-5 lp, shell over shell, (ch 5, sc in next ch-5 lp) twice, ch 5, ** shell over shell; rep from * around; join last ch-5 to top of beg ch-3.

Rnd 29: Sl st in next dc and into next ch, sc in same lp, (ch 5, sc in next ch-3 lp) twice; * ch 5, sc in center ch of ch-5 lp, ch 5, shell over shell, ch 6, (sc in ch-3 lp; in next sc work dc, ch 3, and dc) 4 times; sc in ch-3 lp; ch 6, shell over shell; ch 5, sc in center ch of ch-5 lp; (ch 5, sc in next ch-3 lp) 3 times; (ch 5, sc in center ch of ch-5 lp) 3 times; (ch 5, ** sc in next ch-3 lp) 3 times; rep from * around; join last ch-5 to beg sc.

continued

Rnd 30: Sl st in next 2 ch, sc in next ch, (ch 5, sc in next ch-5 lp) 3 times; * ch 5, shell over shell; ch 7, (sc in ch-3 lp; in next sc work dc, ch 3, and dc) 3 times, sc in ch-3 lp, ch 7, shell over shell; (ch 5, sc in next ch-5 lp) 12 times; rep from * around; join last ch-5 to beg sc.

Rnd 31: Sl st in next 2 ch, sc in next ch, (ch 6, sc in next ch-5 lp) 3 times; * ch 6, shell over shell, ch 7, (sc in next ch-3 lp, in next ch-3 lp work dc, ch 3, and dc) 2 times; sc in next ch-3 lp; ch 7, shell over shell; (ch 6, sc in next ch-5 lp) 13 times; rep from * around; join last ch-6 to beg sc.

Rnd 32: Sl st in next 2 ch, sc in next ch; (ch 6, sc in next ch-6 lp) 3 times; * ch 6, shell over shell, ch 7, sc in next ch-3 lp, in next sc work dc, ch 3, and dc; sc in next ch-3 lp, ch 7, shell over shell, (ch 6, sc in next ch-6 lp) 14 times; rep from * around; join last ch-6 to beg sc.

Rnd 33: Sl st in next 2 ch, sc in next ch; (ch 6, sc in next ch-6 lp) 3 times, * ch 6, shell over shell, ch 7, sc in ch-3 lp, ch 7, shell over shell; (ch 6, sc in next ch-6 lp) 15 times; rep from * around; join last ch-6 to beg sc.

Rnd 34: Sl st in next 2 ch, sc in next ch; (ch 7, sc in next ch-6 lp) 3 times; * ch 7, shell over shell, ch 5, sc in sc, ch 5, shell over shell, (ch 7, sc in next ch-6 lp) 16 times; rep from * around; join last ch-7 to beg sc.

Rnd 35: Sl st in next 3 ch, sc in next ch; (ch 7, sc in next ch-7 lp) 3 times; * ch 7, shell over shell; ch 7, shell over shell; (ch 7, sc in next ch-7 lp) 17 times; rep from * around; join last ch-7 to beg sc.

Rnd 36: Sl st in next 3 ch, sc in next ch, (ch 7, sc in ch-7 lp) 3 times; * ch 7, dc in ch-3 lp of shell, shell in fourth ch of ch-7 lp, dc in ch-3 lp of next shell, (ch 7, sc in next ch-7 lp) 18 times; rep from * around; join last ch-7 to beg sc.

Rnd 37: Sl st in next 3 ch, sc in next ch, (ch 7, sc in next ch-7 lp) 2 times; * ch 7, sc in ch-3 lp; (ch 7, sc in next ch-7 lp) 19 times; rep from * around; join last ch-7 to beg sc.

Rnd 38: Sl st in next 3 ch, sc in next ch; * ch 7, sc in next ch-7 lp; rep from * around; join last ch-7 to beg sc.

Rnds 39 and 40: Rep Rnd 38.

Rnd 41: Sl st into next 3 ch, ch 3, in same lp work dc, ch 3, and 2 dc; in *each* ch-7 lp around work shell of 2 dc, ch 3, and 2 dc; join to top of beg ch-3.

Rnd 42: Sl st into next dc and 2 ch of ch-3 lp; ch 6, dc in same lp; * ch 5, sc in ch-3 lp of shell, ch 5, in ch-3 lp of next shell work dc, ch 3, and dc; rep from * around; end ch 5, sc in last ch-3 lp, ch 5, join to third ch of beg ch-6.

Note: To work double treble crochet (dtr) in next round, yo hook 3 times, and complete stitch by working 2 lps off hook until 1 lp remains.

To work triple treble crochet (ttr), yo hook 4 times, and complete stitch by working 2 lps off hook until 1 lp remains.

Rnd 43: **Ch 6, holding back last lp of next 3 sts, work dtr, trc, and dc in same ch as join, yo, draw through all lps on hook—beg petal made;** * ch 5, work ttr in center ch of ch-3 lp, ch 5, dc around post of ttr, ch 5, **holding back last lp of each st, work ttr, dtr, trc, and dc in next dc, yo, draw through all lps on hook—petal made;** ch 1, ** petal in next dc; rep from * around; join last ch-1 to top of beg petal.

Rnd 44: Sl st in next 5 ch and dtr and work a beg petal; * ch 5, ttr in center ch of ch-5 lp, ch 5, dc around post of ttr; ch 5, petal in next dc, ch 1, petal in next ttr; rep from * around; join last ch-1 to top of beg petal.

Rnd 45: Sl st in next 2 ch, sc in next ch, ch 2; * in next ch-5 lp work 3 dc, ch 3, and 3 dc; ch 2, sc in center ch of next ch-5 lp, ch 9, sc in center ch of next ch-5 lp, ch 2; rep from * around; join last ch-9 to sc at beg of rnd.

Rnd 46: Sl st in next 6 st, sc in center ch of ch-3 lp; * ch 9, sc in fifth ch of ch-9 lp; ch 9, sc in second ch of next ch-3 lp; rep from * around; end ch 4, dtr to beg sc.

Rnd 47: Ch 3, in same lp work dc, ch 3, and 2 dc; * ch 3, in next ch-9 lp work 2 dc, ch 3, and 2 dc; rep from * around; join last ch-3 to top of beg ch-3.

Rnd 48: Sl st in next dc and first ch; ch 3, in same lp work 2 dc, **ch 4, sl st in third ch from hook— picot made;** ch 1, work 3 dc in same lp; work 3 dc, picot, and 3 dc in *each* ch-3 lp of every shell around; join to top of beg ch-3; fasten off.

PILLOW ASSEMBLY: Cut two circles of fabric to fit pillow form. With right sides together, sew circles together, leaving opening for turning. Clip curves; turn and press. Insert pillow form into opening and stitch opening closed. Center crochet piece on top of form and tack base of Rnd 48 along outside edge of pillow seam, allowing picot edge to extend beyond the seam. If desired, make a crocheted back for the pillow. Work rnds 1–47. Hand-sew crocheted pieces together matching Rnd 47.

POPCORN PINEAPPLE PILLOW

Shown on pages 6 and 7.

Finished pillow measures 16 inches in diameter.

MATERIALS

DMC Cebelia crochet cotton, Size 20 (50-gram ball): 2 balls of ecru
Size 11 steel crochet hook
16-inch pillow form
½ yard of 44-inch-wide fabric to cover form

Abbreviations: See page 186.
Gauge: First 7 rounds = diameter of 3½ inches.

INSTRUCTIONS

Note: To work dtr, yo hook 3 times, draw up lp in st, (yo, draw through 2 lps on hook) 4 times.

Beg in center, ch 5, join with sl st to form ring.

Rnd 1: Ch 6, (dtr, ch 1) 23 times; join with sl st to fifth ch of beg ch-6—24 dtr.

Rnd 2: Sl st into ch-1 sp, ch 1, 2 sc in same sp; work 2 sc in each ch-1 sp around; join with sl st to first sc—48 sc around.

Rnd 3: Ch 4, trc in same st as join; * trc in next 3 sc, sk sc, in next sc work trc, ch 2, and trc; sk sc, trc in next sc **; 2 trc in next sc; rep from * around ending the last rep at the **; join to top of beg ch-4.

Note: In the instructions that follow, ** indicates the point where the *last* repeat ends in the round. Then join the last ch-lp to the beg ch.

Rnd 4: Sl st into next trc; **ch 4, work 7 trc in same trc, drop hook from work, insert hook in top of beg ch-4 and draw the dropped lp through—beg popcorn (pc) made;** ch 2, **work 8 trc in next trc, drop hook from work, insert hook in top of first trc of 8-trc grp and draw the dropped lp through—pc made;** ch 2, * sk 3 trc, in ch-2 sp work 10 trc; ch 2, ** sk 3 trc, (pc in next trc, ch 2) twice; rep from * around; join last ch-2 to top of beg pc.

Rnd 5: Sl st into ch-2 sp, ch 4, work 2 trc in same sp, * pc in next ch-2 sp, ch 2, (trc bet next 2 trc, ch 1) 8 times, trc bet last 2 trc, ch 2; pc in ch-2 sp, ** 3 trc in next ch-2 sp; rep from * around; join to top of beg ch-4.

Rnd 6: Sl st into next trc, ch 4, 2 trc in same st; * ch 1, pc in next ch-2 sp; ch 2, sk ch-1 sp, sc in next ch-1 sp; (ch 4, sc in next ch-1 sp) 5 times; ch 2; pc in next ch-2 sp; ch 1, ** 3 trc in center trc of 3-trc grp; rep from * around; join last ch-1 to top of beg ch-4—5 ch-4 lps in each pineapple grp.

Rnd 7: Ch 4, * 2 trc in next trc, trc in next trc, ch 2, pc in next ch-2 lp, ch 2, sc in next ch-4 lp; (ch 4, sc in next ch-4 lp) 4 times; ch 2; pc in next ch-2 lp, ch 2, ** trc in next trc; rep from * around; join last ch-2 to top of beg ch-4.

Rnd 8: Ch 4, trc in same st as join; * trc in next trc; ch 3, trc in next trc, 2 trc in next trc; ch 1, in next ch-2 sp work **2 trc, ch 1, and 2 trc—shell made;** ch 1, pc in next ch-2 sp, ch 2, sc in next ch-4 lp; (ch 4, sc in next ch-4 lp) 3 times; ch 2, pc in next ch-2 sp, ch 1, shell in next ch-2 sp, ch 1, ** 2 trc in next trc; rep from * around; join last ch-1 to top of beg ch-4.

Rnd 9: Turn, sl st back to second ch-1 sp, turn, ch 4, in same sp work trc, ch 1, and 2 trc; * ch 2, work 8 trc in next ch-3 lp; ch 2, sk next ch-1 sp, **work shell in ch-1 sp of next shell—shell over shell;** ch 1, pc in next ch-2 sp, ch 2, sc in ch-4 lp; (ch 4, sc in next ch-4 lp) 2 times; ch 2, pc in ch-2 sp, ch 1, ** shell over shell; rep from * around; join last ch-1 to top of beg ch-4.

Rnd 10: **Sl st into next trc and ch-1 sp, ch 4, in same sp work trc, ch 1, and 2 trc—beg shell made;** * ch 2, trc in first trc of 8-trc grp; (ch 1, trc in next trc) 7 times; ch 2, work shell over shell; ch 2, pc in next ch-2 sp; ch 2, sc in ch-4 lp, ch 4, sc in next lp, ch 2, pc in next ch-2 lp, ch 2, ** work shell over shell; rep from * around; join last ch-2 to top of beg ch-4.

Rnd 11: Work beg shell; * ch 2, 2 trc in first trc of 8-trc grp, (ch 1, 2 trc in next trc) 7 times; ch 2, work shell over shell, ch 2, sk ch-2 lp, pc in next ch-2 lp, ch 2, dc in ch-4 lp, ch 2, pc in ch-2 lp, ch 2, ** work shell over shell; rep from * around; join last ch-2 to top of beg ch-4.

Rnd 12: Work beg shell; * ch 4, sk ch-2 sp, sc in next ch-1 sp; (ch 4, sc in next ch-1 sp) 6 times; ch 4, work shell over shell, ch 3, work shell in dc bet pcs; ch 3, ** work shell over shell; rep from * around; join last ch-3 to top of beg ch-4.

Rnd 13: Work beg shell; * ch 5, sk ch-4 lp, sc in next ch-4 lp; (ch 4, sc in next lp) 5 times, ch 5, work shell over shell; ch 3, in ch-1 sp of next shell work 2 trc, ch 2, and 2 trc; ch 3, ** work shell over shell; rep from * around; join last ch-3 to top of beg ch-4.

Rnd 14: Work beg shell; * ch 5, sc in ch-4 lp, (ch 4, sc in next ch-4 lp) 4 times; ch 5, work shell over shell; ch 3, work 6 trc in ch-2 sp, ch 3, ** work shell over shell; rep from * around; join last ch-3 to top of beg ch-4.

continued

Rnd 15: Work beg shell; * ch 5, sc in ch-4 lp; (ch 4, sc in next ch-4 lp) 3 times; ch 5, work shell over shell, ch 3, trc in first trc of 6-trc grp; (ch 1, trc in next trc) 5 times; ch 3, ** work shell over shell; rep from * around; join last ch-3 to top of beg ch-4.

Rnd 16: Sl st into next trc and ch-1 sp, ch 4, in same sp work trc, ch 2, and 2 trc; * ch 5, sc in ch-4 lp, (ch 4, sc in next ch-4 lp) twice; ch 5, in ch-1 sp of next shell work 2 trc, ch 2, and 2 trc; ch 4, trc in first trc of 6-trc grp, (ch 1, in next trc work trc, ch 1, and trc) 4 times; ch 1, trc in last trc, ch 4, ** in ch-1 sp of next shell work 2 trc, ch 2, and 2 trc; rep from * around; join last ch-4 to top of beg ch-4.

Rnd 17: Work beg shell, * ch 5, sc in ch-4 lp, ch 4, sc in next ch-4 lp, ch 5; in ch-2 sp work 2 trc, ch 1, 4 trc, ch 1, and 2 trc; ch 4, sc in next ch-1 sp; (ch 4, sc in next ch-1 sp) 8 times; ch 4, ** in ch-2 sp work 2 trc, ch 1, 4 trc, ch 1, and 2 trc; rep from * around; then work shell in beg ch-2 sp; join to top of beg ch-4.

Rnd 18: Work beg shell, * ch 4, dc in ch-4 lp at tip of pineapple, ch 4, shell in next ch-1 sp; ch 3, shell in next ch-1 sp; ch 4, sk next lp, sc in next ch-4 lp; (ch 4, sc in next lp) 7 times; ch 4, shell in next ch-1 sp, ch 3; ** shell in next ch-1 sp; rep from * around; join last ch-3 to top of beg ch-4.

Rnd 19: Work beg shell, * shell over next shell, ch 3, in next ch-3 lp work 2 trc, ch 1, 4 trc, ch 1, and 2 trc; ch 3, shell over shell, ch 4, sk ch-4 lp, sc in next ch-4 lp; (ch 4, sc in next lp) 6 times; ch 4, shell over shell, ch 3, in next ch-3 lp work 2 trc, ch 1, 4 trc, ch 1, and 2 trc; ch 3, ** shell over shell; rep from * around; join last ch-3 to top of beg ch-4.

Rnd 20: Sl st in next trc and into ch-1 sp; ch 4, trc in same sp; * 2 trc in ch-1 sp of next shell; ch 3, shell in next ch-1 sp; sk trc, 2 trc in next trc, ch 1, 2 trc in next trc, shell in next ch-1 sp; ch 3, shell over shell, ch 4, sk ch-4 lp, sc in next ch-4 lp; (ch 4, sc in next ch-4 lp) 5 times; ch 4, shell over next shell, ch 3, shell in next ch-1 sp, sk trc, 2 trc in next trc, ch 1, 2 trc in next trc, shell in next ch-1 sp, ch 3, ** 2 trc in ch-1 sp of next shell; rep from * around; join last ch-3 with sl st to top of beg ch-4.

Rnd 21: Sl st in next trc, ch 7, * (shell in next ch-1 sp, ch 3) 3 times; shell over shell, ch 4, sk ch-4 lp, sc in next ch-4 lp, (ch 4, sc in next ch-4 lp) 4 times, ch 4, shell over shell, (ch 3, shell in next ch-1 sp) 3 times; ch 3, ** trc in sp between next 2 trc groups; ch 3; rep from * around; join last ch-3 to fourth ch of beg ch-7.

Rnd 22: Ch 4, in same st as join work trc, ch 1, and 2 trc; * (ch 3, shell over shell) 4 times; ch 4, sk ch-4 lp, sc in next lp, (ch 4, sc in next lp) 3 times; ch 4, shell over shell; (ch 3, shell over shell) 3 times; ch 3, ** shell in trc between trc grp; rep from * around; join last ch-3 to top of beg ch-4.

Rnd 23: Work beg shell, (ch 3, shell over shell) 4 times; * ch 4, work 2 lp over pineapple, ch 4, shell over shell; (ch 3, shell over shell) 8 times; rep from * around; join last ch-3 to top of beg ch-4.

Rnd 24: Work beg shell, (ch 4, shell over shell) 4 times, * ch 4, sk ch-4 lp, sc in next ch-4 lp; ch 4, sc in next ch-4 lp; (ch 4, shell over shell) 9 times; rep from * around; join last ch-4 to top of beg ch-4.

Rnd 25: **Sl st in next trc and into ch-1 sp; ch 4, in same sp work 2 trc, ch 1, and 3 trc—beg 6-trc shell made;** * (ch 4, shell over shell) 4 times, ch 2, dc in ch-4 lp at top of pineapple; ch 2, shell over shell, (ch 4, shell over shell) 3 times, ch 4; ** in ch-1 sp of next shell work 3 trc, ch 1, and 3 trc; rep from * around; join last ch-4 to top of beg ch-4.

Rnd 26: Sl st in next 2 trc and ch-1 sp; ch 4, in same sp work 2 trc, ch 2, and 3 trc; * ch 3, in ch-1 sp of next shell work **3 trc, ch 2, and 3 trc—6-trc shell made;** rep from * around; join last ch-3 to top of beg ch-4.

Rnd 27: Sl st in next 2 trc and into ch-2 sp; ch 4, in same sp work 3 trc, ch 2, and 4 trc; * ch 1, in ch-2 sp of next shell work **4 trc, ch 2, and 4 trc—8-trc shell made;** rep from * around; join last ch-1 to top of beg ch-4.

Rnd 28: Sl st in next 3 trc and into ch-2 sp; ch 4, in same sp work 3 trc, ch 2, and 4 trc; * in next ch-1 sp work 2 trc, ch 1, and 2 trc; in next ch-2 sp work 8-trc shell; rep from * around; join to top of beg ch-4.

Rnds 29 and 30: Sl st in next 3 trc and into ch-2 sp; ch 4, in same sp work 3 trc, ch 2, and 4 trc; work 8-trc shells over previous 8-trc shells and 6-trc shells over 4-trc shells; join as before.

Rnd 31: Work 8-trc shells over all shells around; join.

Rnd 32: Sl st into ch-2 sp of shell; * ch 8, sc in ch-2 sp of next shell; rep from * around; join to beg ch.

Rnd 33: Sl st to center of ch-8 lp; * ch 8, sc in next ch-8 lp, rep from * around; join, fasten off.

EDGING: *Rnd 1:* Working in ch-8 lps on Rnd 32, work dc on either side of the sc of Rnd 32 as follows: Join thread to the right of any sc of any lp on Rnd 32, ch 3, dc in same side of lp; * ch 4, 2 dc in left side of lp, ch 4, 2 dc in right side of next lp, rep from * around; join to top of beg ch-3; fasten off.

PILLOW ASSEMBLY: Cut two circles of fabric to fit pillow form. With right sides together, sew circles together, leaving opening for turning. Clip curves; turn and press. Insert pillow form into opening and stitch opening closed. Center crochet piece on top of form, stretching to fit and positioning Rnd 32 along the pillow edge. Tack Rnd 33 along edge of pillow back.

GRAPE FILET TABLECLOTH

Shown on page 9.

Cloth measures 68x76 inches, including edging.

————MATERIALS————
DMC Cebelia crochet cotton,
    Size 10 (50-gram ball): 15
    balls of ecru or white
Size 11 steel crochet hook
Tapestry needle

Abbreviations: See page 186.
Gauge: 4 spaces = 1 inch; 5 rows = 1 inch.

————INSTRUCTIONS————
Note: See page 88 for additional information for working filet crochet designs. The chart on pages 20 and 21 represents one-fourth of the design. When working from this chart, always begin *each* row at the right side of the chart;

work across to the centerline. Then read the same row of the chart from right to left to complete the second half of the row.

Always ch 5 to turn at the end of each row to count as the first dc and ch-2 sp.

Beg at lower edge, ch 863.

Row 1: Dc in eighth ch from hook; * ch 2, sk 2 ch, dc in next ch—sp made; rep from * across—286 sps across row; ch 5, turn.

Rows 2–10: Sk first dc, dc in next dc; * ch 2, dc in next dc; rep from * across; end ch 2, sk 2 ch of turning ch, dc in next ch—286 sps across row; ch 5, turn.

Rows 11–173: Work from chart.

Rows 174–346: Work the mirror image of the chart, working rows 173–1; fasten off at end of Row 346.

EDGING: Ch 50.
Note: When reading rows from chart, *top right,* always read odd-numbered rows from right to left and even-numbered rows from left to right.

Row 1: Dc in eighth ch from hook; ch 2, sk 2 ch, dc in next 4 ch; (ch 2, sk 2 ch, dc in next ch) 12 times; ch 5, turn.

Row 2: Sk first dc, dc in next dc; (ch 2, dc in next dc) 11 times; dc in next 3 dc; ch 2, dc in next dc, ch 2, sk 2 ch of turning ch, dc in next ch; ch 5, turn.

Row 3: Sk first dc, dc in next dc; ch 2, dc in next 4 dc; (ch 2, dc in next dc) 5 times; 2 dc in ch-2 sp, dc in next dc; (ch 2, dc in next dc) 6 times; *** yo, draw up lp at base of last dc made, yo, draw through 1 lp on hook—base for next st; (yo, draw through 2 lps on hook) twice; rep from * 5 times more—6 dc and 2 bls increased at end of row;** ch 8, turn.

Row 4: Dc in fourth, fifth, sixth, seventh, and eighth chs from hook—6 dc increased at beg of

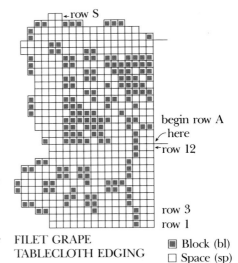

FILET GRAPE
TABLECLOTH EDGING
■ Block (bl)
□ Space (sp)

row; dc in next dc; (ch 2, sk 2 dc, dc in next dc) twice; (ch 2, dc in next dc) twice; 2 dc in ch-2 sp, dc in next dc; complete row working from chart, *above;* ch 5, turn.

Rows 5–12: Work from chart as established.

Rep rows 3–12 thirty-three times more; then rep rows 3–6 once—346 rows completed to fit along left edge of cloth.

For corner, work rows A–S; fasten off.

Join thread in same place as A on chart to begin the edging along the top edge of cloth. Work Row 1 across 15 sps (bls) along straight edge at corner. Continue to follow chart as established, working rows 1–12 once; then rep rows 3–12 twenty-seven times more; rep rows 3–6—286 rows completed. Work corner from rows A–S; fasten off.

Continue to work as established to make two more sides to match the length and width of cloth; fasten off. Whipstitch Row 1 and last corner straight edge together.

Carefully pin, then sew edging to cloth, matching rows as you stitch. Block cloth to complete.

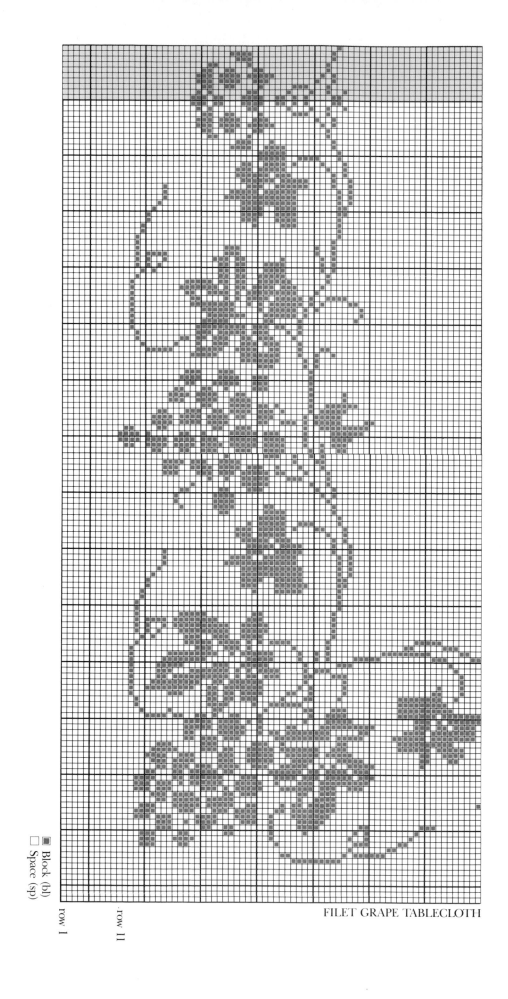

row 1

row 11

FILET GRAPE TABLECLOTH

TABLE RUNNER

Shown on page 8.

Finished runner measures 15x35 inches using Size 30 thread and Size 12 hook or 18½x44 inches using Size 20 thread and Size 11 hook.

MATERIALS
DMC Cebelia crochet cotton, Size 30 or Size 20 (50-gram ball): 4 balls of white or ecru
Size 12 or Size 11 steel crochet hook or size to obtain gauge cited below

Abbreviations: See page 186.
Gauge: Block measures 6¾ inches square using Size 30 thread and Size 12 hook; and 8½ inches square using Size 20 thread and Size 11 hook.

INSTRUCTIONS
Note: In the instructions that follow, the ** indicates the point where the last repeat ends in the round. Then work the ending instructions as given and join work to beginning chain.

BLOCK: Ch 5, join with sl st to form ring.

Rnd 1: Ch 3, in ring work 3 dc; (ch 2, in ring work 4 dc) 3 times; ch 2, join with sl st to top of ch-3 at beg of rnd.

Rnd 2: Ch 3, dc in next 3 dc; (in ch-2 sp work 3 dc, ch 3, and 3 dc; dc in next 4 dc) 3 times; in last ch-2 sp work 3 dc, ch 3, 3 dc; join to top of beg ch-3.

Rnd 3: Ch 5, (sk next 2 dc, dc in next dc, ch 2) twice; * in center ch of ch-3 lp work dc, ch 3, and dc; ch 2, dc in next dc; ** (ch 2, sk 2 dc, dc in next dc) 3 times, ch 2; rep from * 3 times more; end ch 2, join to third ch of beg ch-5.

Rnd 4: Ch 5, dc in next dc, ch 2, dc in next dc; * 2 dc in ch-2 lp, dc in next dc, in ch-3 lp work 3 dc, ch 3, and 3 dc; dc in next dc, 2 dc in ch-2 lp, dc in next dc, ** (ch 2, dc in next dc) 3 times; rep from * 3 times more; then ch 2, join to third ch of beg ch-5.

Rnd 5: Ch 5, * dc in next dc; 2 dc in ch-2 sp, dc in 7 dc; in ch-3 lp work 3 dc, ch 3, and 3 dc; dc in next 7 dc; 2 dc in ch-2 sp, ** dc in dc, ch 2; rep from * 3 times more; join to third ch of beg ch-5.

Rnd 6: Ch 5, * dc in next dc, (ch 2, sk 2 dc, dc in next dc) 4 times; ch 2, in center ch of ch-3 lp work dc, ch 3, and dc; ch 2, dc in next dc, (ch 2, sk 2 dc, dc in next dc) 4 times, ch 2; rep from * 3 times more; when working bet the *s for the third time, rep bet last set of ( )s 3 times instead of 4, ch 2; join to third ch of beg ch-5.

Rnd 7: Ch 5, dc in next dc; (ch 2, dc in next dc) 3 times; * (2 dc in ch-2 lp, dc in next dc) twice; in ch-3 lp work 3 dc, ch 3, and 3 dc; dc in next dc; (2 dc in ch-2 sp, dc in dc) twice; ** (ch 2, dc in next dc) 7 times; rep from * 3 times more; then (ch 2, dc in next dc) twice; ch 2, join to third ch of beg ch-5.

Rnd 8: Ch 5, dc in next dc, (ch 2, dc in next dc) 2 times; * 2 dc in ch-2 sp, dc in next 10 dc; in ch-3 lp work 3 dc, ch 3, and 3 dc; dc in 10 dc; 2 dc in ch-2 lp, dc in dc, ** (ch 2, dc in next dc) 5 times; rep from * 3 times more; then ch 2, dc in dc, ch 2, join to third ch of beg ch-5.

Rnd 9: Ch 5, dc in next dc; (ch 2, dc in next dc) twice; * (ch 2, sk 2 dc, dc in next dc) 5 times; ch 2, in center ch of ch-3 lp work dc, ch 3, and dc; ch 2, dc in next dc; (ch 2, sk 2 dc, dc in next dc) 5 times, ** (ch 2, dc in next dc) 5 times; rep from * 3 times more; then ch 2, dc in next dc, ch 2, join to third ch of beg ch-5.

Rnd 10: Ch 5, dc in next dc; (ch 2, dc in next dc) 5 times; * (2 dc in ch-2 lp, dc in next dc) 3 times; in ch-3 lp work 3 dc, ch 3, and 3 dc; dc in next dc, (2 dc in ch-2 lp, dc in next dc) 3 times; ** (ch 2, dc in next dc) 11 times; rep from * 3 times more; then (ch 2, dc in next dc) 4 times, ch 2, join to third ch of beg ch-5.

Rnd 11: Ch 5, dc in next dc, (ch 2, dc in next dc) 4 times; * 2 dc in ch-2 sp, dc in next 13 dc; in ch-3 lp work 3 dc, ch 3, and 3 dc; dc in next 13 dc; 2 dc in ch-2 sp, dc in next dc; ** (ch 2, dc in next dc) 9 times; rep from * 3 times more; then (ch 2, dc in next dc) 3 times, ch 2; join to third ch of beg ch-5.

Rnd 12: Ch 5, dc in next dc; (ch 2, dc in next dc) 4 times, * (ch 2, sk 2 dc, dc in next dc) 6 times; ch 2, in center ch of ch-3 lp work dc, ch 3, and dc; ch 2, dc in next dc; (ch 2, sk 2 dc, dc in next dc) 6 times; ** (ch 2, dc in next dc) 9 times; rep from * 3 times more; then (ch 2, dc in next dc) 3 times; ch 2, join to third ch of beg ch-5.

Rnd 13: Ch 3, * 2 dc in ch-2 lp, dc in next dc; (ch 2, dc in next dc) 7 times; (2 dc in ch-2 lp, dc in next dc) 4 times; 3 dc, ch 3, and 3 dc in corner ch-3 lp; dc in next dc, (2 dc in ch-2 lp, dc in next dc) 4 times; (ch 2, dc in next dc) 7 times; rep from * 3 times more; when working bet the *s for the third time, rep bet last set of ( )s 6 times instead of 7; then ch 2, join to top of beg ch-3.

Rnd 14: Ch 5, sk 2 dc, dc in next dc; * 2 dc in ch-2 sp, dc in next dc; (ch 2, dc in next dc) 5 times; 2 dc in ch-2 sp, dc in next 16 dc, 3 dc, ch 3, and 3 dc in corner lp, dc in next 16 dc; 2 dc in ch-2 sp, dc in next dc; (ch 2, dc in next dc) 5 times; 2 dc in ch-2 sp, ** dc in next dc, ch 2, sk 2 dc, dc in next dc; rep from * 3 times more; join to third ch of beg ch-5.

Rnd 15: Ch 3, 2 dc in ch-2 lp, dc in next dc, ch 2, sk 2 dc, dc in next dc; * 2 dc in ch-2 lp, dc in next dc, (ch 2, dc in next dc) 4 times; (ch 2, sk 2 dc, dc in next dc) 7 times, ch 2, in center ch of ch-3 lp work dc, ch 3, and dc; ch 2, dc in next dc; (ch 2, sk 2 dc, dc in next dc) 7 times, (ch 2, dc in next dc) 4 times; ** (2 dc in ch-2 lp, dc in next dc, ch 2, sk 2 dc, dc in next dc) twice; rep from * 3 times more; 2 dc in ch-2 lp, dc in next dc, ch 2, join to top of beg ch-3.

Rnd 16: Ch 5, (sk next 2 dc, dc in next dc, 2 dc in ch-2 lp, dc in next dc, ch 2) twice; (dc in next dc, ch 2) 6 times; dc in next dc; * (2 dc in ch-2 lp, dc in next dc) 4 times; in corner ch-3 lp work 3 dc, ch 3, and 3 dc; dc in next dc, (2 dc in ch-2 lp, dc in next dc) 4 times; (ch 2, dc in next dc) 7 times; ** (2 dc in ch 2 lp, dc in next dc, ch 2, sk 2 dc, dc in next dc) 3 times, 2 dc in ch-2 lp, dc in next dc, (ch 2, dc in next dc) 7 times; rep from * 3

times more; then 2 dc in ch-2 lp, dc in next dc, ch 2, sk 2 dc, dc in next dc, 2 dc in ch-2 lp; join to third ch of beg ch-5.

Rnd 17: Ch 3, (2 dc in ch-2 lp, dc in next dc, ch 2, sk 2 dc, dc in next dc) twice; 2 dc in ch-2 sp, dc in next dc; * (ch 2, dc in next dc) 5 times; 2 dc in ch-2 lp, dc in next 16 dc; in ch-3 corner lp work 3 dc, ch 3, and 3 dc; dc in next 16 dc, 2 dc in ch-2 lp, dc in next dc; (ch 2, dc in next dc) 5 times; ** (2 dc in ch-2 sp, dc in next dc, ch 2, sk 2 dc, dc in next dc) 4 times, 2 dc in next lp, dc in next dc; rep from * 3 times more; then (2 dc in ch-2 sp, dc in next dc, ch 2, sk 2 dc, dc in next dc) twice, join last ch-2 to top of beg ch-3.

Rnd 18: Ch 5, sk 2 dc, dc in next dc, (2 dc in ch-2 lp, dc in next dc, ch 2, sk 2 dc, dc in next dc) twice; 2 dc in ch-2 sp, dc in next dc; * (ch 2, dc in next dc) 4 times; (ch 2, sk 2 dc, dc in next dc) 7 times; ch 2, in center ch of ch-3 lp work dc, ch 3, and dc; ch 2, dc in next dc; (ch 2, sk 2 dc, dc in next dc) 7 times; (ch 2, dc in next dc) 4 times, ** (2 dc in ch-2 lp, dc in next dc, ch 2, sk 2 dc, dc in next dc) 5 times; 2 dc in ch-2 lp, dc in next dc; rep from * 3 times; then (2 dc in ch-2 lp, dc in next dc, ch 2, sk 2 dc, dc in next dc) twice; 2 dc in ch-2 sp, join to third ch of beg ch-5.

Rnd 19: Ch 3, 2 dc in ch-2 lp, dc in next dc; (ch 2, sk 2 dc, dc in next dc, 2 dc in ch-2 lp, dc in next dc) 3 times; * (ch 2, dc in next dc) 7 times; (2 dc in ch-2 sp, dc in next dc) 4 times; in ch-3 corner lp work 3 dc, ch 3, and 3 dc; dc in next dc, (2 dc in ch-2 sp, dc in next dc) 4 times; (ch 2, dc in next dc) 7 times; ** (2 dc in ch-2 sp, dc in next dc, ch 2, sk 2 dc, dc in next

dc) 6 times; 2 dc in ch-2 sp, dc in next dc; rep from * 3 times more; then (2 dc in ch-2 sp, dc in next dc, ch 2, sk 2 dc, dc in next dc) twice; 2 dc in last ch-2 sp; dc in next dc, ch 2; join to top of beg ch-3.

Rnd 20: Ch 5, sk 2 dc, dc in next dc, (2 dc in next ch-2 sp, dc in next dc, ch 2, sk 2 dc, dc in next dc) 3 times; 2 dc in ch-2 sp, dc in next dc; * (ch 2, dc in next dc) 5 times; 2 dc in ch-2 sp, dc in next 16 dc; in ch-3 corner lp work 3 dc, ch 3, and 3 dc; dc in next 16 dc, 2 dc in ch-2 sp, dc in next dc, (ch 2, dc in next dc) 5 times; ** (2 dc in ch-2 sp, dc in next dc, ch 2, sk 2 dc, dc in next dc) 7 times, 2 dc in ch-2 sp, dc in next dc, rep from * 3 times more; then (2 dc in ch-2 sp, dc in next dc, ch 2, sk 2 dc, dc in next dc) 3 times; 2 dc in ch-2 sp; join to third ch of beg ch-5; fasten off.

Make 10 blocks. Whipstitch blocks together into two rows, each row with 5 blocks; whipstitch rows together.

EDGING: *Rnd 1:* Join thread in center ch of any ch-3 corner lp, ch 6, dc in same ch; ch 2, dc in next dc, * (ch 2, sk 2 dc, dc in next dc) 7 times (ch 2, dc in next dc) 5 times; (ch 2, sk 2 dc, dc in next dc, ch 2, dc in next dc) 8 times; (ch 2, dc in next dc) 4 times; (ch 2, sk 2 dc, dc in next dc) 7 times, ch 2, dc in join between blocks, ch 2, dc in next dc; rep from * around working dc, ch 3, and dc in center ch of ch-3 corner lp; join to third ch of beg ch-6.

Rnd 2: Sl st into center ch of ch-3 lp, ch 3, in same lp work 3 dc; ch 2, dc in next dc; * 2 dc in ch-2 sp,
continued

dc in next dc, ch 2, dc in next dc; rep from * around working 4 dc in center ch of *each* ch-3 corner lp; end ch 2, join to top of beg ch-3.

Rnd 3: Ch 7, sk 2 dc, dc in next dc; * 2 dc in ch-2 sp, dc in next dc, ch 2, sk 2 dc, dc in next dc; rep from * around working ch-4 lp across *each* corner; work 2 dc in last ch-2 lp; join with sl st to third ch of beg ch-7.

Rnd 4: Sl st into ch-4 lp, ch 4, in same lp work trc, **ch 3, sl st in third ch from hook—picot made;** in same lp work (2 trc, picot) twice and 2 trc; * in next ch-2 lp work 2 trc, picot, and 2 trc; rep from * around, working (2 trc, picot) 3 times and 2 trc in each ch-4 corner lp; join to top of beg ch-4; fasten off. Block runner to size and press.

ROSE ANTIMACASSAR

Shown on page 10.

Antimacassar measures 25½ inches wide and 23 inches long.

MATERIALS
DMC Cebelia crochet cotton, Size 10 (282-yard ball): 4 balls of white
Size 10 steel crochet hook

Abbreviations: See page 186.
Gauge: 4 spaces = 1 inch; 4 rows = 1¼ inches.

INSTRUCTIONS
Note: Antimacassar is worked following the chart, *opposite,* and is worked from the top of the design toward the bottom. This piece is worked using the filet crochet technique, except the filet design is created using treble crochets instead of double crochets. For additional information for working filet crochet patterns, refer to the tip box on page 88.

Beginning along the top edge, ch 295.

Row 1: Trc in fifth ch from hook and in next 2 ch; * ch 2, sk 2 ch, trc in next 4 ch; rep from * across row—49 blocks and 48 spaces made; ch 4, turn.

Row 2: Trc in next 3 trc, * ch 2, trc in next trc, ch 2, sk 2 trc, trc in next trc; rep from * across row—95 spaces made; trc in last 2 trc and top of turning ch-4; ch 4, turn.

Rows 3–34: Work from chart, *opposite.*

Row 35: Following chart, continue to work trc filet pattern across row until the 6-bl unit is completed; **ch 5, sk 5 trc, trc in next trc—ch-5 lp made;** ch 2, sk 2 trc, trc in next trc, complete row following chart.

Rows 36–64: Continue to work from chart. Note how the ch-5 lps form a honeycomb design around the vase. Work the treble crochets at the beginning and end of the ch-5 lps in the *center* chain of the lp of the previous row to make the pattern. When pattern is offset by a short lp to maintain the pattern consistency, work ch-2 lps instead of ch-5 lps.

Rows 65–68: Work first scallop over 58 sts following chart; fasten off at end of Row 68.

As blocks decrease at beginnings of rows, do not work chains to turn; simply turn work, sl st over to starting point, then ch 4, and complete the beginning block.

Join thread and work second scallop over 142 sts following chart; fasten off at end of Row 75.

Join thread and work third scallop over 58 sts; fasten off at end of Row 68. Block and press finished piece.

GRANNY AFGHAN WITH RUFFLES

Shown on page 11.

Afghan measures 47x57 inches.

MATERIALS
Unger Roly Poly worsted-weight yarn (3.5-ounce skein): 6 skeins of grape (No. 9847); 2 skeins of fuchsia (No. 7665)
Unger Utopia (3.5-ounce skein): 4 skeins of green (No. 143); 2 skeins of burgundy (No. 304)
Size G aluminum crochet hook
Tapestry needle

Abbreviations: See page 186.
Gauge: One block = 4½ inches square.

INSTRUCTIONS
SQUARE MOTIF: With fuchsia, ch 5, join with sl st to form ring.

Rnd 1: Ch 3, work 15 dc in ring; join with sl st to front lp at top of beg ch-3—16 dc.

Rnd 2: Ch 1, in same front lp work sc, dc, and sc; in *front* lp of *each* dc around work **sc, dc, and sc—scallop made;** join with sl st to *back* lp at top of beg ch-3 of Rnd 1—16 scallops made.

continued

ROSE ANTIMACASSAR

row 1

row 35

row 64

row 68

row 75

■ Block (bl)
□ Space (sp)
☐ Ch-5 loop (lp)

Rnd 3: Ch 4, folding scallops forward toward center of circle, * dc in *back* lp of next dc of Rnd 1, ch 1; rep from * around; join last ch-1 to third ch of beg ch-4—16 dc and 16 ch-1 sp around; fasten off.

Rnd 4: Join green in *back* lp of any ch-1 st with sc; sc in *back* lp of each dc and ch around; join with sl st to first sc—32 sc around.

Rnd 5: **Ch 3, holding back last lp of each dc on hook, work 2 dc in same st as join, yo, draw through 3 lps on hook—beg cluster (cl) made;** ch 2, **holding back last lp of each dc, work 3 dc in same st as beg cl; yo, draw through 4 lps on hook—cl made;** * (ch 2, sk sc, cl in next sc) 3 times; ch 2, sk sc; in next sc work cl, ch 2, and cl—corner made; rep from * 2 times more; then (ch 2, sk sc, cl in next sc) 3 times; ch 2, join to top of beg cl; fasten off green—20 cls around.

Rnd 6: With grape lp on hook, join yarn in any ch-2 corner sp with sc; work 2 sc in same sp; * (2 sc in next ch-2 sp) 4 times; 3 sc in ch-2 corner sp; rep from * 2 times more; then (2 sc in next ch-2 sp) 4 times; join to first sc.

Rnd 7: Ch 3; * in next sc work dc, ch 1, dc, ch 1, and dc; dc in next 10 sc; rep from * around, working dc in last 9 sc instead of 10 on last rep; join with sl st to top of beg ch-3; fasten off.

Make 63 blocks, working 32 with fuchsia centers and 31 with burgundy centers. With grape, use tapestry needle to whipstitch blocks together, stitching through the back lps to join. Assemble squares into nine rows, each row with 7 blocks, and alternating fuchsia and burgundy centers across each row.

BORDER: *Rnd 1:* Join grape in dc in any corner, ch 3, in same st work 4 dc; dc in each st around, working 5 dc in each corner st; join to top of beg ch-3.

Rnd 2: Ch 3, dc in next st; * **dc around post from front of next 2 dc—2 raised dc made;** dc in next 2 st; rep from * around, working 5 dc in each corner st; join to top of beg ch-3.

Rnds 3–5: Ch 3, working in pat as established, work a raised dc over each raised dc, dc over each dc, and 5 dc in each corner st; join to top of beg ch-3. *Note:* Keeping to pat, add raised dc in corner sts as work increases.

Rnd 6: Ch 3, * sk 2 st, sc in next st, sk 2 st, dc in next st; in next st work dc, 3 trc, and dc; dc in next st; rep from * around working dc, 5 trc, and dc in each corner st; end with dc, 3 trc, and dc in last st; join to top of beg ch-3.

Rnd 7: * Sk next sc, sc in next 3 st; in center trc work hdc, ch 2, and hdc; sc in next 3 st; rep from * around, working sc in 4 st up to trc at corner; in corner trc work 2 hdc, ch 2, and 2 hdc; join with sl st to first sc; fasten off.

Weave in all ends and block.

WATER LILY BEDSPREAD

Shown on page 13.

One hexagon measures 14 inches across.

MATERIALS

Coats & Clark South Main mercerized cotton (400-yard ball): 44 balls of white or ecru for Single-Size Spread; 55 balls for Double-Size Spread
Size 7 steel crochet hook
Tapestry needle

Abbreviations: See page 186.

INSTRUCTIONS

For single-size spread, make 38 hexagon motifs and 4 half motifs. For double-size spread, make 53 hexagon motifs and 6 half motifs.

HEXAGON MOTIF: Starting at center, ch 9; join with sl st to form ring.

Rnd 1: Ch 1, 18 sc in ring; join with sl st to first sc.

Rnd 2: **Ch 3, 4 dc in back lp of next st, drop lp from hook, insert hook in top of ch-3 and draw dropped lp through—beg popcorn (pc) made;** * ch 2, sk sc; **5 dc in back lp of next sc, drop lp from hook, insert hook in first dc of the 5-dc grp and draw dropped lp through—pc st made;** rep from * around; end ch 2; join with sl st to top of beg pc.

Rnd 3: Ch 5, * dc in next ch-2 lp, ch 2, dc in next pc, ch 2; rep from * around; end ch 2; join to third ch of beg ch-5.

Rnd 4: Ch 1, 3 sc in same st as join; * sc in next sp, 3 sc in next dc; rep from * around; join to back lp of beg sc.

Note: Hereafter, work in the *back* lp only of each sc.

Rnds 5–16: Ch 1, sc in same st as join; * **3 sc in next sc—3-sc grp made;** sc in each sc to center sc of next grp; rep from * around; join to first sc—18 3-sc grps.

At end of last rnd fasten off. Mark center st *between* each 3-sc grp with contrasting thread.

Rnd 17: Overlap the 5 sc following any marked sc over the 5 sc before same marked sc; with lp on hook and working through both thicknesses, sc in the 5 sc, ch 4, * overlap the 5 sc following next marked sc; working through both thicknesses, sc in the 5 sc, ch 4; rep from * around; join.

Rnd 18: Working in *back* lp only, * sc in next 2 sc, 3 sc in next sc, sc in next 2 sc, sc in next 4 ch; (sc in next 5 sc, sc in next 4 ch) twice; sc in 2 sc; rep from * around; end with sc in last 4 ch; join to beg sc.

Rnds 19–22: Working in *back* lp only, sc in each sc around making 3 sc in center sc of each 3-sc grp; join. At end of Rnd 22 fasten off.

Rnd 23: Join thread to center sc of any 3-sc grp, working through *both* lps of sc, ch 4, dc in same st; * (ch 1, sk sc, dc in next sc) 18 times; ch 1, in center sc of next 3-sc grp make dc, ch 1, and dc; rep from * around; end with ch 1, join to third ch of beg ch-4—120 sps.

Rnd 24: Sc into next sp, ch 4, dc in same sp; * (ch 1, dc in next sp) 19 times; ch 1, in next sp work dc, ch 1, and dc; rep from * around; end with ch 1, join to third ch of beg ch-4—126 sps.

Rnd 25: Working in *back* lps only and counting each ch-1 as st, * make 3 sc in next st, sc in next 41 st; rep from * around; join—43 sc between point st.

Rnd 26: Sl st to center sc of first 3-sc grp, working in *back* lp only, * 3 sc in center sc, sc in 3 sc, (pc in next sc, sc in next 5 sc) 6 times; pc in next sc, sc in 3 sc; rep from * around; join.

Rnd 27: 3 sc in center sc, sc in each st around making 3 sc in center sc of each 3-sc grp; join.

Rnd 28: Sl st to center sc of first 3-sc grp, working in *back* lp only, * 3 sc in center sc, sc in next 2 sc, (pc in next sc, sc in next 5 sc) 7 times; pc in next sc, sc in next 2 sc; rep from * around; join.

Rnd 29: Rep Rnd 27.

Rnd 30: Working through *both* lps, in center sc make sl st, ch 4, and dc; * (ch 1, sk sc, dc in next sc) 25 times; ch 1; in center sc of next 3-sc grp make dc, ch 1, and dc; rep from * around; end with ch 1; join to third ch of beg ch-4.

Unless stated otherwise, work in back lps of st only.

Rnd 31: Rep Rnd 24.

Rnd 32: Rep Rnd 25—57 sc between points.

Rnd 33: Sl st to center sc, * 3 sc in center sc, sc in next 4 sc; (pc in next sc, sc in next 5 sc) 8 times; pc in next sc, sc in next 4 sc; rep from * around; join.

Rnd 34: Rep Rnd 27.

Rnd 35: * 3 sc in corner st, sc in 3 sc; (pc in next sc, sc in next 5 sc) 9 times; pc in next sc, sc in next 3 sc; rep from * around; join.

Rnd 36: Rep Rnd 27.

Rnd 37: * 3 sc in center sc, sc in next 2 sc; (pc in next sc, sc in next 5 sc) 10 times; pc in next sc, sc in 2 sc; rep from * around; join.

Rnd 38: Rep Rnd 27—69 sc between points.

Rnd 39: Working through *both* lps, sl st in center sc, ch 4, dc in same place; * (ch 1, sk sc, dc in next sc) 34 times; ch 1, in center sc of next 3-sc grp make dc, ch 1, and dc; rep from * around; end ch 1, join.

Rnd 40: Sl st into sp, ch 4, dc in same sp; * (ch 1, dc in next sp) 35 times; ch 1, in next sp make dc, ch 1, and dc; rep from * around; end ch 1, join; fasten off.

HALF MOTIF: Starting at center of long edge, ch 7; join with sl st to form ring.

Row 1: Ch 1, work 12 sc in ring; turn.

Row 2: Ch 5, (sk sc, pc in next sc, ch 2) 4 times; sk sc, pc st in next sc, ch 5, 3 sc in ring, ch 3; join to third ch of beg ch-5.

Row 3: Ch 4, dc in same st as join; ch 1, dc in next sp, ch 1, dc in pc, ch 1, dc in next sp; * ch 1, in next pc work dc, ch 1, and dc; ch 1, dc in next sp, ch 1, dc in pc, ch 1, dc in next sp; rep from * once; end ch 1, dc in third ch of ch-5 lp; ch 1, dc in same ch; ch 4, turn.

Row 4: Dc in next sp, * (ch 1, dc in next sp) 4 times; ch 1; in next sp make dc, ch 1, and dc; rep from * twice more; end ch 1, dc in third ch of turning ch; ch 1, turn.

Row 5: Working in *back* lp only and counting ch as st, sc in first 13 st; 3 sc in next st, sc in next 11 st, 3 sc in next st, sc in next 11 st, 2 sc around turning ch; fasten off.

Row 6: Fasten thread in sc at beginning of Row 5, ch 1; working in back lp *only,* work 2 sc in same st; sc in next 2 sc; (pc in next st, sc in next 3 sc) twice; pc in next st, * sc in next 2 sc, 3 sc in next st; sc in next 2 sc, (pc in next sc, sc in 3 sc) 2 times; pc in next st, rep from * once more; sc in next 2 sc; end with 2 sc in last sc; ch 1, turn.

Row 7: Working in *back* lps only, work 2 sc in first st, * sc in each st to center sc of next 3-sc grp, 3 sc in center sc; rep from * across; end with 2 sc in last sc; ch 1, turn—15 sc bet each 3-sc grp.

continued

Row 8: Working in *back* lp only, work 2 sc in first sc, sc in next 2 st; (pc in next st, sc in next 3 sc) 3 times; pc in next st, * sc in next 2 sc, 3 sc in next st; sc in next 2 sc, (pc in next sc, sc in 3 sc) 3 times; pc in next st, rep from * once more; sc in next 2 sc; end with 2 sc in last sc; ch 1, turn.

Row 9: Rep Row 7—21 st in each section plus the increased sts; ch 4, turn.

Row 10: Dc in same st; * (ch 1, sk sc, dc in next sc) 10 times; ch 1, in center sc of next 3-sc group make dc, ch 1, and dc; rep from * across; end ch 1, work dc, ch 1, and dc in last sc; ch 4, turn.

Row 11: Dc in first sp; * (ch 1, dc in next sp) 11 times; ch 1; in next sp make dc, ch 1, and dc; rep from * across; end with ch 1, work dc, ch 1, and dc in turning sp; ch 1, turn.

Row 12: Working in *back* lps and counting ch-1s as st, sc in first st; * sc in each st to corner, 3 sc in corner st; rep from * across; end sc in each of first 2 st of turning ch; fasten off.

Row 13: Join thread at beg of Row 12, and working in back lps, work 2 sc in same st; * sc in each st to corner, 3 sc in corner st; rep from * across, end with 2 sc in last st; fasten off.

Rows 14–17: Working in *back* lps only, join thread to first sc, ch 1, work 2 sc in first and last sc and 3 sc in center sc of the 3-sc grp, sc in each sc across; at end of Row 17, ch 4, turn.

Row 18: Rep Row 10, except there will be 19 ch-1 sps between each corner sp.

Row 19: Rep Row 11, except there will be 20 ch-1 sps bet each corner sp.

Row 20: Rep Row 12; fasten off.

Beginning and ending rows on half motif as established and starting with Rnd 25 of hexagon motif, continue working in rows in same pat as for hexagon. Work the last 2 rows on the fourth side of the half motif.

TO ASSEMBLE SPREAD: Refer to photograph, page 13, for placement of hexagon motifs and half motifs. A single-size spread requires 3 rows of 8 hexagons and 2 rows of 7 hexagons. A double-size spread requires 4 rows of 8 hexagons and 3 rows of 7 hexagons. With right sides facing, whipstitch hexagons together using the crochet cotton and sewing through the top lps only. Fill in spaces at top and bottom of spread with half motifs.

FOR THE FRINGE: Cut five strands of thread, each 10 inches long. Double these strands to form a loop. Insert hook in sp on edge of spread and draw loop through. Draw loose ends through loop and pull up tightly to form a knot. Knot five strands as before in every other space or every ½ inch around 3 sides, leaving one narrow edge free (top edge of spread). Trim fringe evenly.

LILY POND AFGHAN

Shown on pages 12 and 13.

Finished afghan measures 53x81 inches.

MATERIALS

Bernat Sweety (50-gram ball): 1 ball *each* of white (No. 2242), blue (No. 2264), yellow (No. 2201), pink (No. 2237), rose (No. 2252), and peach (No. 2247)

3 skeins teal (No. 2288)
9 skeins mint green (No. 2280)
Size H aluminum crochet hook or size to obtain gauge cited below
Tapestry needle

Abbreviations: See page 186.
Gauge: Hexagon motif = 7 inches across two parallel sides.

INSTRUCTIONS

Note: The afghan shown on pages 12 and 13 uses six yarn colors for the flowers (rnds 1 and 2 of following instructions). The hexagons are arranged in alternating rows of seven and six hexagons. The first, third, fifth, seventh, ninth, and 11th rows have seven hexagons in *each* row; the even-numbered rows *each* have six hexagons. The first two rnds of each hexagon, we made 14 flowers each from blue and rose, and 11 flowers each from pink, yellow, white, and peach.

The bottom row, beginning at the left corner, begins with a blue flower, followed with pink, yellow, rose, white, peach, and blue. The flower colors run diagonally across the afghan in all subsequent rows. The second row begins with peach, the third begins with rose, the fourth begins with yellow, the fifth begins with blue, and all the remaining rows follow this sequence.

HEXAGON MOTIF (make 72): With flower color, ch 6; join with sl st to form ring.

Rnd 1: Ch 4—counts as dc and ch-1 sp; in ring work (dc, ch 1) 11 times; join with sl st to third ch of beg ch-4—12 dc.

Rnd 2: Sl st into ch-1 sp; ch 4—counts as hdc and ch-2 sp; in same ch-1 sp work hdc, ch 2, and hdc—beg petal made; ch 2; * in next ch-1 sp work (hdc, ch 2) 2 times, in same same sp work hdc; ch 2; rep from * around—36 hdc around; fasten off.

Rnd 3: Holding petals toward center of work, join teal with sc around post of any dc in Rnd 1; * ch 3, sk next dc on Rnd 1, sc around post of next dc; rep from * 5 times more; join last ch-3 with sl st to beg sc—6 ch-3 sps around.

Rnd 4: Sl st into next ch-3 sp; **ch 3, holding back last lp of each dc on hook, work 2 dc in same sp, yo, draw through all 3 lps on hook—beg cluster (cl) made;** ch 2, **holding back last lp of each dc on hook, work 3 dc in same sp, yo, draw through all 1 lps on hook—cl made;** ch 3; * in next ch-3 sp work cl, ch 2, and cl; ch 3; rep from * 4 times more; join last ch-3 to top of beg cl—12 cls around; fasten off.

Rnd 5: Join mint green into any ch-2 sp bet cls of Rnd 4; work beg cl in same sp; ch 2, in same sp work cl, ch 2, and cl; * ch 3, sk next ch-3 sp; in next ch-2 sp work (cl, ch 2) twice, and cl; rep from * 4 times more; end ch 3, join to top of beg cl—18 cls around.

Rnd 6: Sl st into ch-2 sp; work beg cl in same sp; ch 2, work cl in same sp; ch 2, in next ch-2 sp work cl, ch 2, and cl; * ch 3, sk ch-3 lp, in next ch-2 sp work cl, ch 2, and cl; ch 2, in next ch-2 sp work cl, ch 2, and cl; rep from * 4 times more; end ch 3, join to top of beg cl—24 cl around.

Rnd 7: Sl st into ch-2 sp; work beg cl in same sp; ch 2, cl in same sp; (ch 2, in next ch-2 sp work cl, ch 2, and cl) twice; * ch 3, (in next ch-2 sp work cl, ch 2, and cl) 3 times; rep from * 4 times more; end ch 3; join to top of beg cl; fasten off.

HALF HEXAGON (make 10): With light green, ch 6, join with sl st to form ring.

Row 1: Ch 4—counts as dc and ch-1 sp; in ring work (dc, ch 1) 6 times; dc in ring; ch 4, turn—8 dc in row; turn.

Row 2: Work beg cl in first ch-1 sp; (ch 3, sk next ch-1 sp; in next ch-1 sp work cl, ch 2, and cl) twice; ch 3, sk next ch-1 sp, work cl in last ch-1 sp, ch 1, dc in third ch of turning ch-4; ch 4, turn.

Row 3: Work beg cl, ch 2, and cl in first ch-1 sp (bet dc and first cl); * ch 3, sk ch-3 sp; in next ch-2 sp work (cl, ch 2) twice and cl; rep from * once more; ch 3, in sp bet last cl and turning ch work cl, ch 2, and cl; ch 4, turn.

Row 4: In first ch-2 sp work beg cl, ch 2, and cl; * ch 3, in next ch-2 sp work cl, ch 2, and cl; ch 2, in next ch-2 sp work cl, ch 2, and cl; rep from * once more; ch 3, work cl, ch 2, and cl in last ch-2 sp; ch 1, dc in third ch of turning ch; ch 4, turn.

Row 5: In ch-1 sp bet dc and first cl work beg cl; ch 2, in next ch-2 sp work cl, ch 2, and cl; * ch 3, (in next ch-2 sp work cl, ch 2, and cl; ch 2) twice; in next ch-2 sp work cl, ch 2, and cl; rep from * once more; ch 3, in last ch-2 sp work cl, ch 2, and cl; ch 2, cl in sp bet last cl and turning ch; ch 1, dc in third ch of turning ch; fasten off.

ASSEMBLY: Arrange hexagons in color arrangement as described in the note at start of instructions. Use tapestry needle to whipstitch hexagons together in rows. Then whipstitch five half hexagons to each side.

BORDER: *Rnd 1:* With right side facing, join mint green in any corner ch-2 sp; in same sp work beg cl, ch 2, and cl; work in same cl pat as established in Rnd 7 of hexagon, working cl, ch 2, and cl in ch-2 sp of each cl; work ch-2 lps bet cl-grps.

When working along sides and at places where two hexagons meet, work 1 cl in first corner; *do not ch 2,* work cl in corner of next hexagon.

When working along sides of half hexagons, work cl, ch 2, and cl in turning-ch rows and work cl, ch 2, and cl in the ch-6 ring; at end of rnd, join last ch-2 to top of beg cl.

Rnd 2: Sl st into ch-2 sp, ch 2, sc in same sp, * ch 3, sc in next sp; rep from * around; join last ch 3 to beg sc.

Rnd 3: Sl st in next 2 ch of first ch-3 lp; ch 1, sc in same lp; * ch 4, sc in next ch-3 lp; rep from * around; end ch 1, dc in sc at beg of rnd.

Rnd 4: Ch 1, sc in same lp; * ch 5, sc in next ch-4 lp; rep from * around; end ch 2, dc in sc at beg of rnd; fasten off.

Weave in all ends, and block.

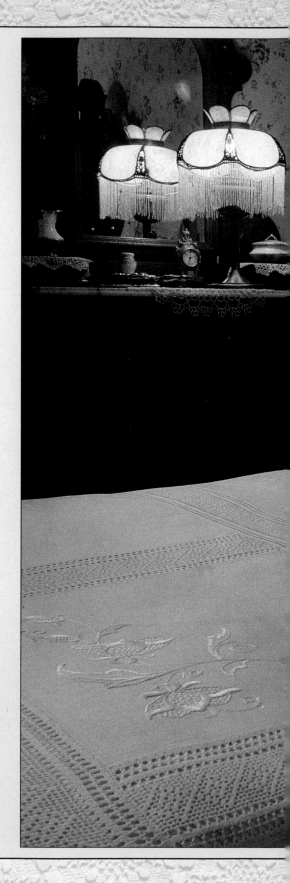

Perennial Borders

A PROFUSION
OF EDGINGS

As airy and elegant as any old-world lace, crocheted edgings evolved during the 19th century as relatively quick-to-make copies of costly antique trims. Some edgings are faithful re-creations of traditional needlepoint and bobbin lace patterns; others use the original designs merely as a point of departure. All are utterly captivating.

Here, two coordinated diamond-pattern crocheted bands are worked in filet crochet with lacet stitches. These bands frame the embroidered blocks of this handsome 84-inch-square coverlet. Instructions begin on page 38.

"*Whether a lady is possessed of few or many personal attractions, it is her duty at all times to appear tidy and to make herself as comely and attractive as circumstances and surroundings permit,*" exhorts a book on deportment published in 1883. If her surroundings include pretty lace-trimmed linens like these, any lady would be happy to comply.

A filet crochet edging in a Maltese cross design, with deep points and squared corners, trims the simple linen curtain *opposite.* You could use the same edging on a matching dresser scarf, or crochet companion strips of lace to trim the shelves of cupboards filled with a collection of antique china cups and plates.

Graceful scallops and an unusual diagonal pattern enhance the sturdy border on the guest towel at *right.* Lace-trimmed items such as these look better if light to medium starch is used after laundering and if the lace is gently stretched while damp, before ironing. Instructions for these two edgings begin on page 40.

This trio of floral-patterned borders can be used in a number of artful ways. *Above,* a filet design encircles a tapestry pattern pillow. Flounced against an under ruffle of rose-colored damask, the lace frames the flowered fabric as a white picket fence surrounds a cottage garden.

The petaled filet edging, *opposite,* is carefully fitted to a fabric-covered frame and trimmed with satin roses. The trim enhances the old-fashioned aura of the family wedding photo. Beside it lies a parlor sachet, a bit of nostalgic whimsy stitched from linen circles, skirted with a gathered band of lace, and stuffed with a medley of sweet-smelling potpourri.

Instructions for these projects are on pages 41–43.

Dainty, lace-trimmed linens were once a part of every bride's trousseau. With this in mind, young girls and their mothers often kept elaborate scrapbooks filled with sample lengths of favorite crocheted edgings. Some were lovingly copied from friends, and others were selected from among the many patterns published in popular women's magazines of the day.

Pictured on these pages are lovely edgings that might easily have been inspired by just such a scrapbook of samples.

Trimming the sheet and pillow slip, *opposite,* are narrow strips of a rose filet edging with matching bands of insertion lace that lend a touch of elegance to company-best linens. Probably inspired by an antique bobbin lace design, the diamond-patterned border edging attached to the store-bought dust ruffle adds a splendid flourish to the charming quilt.

At *right,* a deep swath of fine spiderweb lace turns a simple linen case into a pillow slip worthy of the most romantic boudoir.

See pages 43–45 for the instructions for these crocheted projects.

BEDSPREAD WITH CROCHETED EDGINGS

Shown on pages 30 and 31.

Finished bedspread measures 84 inches square. Straight edging measures 6 inches wide. Zigzag edging measures 4 inches deep at its widest point.

MATERIALS

DMC Cebelia crochet cotton, Size 20 (405-yard ball): 1 ball makes approximately 34 inches of the straight edging or 70 inches of the zigzag edging
Size 11 steel crochet hook
Needle and sewing thread
4 yards of 44-inch-wide white linen fabric or fabric of your choice
DMC embroidery floss to match fabric

Abbreviations: See page 186.
Gauge: 5 spaces = 1 inch; 6 rows = 1 inch.

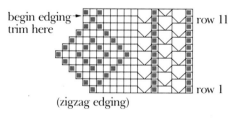

begin edging trim here → row 11
row 1
(zigzag edging)

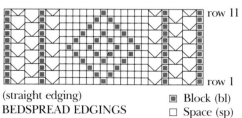

row 11
row 1
(straight edging)
BEDSPREAD EDGINGS

- ■ Block (bl)
- □ Space (sp)
- ⋈ Lacet st
- ▭ Ch-5 Loop

INSTRUCTIONS

The instructions for the edgings follow. The straight edging is for the strips that border the fabric squares in the center of the spread. The zigzag edging is for the borders along the outside edges of the spread. It is best to add 2 or 3 inches to the strip measurements to allow for shrinkage. Wash the strips in hot water, block, and press prior to assembling the strips onto the fabric.

For the straight edging
Make 2 strips, each 76 inches long; 3 strips, each 46 inches; and 2 strips, each 20 inches.
Beg along narrow edge, ch 90.
Row 1: Dc in fourth ch from hook and in next 2 ch; **ch 3, sk 2 ch, sc in next ch, ch 3, sk 2 ch, dc in next ch—lacet st made;** ch 5, sk 5 ch, dc in next 4 ch, work lacet st; (ch 2, sk 2 ch, dc in next ch) 6 times; dc in next 3 ch; (ch 2, sk 2 ch, dc in next ch) 6 times; work lacet st, dc in 3 ch, ch 5, sk 5 ch, dc in next ch, work lacet st, dc in next 3 ch; ch 3, turn.
Row 2: Sk first dc, dc in 3 dc, ch 5, dc in next dc, **ch 3, sc in third ch of ch-5 lp, ch 3, dc in next dc—lacet st over ch-5 lp made;** dc in next 3 dc, ch 5, dc in next dc; (ch 2, dc in next dc) 5 times; 2 dc in ch-2 sp, dc in next dc, ch 2, sk 2 dc, dc in next dc, 2 dc in ch-2 sp, dc in next dc; (ch 2, dc in next dc) 5 times; ch 5, dc in next 4 dc, work lacet st, ch 5, dc in next 3 dc and in top of turning ch; ch 3, turn.
Rows 3–11: Work from chart, *bottom left.* When working from chart, always read odd-numbered rows from right to left and even-numbered rows from left to right. For additional information for working filet designs, see the tip box on page 88.

Rep rows 2–11 for desired length and for the required number of strips as cited for the straight edging.

For the zigzag edging
Make 4 strips, each 76 inches long.
Beg along narrow edge, ch 48.
Row 1: Dc in fourth ch from hook and in next 2 ch; **ch 3, sk 2 ch, sc in next ch, ch 3, sk 2 ch, dc in next ch—lacet st made;** ch 5, sk 5 ch, dc in next 4 ch, work lacet st; (ch 2, sk 2 ch, dc in next ch) 6 times; dc in next 3 ch; ch 5, turn.
Row 2: **Dc in fourth and fifth ch from hook, dc in next dc—bl inc at beg of row;** ch 2, sk 2 dc, dc in next dc, 2 dc in ch-2 lp, dc in next dc; (ch 2, dc in next dc) 5 times; ch 5, dc in next 4 dc, work lacet st over ch-5 lp; ch 5, dc in next 3 dc and in top of turning ch; ch 3, turn.
Rows 3–11: Work from chart, *below left, top.* Read odd-numbered rows from right to left and even-numbered rows from left to right.
To increase a block at beg of rows 2, 4, and 6: Ch 5, turn at end of previous row, then dc in fourth and fifth ch from hook, dc in next dc. Complete row following chart.
To increase a block at end of rows 3 and 5: (Yo hook, draw up lp at base of last dc made, yo, draw through 1 lp on hook—base ch for next dc; complete st as for dc) 3 times; ch 5, turn.
To decrease a block at end of rows 7 and 9: Work across Row 6 or Row 8 and complete last dc, turn, sl st in second, third, and fourth dc; ch 3, work 2 dc in ch-2 sp, dc in next dc; complete row from chart.
Work from chart through Row 11; then rep rows 2–11 for pat for the required length or as cited above for the zigzag edging.
continued

EMBROIDERY STITCHES

Buttonhole stitch

Herringbone stitch

Feather stitch

Outline stitch

French knot stitch

Satin stitch

BEDSPREAD EMBROIDERY

—— Outline stitch

:·:·:· French knots

▨ Satin stitch

ᕤᕐᕤ Feather stitch

ʟʟʟʟ Buttonhole stitch

✕✕✕ Open Herringbone stitch

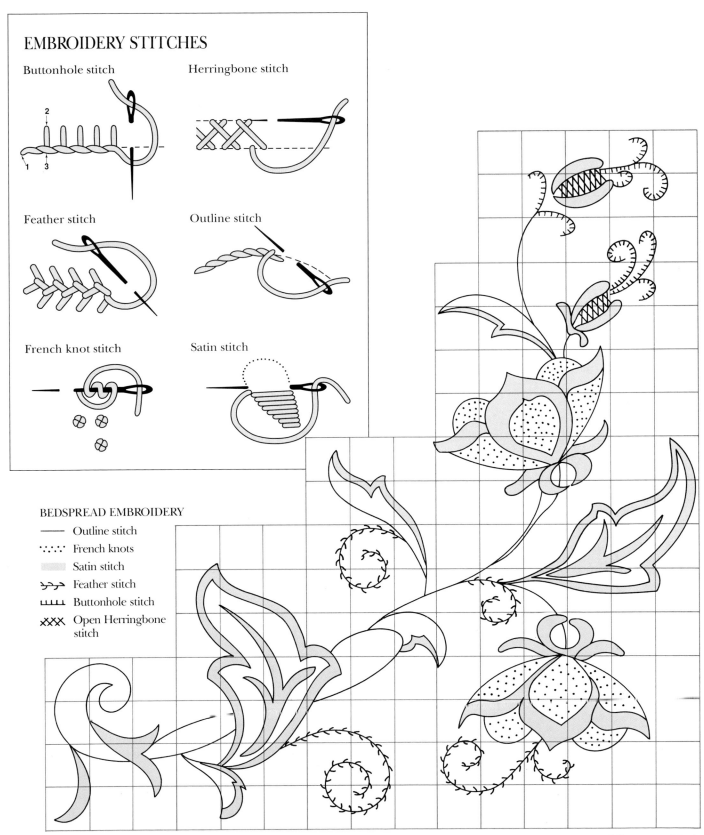

1 Square = 1 Inch

To trim the zigzag edge: Join thread at top of strip on zigzag side as shown on chart, ch 3, * sc in dc at end of next block; (ch 4, sc in dc at end of next block in row below) 4 times, ch 3, dc around side (post) of st, ch 3, sc in *base* of same dc; (ch 4, sc in dc at end of next block in row below) 4 times; ch 3, rep from * across strip; ch 4, turn.

Row 2: Sc in next ch-4 lp; * **ch 4, sl st in third ch from hook—picot made;** ch 3, sc in next ch-lp; rep from * across strip; fasten off.

For the spread
Prewash fabric before assembling into spread. Cut the fabric into four 21-inch squares, two 47x10-inch strips, and two 77x10-inch strips. (Cutting directions include ½-inch seam allowances.)

Enlarge the embroidery design on page 39 onto graph paper. Flopping the pattern, transfer the design into corners of the four 21-inch squares (see photo on pages 30 and 31 for placement). Use three strands of floss to work the embroidery following the stitching guide on the pattern. Turn under ¼ inch twice to hem each square.

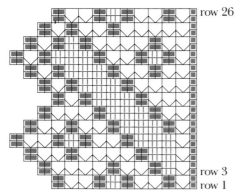

HAND-TOWEL EDGING

7 dc
Lacet st
Ch-5 Loop
Mesh

To assemble the spread, hand-sew one 20-inch straight edging between two squares; repeat for the other two squares. Sew these two units together, with a 46-inch straight edging between. Sew two 46-inch edgings to opposite sides of the assembled square. Hem, then sew the two 47x10-inch fabric strips to the last crocheted edges. Sew the 76-inch straight edgings to opposite sides of the other two ends. Hem, then sew the two 77x10-inch fabric strips along these same sides. Sew the zigzag edgings to each of the four sides to complete the spread.

HAND-TOWEL EDGING

Shown on page 33.

Edging measures 4¾ inches wide across the widest point.

——MATERIALS——
DMC Cordonnet Special cotton thread, Size 40 (249-yard ball): 1 ball makes 24 inches
Size 12 steel crochet hook

Abbreviations: See page 186.
Gauge: 3 lacet stitches = 1 inch; 6 rows = 1 inch.

——INSTRUCTIONS——
Beg along narrow edge, ch 66.
Row 1: Dc in fourth ch from hook and in next 2 ch; **ch 3, sk 2 ch, sc in next ch, ch 3, sk 2 ch, dc in next ch—lacet st made;** dc in next 6 ch; make 2 lacet sts; dc in next 6 ch; **(ch 1, sk ch, dc in next ch) 3 times—mesh made;** dc in next 6 ch, work 2 lacet sts; dc in last 6 ch; ch 3, turn.
Row 2: Sk first dc, dc in 6 dc; (ch 5, dc in next dc) twice; dc in 6 dc; **(ch 1, dc in next dc) 3 times—mesh over dc made;** dc in 6 dc;

(ch 5, dc in next dc) twice, dc in 6 dc, ch 5, dc in next 3 dc, dc in top of turning ch; ch 3, turn.
Row 3: Sk first dc, dc in next 3 dc; **ch 3, sc in center ch of ch-5 lp, ch 3, dc in next dc—lacet st over ch-5 lp made;** (ch 1, sk dc, dc in next dc) 3 times; 5 dc in ch-5 lp; dc in next dc; work lacet st over ch-5 lp, ch 3, sk 2 dc, sc in next dc; ch 3, sk 2 dc, dc in next dc; (dc in ch-1 sp, dc in next dc) 3 times; ch 3, sk 2 dc, sc in next dc, ch 3, sk 2 dc, dc in next dc; (work lacet st over next ch-5 lp) twice; ch 3, sk 2 dc, sc in next dc, ch 3, sk 2 dc, dc in top of turning ch; (**yo hook, draw up loop at base of last dc made; yo, draw through 1 lp on hook—base chain for next dc; complete st as for dc) 6 times—6 sts inc at end of row;** ch 3, turn.
Rows 4–26: Refer to chart, *bottom left,* and work as established. Rep rows 3–26 for desired length plus 2 or 3 inches to allow for shrinkage. Wash and press edging. Use sewing thread to sew edging to towel or desired item.

CURTAIN EDGING

Shown on page 32.

Edging measures 4¾ inches across its widest point.

——MATERIALS——
DMC Cordonnet Special cotton thread, Size 40 (249-yard ball): 1 ball makes 18 inches
Size 14 steel crochet hook

Abbreviations: See page 186.
Gauge: 6 sp = 1 inch; 7 rows = 1 inch.

——INSTRUCTIONS——
Beg at narrow edge, ch 65.
Row 1: Dc in eighth ch from

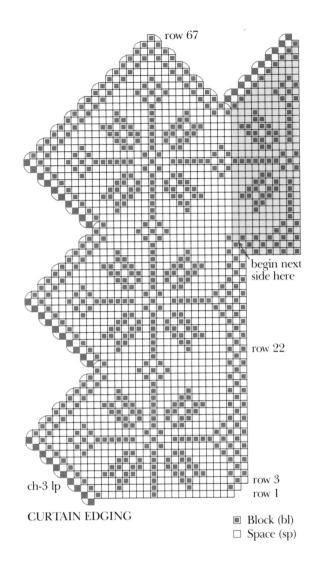

row 67

begin next side here

row 22

row 3
row 1

ch-3 lp

CURTAIN EDGING

☐ Block (bl)
☐ Space (sp)

Row 4: Sk 3 dc, dc in next dc, in ch-3 lp work 3 dc, ch 3, and 3 dc; dc in next dc; work across row referring to chart, *left.*

Rows 5–22: Work from chart.

Rep rows 3–22 for desired length of curtain minus the width of the edging plus 3 inches. (Our curtain has 15 motifs along each side.)

Rows 23–67: Work from chart. Note how rows 37 and 38 decrease to establish placement for next side. The shaded portion of the chart shows the placement of the stitches for the *next* side. When working the corner, only work the unshaded portions.

To begin next side, rep Row 1 of chart, fitting it across side of edging as shown on chart. Work as for first side to complete this side and remaining side.

Use sewing thread to whipstitch edging to curtain.

SACHET PILLOW EDGING

Shown on page 35.

Edging measures 4 inches across the widest point.

MATERIALS
DMC Cordonnet Special cotton thread, Size 40 (249-yard ball): 1 ball makes 25 inches
Size 14 steel crochet hook
Two 5-inch-diameter circles cut from 2 white linen handkerchiefs
¾ yard each of pink (2 lengths) and white (1 length) ¼-inch-wide ribbons
Polyester fiberfill

Abbreviations: See page 186.
Gauge: 7 sp = 1 inch; 7 rows = 1 inch.

hook; (ch 2, sk 2 ch, dc in next ch) 10 times; dc in next 3 ch; (ch 2, sk 2 ch, dc in next ch) 7 times; dc in next 3 ch; ch 3, 4 dc in same ch as last dc; ch 3, turn.

Row 2: Sk 3 dc, dc in next dc, in ch-3 lp work 3 dc, ch 3, and 3 dc; dc in next dc, ch 2, sk 2 dc, dc in next dc; (ch 2, dc in next dc) twice; 2 dc in ch-2 sp, dc in next dc; (ch 2, dc in next dc) 4 times, dc in 3 dc; (ch 2, dc in next dc) 4 times, 2 dc in ch-2 sp, dc in next dc; (ch 2, dc in next dc) 5 times, 2 dc in ch-2 lp, dc in next ch; **ch 2, trc in base of last dc—sp inc at end of row;** ch 7, turn.

Row 3: Dc in trc, 2 dc in ch-2 lp, dc in next dc, ch 2, sk 2 dc, dc in next dc; (ch 2, dc in next dc) 5 times; dc in 3 dc, 2 dc in next lp, dc in next dc; (ch 2, dc in next dc) 3 times, dc in next 3 dc; (ch 2, dc in next dc) 3 times; 2 dc in next lp, dc in next 4 dc; (ch 2, dc in next dc) 3 times; ch 2, sk 2 dc, dc in next dc, in ch-3 lp work 3 dc, ch 3, and 3 dc; dc in first dc of 4-dc grp in row below; ch 3, turn.

continued

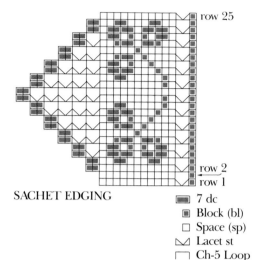

SACHET EDGING

■ 7 dc
■ Block (bl)
□ Space (sp)
⋈ Lacet st
☐ Ch-5 Loop

INSTRUCTIONS

Beg along narrow edge, ch 45.

Row 1: Dc in fourth ch from hook and in next 2 ch; **ch 3, sk 2 ch, sc in next ch, ch 3, sk 2 ch, dc in next ch—lacet st made;** (ch 2, sk 2 ch, dc in next ch) 11 times; ch 5, turn.

Row 2: Sk first dc, dc in next dc; (ch 2, dc in next dc) 10 times; ch 5, dc in next 3 dc and top of turning ch; ch 3, turn.

Row 3: Sk first dc, dc in next 3 dc, work lacet st; (ch 2, dc in next dc) 10 times; ch 2, sk 2 ch of turning ch, dc in next ch; **(yo, draw up lp in base of last dc made, yo, draw through 1 lp on hook—ch-1 made for base for next st; complete st as for dc) 6 times—2 bl inc made at end of row;** ch 3, turn.

Row 4: Sk first dc, dc in next 6 dc; work from chart *above*, and read chart from left to right.

Rows 5–25: Work from chart. Always read odd-numbered rows from right to left and even-numbered rows from left to right.

Rep rows 2–25 for pat repeat until 5 points are completed to make sachet edging as shown in photo on page 35.

With right sides facing, gather and baste edging to fit around one linen circle. With right sides facing, sew linen circles together using ¼-inch seams and leaving opening for stuffing. Turn pillow; stuff and sew opening closed.

Mark three points that are equal distance apart along pillow edging. Weave three ribbons through lacet stitches, beginning each one at a marked point; tie into bows.

PICTURE-FRAME EDGING

Shown on page 35.

Edging measures 3½ inches wide.

MATERIALS

DMC Cordonnet Special crochet cotton, Size 40 (249-yard ball): 1 ball makes 25 inches
Size 14 steel crochet hook
Purchased frame with 4¼ x 6¼-inch opening
1 yard of ⅛-inch-wide ribbon
½ yard of chintz or fabric of your choice to cover frame
Purchased satin roses

Abbreviations: See page 186.
Gauge: 7 sp = 1 inch; 7 rows = 1 inch.

INSTRUCTIONS

Beg along narrow edge, ch 57.

Row 1: Dc in fourth ch from hook and in next 2 ch; (ch 2, sk 2 ch, dc in next ch) 5 times—5 sp made; dc in next 36 ch—12 bl made; **ch 3, sl st in third ch from hook—picot made;** ch 5, turn.

Row 2: **Dc in fourth and fifth ch from hook, dc in next dc—bl inc made;** (ch 2, sk 2 dc, dc in next dc) twice; dc in next 6 dc; (ch 2, sk 2 dc, dc in next dc) 4 times; dc in next 9 dc; ch 2, sk 2 dc, dc in next dc; (ch 2, dc in next dc) 4 times; 2 dc in ch-2 sp, dc in next dc; ch 2, sk 2 dc, dc in top of turning ch; ch 3, turn.

Rows 3–33: Work from chart *below*. Read all even-numbered rows from left to right and odd-numbered rows from right to left. At the end of rows 11, 13, 15, 27, 29, and 31, work picot, turn and sl st to fourth dc, ch 3, and continue to work rows from chart.

Rep rows 2–33 for pat until 17 repeats are made, ending with Row 32 of chart. Use sewing thread to hand-sew beginning and last rows together.

Cover frame with fabric. Pin edging to frame, evenly distributing excess lace to fall into corners to form pleats. Use sewing thread to hand-sew the edging to the inside edge of frame. Trim the lace with ribbon, weaving it through the space blocks and tying it into a bow at one corner. Tack purchased satin roses atop tied bow.

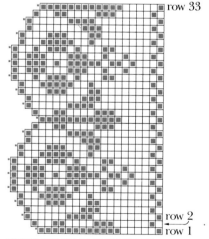

PICTURE FRAME EDGING

▨ Block (bl)
□ Space (sp)
⊡ Picot

FILET DIAMOND PILLOW EDGING

Shown on page 34.

Edging is 6 inches wide at widest point.

MATERIALS

DMC Cordonnet Special crochet cotton, Size 40 (249-yard ball): 1 ball makes 17 inches
Size 14 steel crochet hook
13x15-inch pillow, covered with tapestry fabric, piping, and 6-inch-wide ruffle in fabric of your choice

Abbreviations: See page 186.
Gauge: 7 sp = 1 inch; 7 rows = 1 inch.

INSTRUCTIONS

Follow the chart, *above right,* when working this pattern. The blue tinted stitches along the zigzag edge are worked after the main part is completed.

Beg along narrow edge, ch 78.

Row 1: Dc in fourth ch from hook and in next 2 ch; (ch 2, sk 2 ch, dc in next ch) 6 times—6 sp made; dc in next 15 ch—5 bl made; ch 2, sk 2 ch, dc in next 16 ch; (ch 2, sk 2 ch, dc in next ch) 4 times; dc in next 9 dc; ch 3, turn.

Row 2: Sk first dc, dc in next 6 dc; ch 2, sk 2 dc, dc in next dc; (ch 2, dc in next dc) 3 times; 2 dc in next sp, dc in next 16 dc; 2 dc in next sp, dc in next 4 dc; (ch 2, sk 2 dc, dc in next dc) 4 times; (ch 2, dc in next dc) 6 times; dc in next 2 dc and top of turning ch; ch 3, turn.

Row 3: Sk first dc, dc in next 3 dc; (ch 2, dc in next dc) 7 times; (2 dc in next lp, dc in next dc) 3 times; dc in next 6 dc; ch 2, sk 2

dc, dc in next 16 dc; (ch 2, dc in next dc) 4 times; (ch 2, sk 2 dc, dc in next dc) twice; **(yo hook, draw up lp at base of last dc made; yo, draw through 1 lp on hook—base ch for next dc; complete st as for dc) 6 times—2 bl inc at end of row;** ch 3, turn.

Rows 4–27: Work from chart *above.*

Rep rows 2–27 for pat until edging measures twice the distance around the pillow or for desired length; end with Row 26 of chart; fasten off.

Use sewing thread to whipstitch ends of edging together.

EDGING TRIM: Trim the jagged edge as follows: Join thread in dc at end of strip in place that corresponds with arrow on chart. Ch 5, sk 5 dc, sc in next dc, ch 5, sk 2 bl, sc in dc 2 rows below, ch 5, sk 6 dc, sc in next dc; ch 5, turn; sc in previous lp made, ch 1, turn; work 6 sc in ch-5 lp just made; sl st in sc. Following chart and this sequence as established, work trim around entire edging; join with sl st to first ch of beg ch-5; fasten off. Gather and sew edging to pillow on top of gathered fabric ruffle.

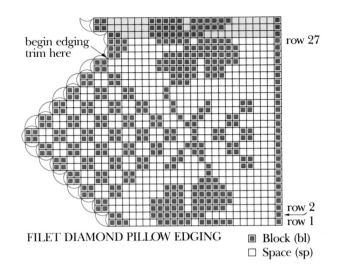

FILET DIAMOND PILLOW EDGING
■ Block (bl)
□ Space (sp)

SPIDERWEB PILLOWCASE EDGING

Shown on page 37.

Edging measures 7 inches across at its widest point.

MATERIALS

DMC Cebelia crochet cotton, Size 20 (405-yard ball): 1 ball makes approximately 31 inches
Size 9 steel crochet hook
Pair of pillowcases
Sewing needle and thread

Abbreviations: See page 186.
Gauge: 2 sp = 1 inch; 5 rows = 1 inch.

INSTRUCTIONS

Beg along narrow edge, ch 78.

Row 1: Dc in eighth ch from hook; (ch 2, sk 2 ch, dc in next ch) 12 times; dc in next 3 ch, ch 2, sk 2 ch, dc in next 4 ch; ch 7, sk 5 ch, sc in next 5 ch, ch 7, sk 5 ch, dc in next 4 ch; ch 2, sk 2 ch, dc in next 4 ch; ch 5, turn.

Row 2: **Dc in fourth and fifth ch from hook, dc in next dc—bl inc at beg of row;** ch 2, sk 2 dc, dc

continued

in next dc, 2 dc in ch-2 lp, dc in dc; ch 2, sk 2 dc, dc in next dc; 3 dc in ch-7 lp, ch 6, sk sc, sc in 3 sc, ch 6, 3 dc at end of ch-7 lp, dc in dc; (ch 2, sk 2 dc, dc in next dc, 2 dc in ch-2 lp, dc in next dc) twice; (ch 2, dc in next dc) 11 times; ch 2, sk 2 ch, dc in next ch; ch 5, turn.

Row 3: Sk first dc, dc in next dc; (ch 2, dc in next dc) 10 times; (2 dc in ch-2 sp, dc in next dc, ch 2, sk 2 dc, dc in next dc) 3 times; 3 dc in ch-6 lp, ch 6, sk sc, sc in next sc; ch 6, 3 dc at end of next ch-6 lp; dc in next dc; (ch 2, sk 2 dc, dc in next dc, 2 dc in ch-2 lp, dc in next dc) twice; ch 2, sk 2 dc, dc in next dc; **(yo hook, draw up lp in base of last dc made, yo, draw through 1 lp on hook—ch made for base of next st; complete st as for dc) 3 times—bl inc at end of row made;** ch 5, turn.

Row 4: Work bl inc for beg of row; * ch 2, sk 2 dc, dc in next dc, 2 dc in ch-2 sp, dc in next dc, ch 5, dc in ch-2 sp, ch 5, sk 3 dc, dc in next dc, 2 dc in next lp, dc in next dc; ch 2, sk 2 dc, dc in next dc; * 3 dc in ch-6 lp, ch 2, 3 dc in next ch-6 lp; dc in next dc; rep bet * once; 2 dc in ch-2 lp, dc in next dc; (ch 2, dc in next dc) 9 times; ch 2, sk 2 ch, dc in next ch; ch 5, turn.

Row 5: Sk first dc, dc in next dc; (ch 2, dc in next dc) 8 times; 2 dc in ch-2 lp, dc in next dc, ch 2, sk 2 dc, dc in next dc; * 2 dc in ch-2 sp, dc in next dc; ch 6, sc at end of ch-5 lp, sc in dc, sc in next ch-5 lp, ch 6, sk 3 dc, dc in next dc; * (2 dc in ch-2 sp, dc in next dc, ch 2, sk 2 dc, dc in next dc) twice; rep bet * once; 2 dc in ch-2 sp, dc in next dc, ch 2, sk 2 dc, dc in next dc; work bl inc; ch 5, turn.

Row 6: Work bl inc; ch 2, sk 2 dc, dc in next dc, 2 dc in ch-2 lp, dc in next dc; * ch 7, sc in ch-6 lp, sc in 3 sc, sc in ch-6 lp, ch 7, sk 3 dc, dc in next dc; 2 dc in ch-2 lp, dc in next dc, ch 2, sk 2 dc, dc in next dc, 2 dc in ch-2 lp, dc in next

dc; rep from * once; (ch 2, dc in next dc) 7 times; ch 2, sk 2 ch, dc in next ch; ch 5, turn.

Row 7: Sk first dc, dc in next dc; (ch 2, dc in next dc) 6 times; (2 dc in next lp, dc in next dc, ch 2, sk 2 dc, dc in next dc) twice; * 3 dc in ch-7 lp, ch 6, sk sc, sc in 3 sc, ch 6, 3 dc in next ch-7 lp, dc in next dc, ch 2, sk 2 dc, dc in next dc, 2 dc in ch-2 lp, dc in next dc, ch 2, sk 2 dc, dc in next dc; rep from * once; work bl inc; ch 5, turn.

Row 8: Work bl inc; * (ch 2, sk 2 dc, dc in next dc, 2 dc in ch-2 sp, dc in next dc) twice; ch 2, sk 2 dc, dc in next dc, 3 dc in ch-6 lp, ch 6, sk sc, sc in next sc, ch 6, 3 dc in ch-6 lp, dc in next dc; rep from * once; rep bet ( )s 3 times; (ch 2, dc in next dc) 5 times; ch 2, sk 2 ch, dc in next ch; ch 5, turn.

Rows 9–21: Keeping to spiderweb design as established (see detail, *above*), work from chart *top*. Rep rows 2–21 for pattern for desired length, ending with Row 20; fasten off. Whipstitch ends together; hand-sew to pillowcase.

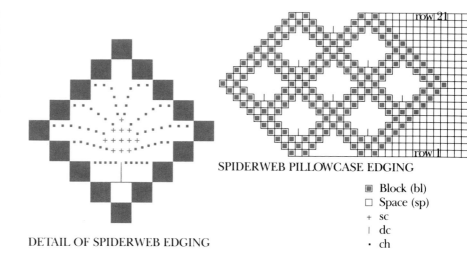

DETAIL OF SPIDERWEB EDGING

SPIDERWEB PILLOWCASE EDGING

■ Block (bl)
□ Space (sp)
+ sc
| dc
· ch

ROSE FILET EDGINGS

Shown on page 36.

Insert edging is 1¾ inches wide. Zigzag edging is 2 inches wide across the widest point.

MATERIALS
DMC Cordonnet Special crochet cotton, Size 60 (324-yard ball): 1 ball makes 60 inches
Size 14 steel crochet hook or size to obtain gauge cited below

Abbreviations: See page 186.
Gauge: 7 blocks = 1 inch; 7 rows = 1 inch.

INSTRUCTIONS
For the zigzag edging
Refer to the tip box on page 88 for additional information for working filet crochet patterns.

Beg along narrow edge, ch 32.

Row 1: Dc in eighth ch from hook, ch 2, sk 2 ch, dc in next 4 ch; ch 2, sk 2 ch, dc in next 7 ch; ch 2, sk 2 ch, dc in next 4 ch, ch 2, sk 2 ch, dc in last ch; ch 10, turn.

Row 2: Dc in eighth ch from hook; (ch 2, dc in next dc) twice; dc in next 3 dc, ch 2, dc in next 4 dc, ch 2, sk 2 dc, dc in next dc, ch 2, dc in next 4 dc; ch 2, dc in next dc, ch 2, sk 2 ch of turning ch, dc in next ch; ch 5, turn.

Row 3: Sk first dc, dc in next dc, ch 2, dc in next 4 dc; (ch 2, dc in next dc) twice; ch 2, sk 2 dc, dc in next dc; ch 2, dc in next dc, ch 2, sk 2 dc, dc in next dc, 2 dc in ch-2 sp, dc in next dc, ch 2, dc in next dc, ch 2, sk 2 ch of turning ch, dc in next ch; ch 7, turn.

Row 4: Dc in first dc, ch 2, dc in next dc, 2 dc in ch-2 lp, dc in next dc, ch 2, sk 2 dc, dc in next dc; (ch 2, dc in next dc) 3 times; (2 dc in ch-2 lp, dc in next dc) twice; ch 2, sk 2 dc, dc in next dc, 2 dc in ch-2 lp, dc in next dc; ch 2, sk 2 ch of turning ch, dc in next ch; ch 5, turn.

Rows 5–13: Keeping to pat as established, work from bottom chart, *below.* Rep rows 2–13 for length across top of sheet or around pillowcase opening, plus 2 or 3 inches to allow for shrinkage; fasten off.

For the insert edging
Beg along narrow edge, ch 44.

Row 1: Dc in eighth ch from hook; (ch 2, sk 2 ch, dc in next ch)

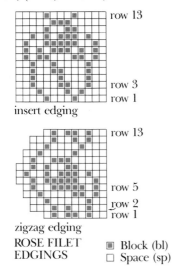

insert edging

zigzag edging
ROSE FILET EDGINGS
■ Block (bl)
□ Space (sp)

3 times; dc in next 3 ch; (ch 2, sk 2 ch, dc in next ch) 3 times, dc in next 3 ch; (ch 2, sk 2 ch, dc in next ch) 4 times; ch 5, turn.

Row 2: Sk first dc, dc in next dc; (ch 2, dc in next dc) twice, 2 dc in ch-2 sp, dc in next dc, ch 2, sk 2 dc, dc in next dc; (ch 2, dc in next dc) twice; 2 dc in ch-2 sp, dc in next dc, ch 2, sk 2 dc, dc in next dc, 2 dc in ch-2 sp, dc in next dc; (ch 2, dc in next dc) twice, ch 2, sk 2 ch of turning ch, dc in next ch; ch 5, turn.

Rows 3–13: Working from top chart, *below left,* rep rows 2–13 for pat for length across top of sheet or around pillowcase opening, plus 2 or 3 inches to allow for shrinkage; fasten off at end of last row.

Wash edgings, press, and use sewing thread to sew edgings to sheet or pillowcase.

DUST RUFFLE EDGING

Shown on page 36.

Edging measures 5¼ inches at the widest point.

——MATERIALS——
DMC Cebelia crochet cotton, Size 20 (405-yard ball): 1 ball makes 50 inches
Size 12 steel crochet hook

Abbreviations: See page 186.
Gauge: 2 lacet stitches = 1 inch; 5 rows = 1 inch.

——INSTRUCTIONS——
Beg along narrow edge, ch 48.

Row 1: Beginning with Row 1 of the chart *above right,* dc in fourth ch from hook and in next 2 ch; **(ch 3, sk 2 ch, sc in next ch, ch 3, sk 2 ch, dc in next ch—**

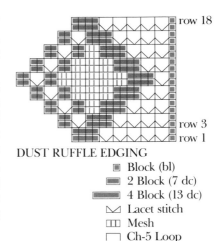

row 18

row 3
row 1

DUST RUFFLE EDGING
■ Block (bl)
▨ 2 Block (7 dc)
▥ 4 Block (13 dc)
⌣ Lacet stitch
⊞ Mesh
☐ Ch-5 Loop

lacet st made) 5 times; dc in next 12 chs; ch 3, turn.

Row 2: Sk first dc, dc in next 12 dc; (ch 5, dc in next dc) 5 times; dc in next 2 dc and in top of turning ch; ch 3, turn.

Row 3: Sk first dc, dc in 3 dc; (ch 3, sc in center ch of ch-5 lp, ch 3, dc in next dc) 4 times; 5 dc in next ch-5 lp, dc in next 7 dc, ch 3, sk 2 dc, sc in next dc, ch 3, sk 2 dc, dc in top of turning ch; **(yo hook, draw up lp at base of last dc made, yo, draw through 1 lp on hook—base chain for next dc made; complete st as for dc) 6 times—2 bl inc at end of row;** ch 3, turn.

Row 4: Sk first dc, dc in next 6 dc, ch 5, dc in next 13 dc; (ch 5, dc in next dc) 4 times; dc in next 2 dc and top of turning ch; ch 3, turn.

Row 5: Working from chart, and reading from left to right, work 1 bl, 3 lacet sts, 5 dc in ch-5 lp, dc in 7 dc; **(ch 1, sk dc, dc in next dc) 3 times—mesh made;** 5 dc in ch-5 lp, dc in next dc, 1 lacet st; inc 2 bl at end of row; ch 3, turn.

Rows 6–18: Work from chart as established. Rep rows 3–18 for pat for desired length; fasten off at end of work. Use sewing thread to sew edging along dust ruffle hem or desired cloth.

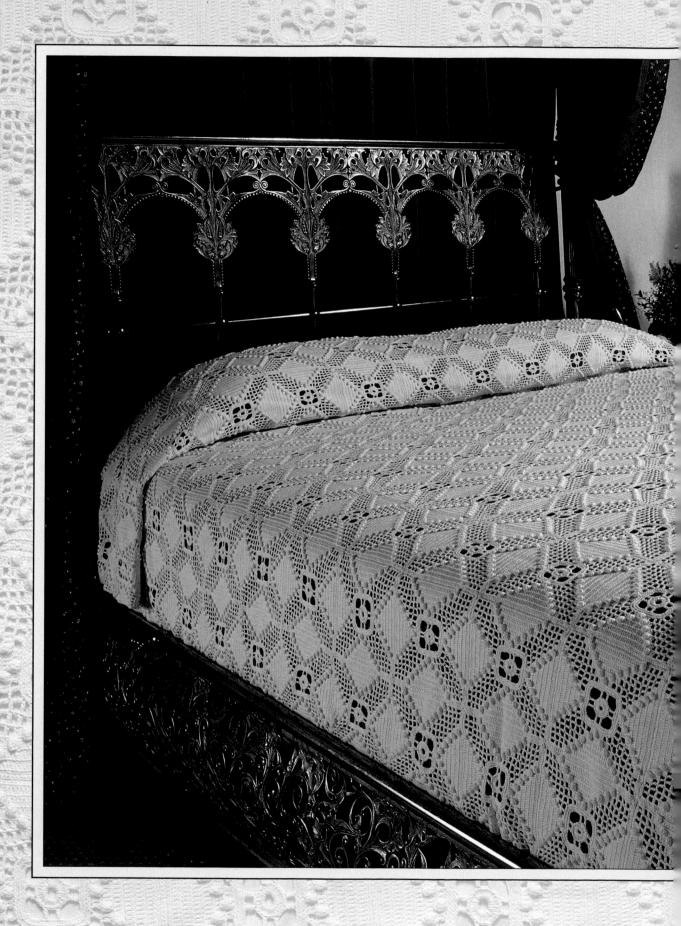

Bedroom Comforts

ABUNDANCE
IN OLD LACE

❧

In the early decades of this century, thread companies published hundreds of pattern booklets every year to meet the public's demand for new and original crochet designs. Lovely, lacy bedspreads—simple or complex, but invariably worked in white or ecru thread—were especially popular, and many of these old designs are considered classics today.

An openwork motif branches into diagonal rays that are outlined with neatly arranged popcorn stitches in this handsome 78x108-inch lattice bedspread design. Instructions begin on page 54.

These two designs make dramatically different uses of a simple diamond-within-a-diamond motif. Both patterns are worked in popcorn stitches.

Above, a simple repeat of a 5-inch block creates a rhythmic, densely textured surface for the 80x100-inch spread.

More complex—and more challenging—is the star pattern, *opposite.* In the shape of 12-inch blocks, this pattern becomes a more fanciful design, combining popcorn stitches with openwork designs to create an intricate white-on-white pattern reminiscent of a pieced patchwork quilt.

Instructions for these spreads begin on page 54.

Bedroom Comforts

*H*istorian, novelist, and
needle artist Rose Lane Wilder called crochet "the art of
making lace in the air." Though patterns may be
repeated, she said, "Each piece has its own individual
character . . . the tension of the thread, the rhythm of the
stitches, the effect of the whole shows you the personality
of the unknown maker."

Exquisite examples of Mrs. Wilder's airy lace are displayed here. An artul mix of spiderweb and popcorn motifs graces the gossamer spread, *opposite,* and delicate bands of ecru lace in complementary patterns trim the pillow slip and sheet in the close-up, *left.*

Fragile though these designs may seem, rest assured that crocheted lace is far more durable than it appears, and with proper care it will last for many years.

When creating trims for sheets, pillowcases, and other items, always crochet an extra inch or two. Then wash both lace and fabric before stitching the trim to the item to adjust for shrinkage.

Instructions for these projects begin on page 57.

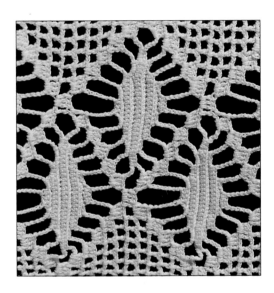

Unlike most crocheted bedspread patterns, which are pieced from individual blocks, the handsome masculine coverlet, *opposite,* is worked in five panel strips. The simplest of stitches—double crochet and chain stitches—and regular repeats make this an ideal project for the novice crocheter who wants to make a bedspread and stitch with thread.

After all five panels are completed and sewn together, the coverlet is bordered with an easy picot edging for a more finished appearance.

The delicate spiderweb insertion sewn into the dust ruffle, *opposite,* and pictured in the close-up, *above,* also could serve as trim for any domestic item from tea towels to table linens.

Instructions for these two projects begin on page 60.

POPCORN LATTICE BEDSPREAD

Shown on pages 46 and 47.

Bedspread measures approximately 78x108 inches.

MATERIALS

DMC Brilliant knitting and crochet cotton in ecru or white (50-gram ball): 66 balls
Size 8 steel crochet hook or size to obtain gauge cited below
Tapestry needle

Abbreviations: See page 186.
Gauge: Each motif measures 6 inches along each side.

INSTRUCTIONS

MOTIF (make 234): Beg at center, ch 6; join with sl st to form ring.

Rnd 1: Ch 3, work 23 dc in ring; join with sl st to top of beg ch-3—24 dc.

Note: In the instructions that follow, work in back lps of st unless specified otherwise.

Rnd 2: Ch 12, * sk 2 dc, dc in next dc, ch 2, sk 2 dc, dc in next dc, ch 9; rep from * twice more; then sk 2 dc, dc in next dc, ch 2; join to third ch of beg ch-12.

Rnd 3: Ch 1, sc in same st as join; * sc in next 4 ch, 3 sc in next ch—corner made; sc in next 4 ch, sc in next dc, sc in next 2 ch, ** sc in next dc; rep from * around; end last rep at **; join with sl st to beg sc.

Rnd 4: Ch 1, sc in same st as join; sc in next 5 sc, 3 sc in next sc; (sc in each 14 sc to next corner, 3 sc in corner st) 3 times; sc in last 8 sc; join with sl st to beg sc—14 sc bet each 3-sc grp.

Rnd 5: Ch 3, dc in next 2 sc; ch 2, sk sc, dc in next sc, ch 2, sk 2 sc; * in corner st work dc, ch 5, and dc; ch 2, sk 2 sc, dc in next sc, ch 2, sk sc, dc in next 3 sc; in next sc **work 5 dc, drop lp from hook, insert hook in top of first dc of 5-dc grp and draw dropped lp through—popcorn (pc) made;** dc in next 3 sc, ch 2, sk 2 sc, dc in next sc, ch 2, sk 2 sc; rep from * twice more; in next st work dc, ch 5, and dc; ch 2, sk 2 sc, dc in next sc, ch 2, sk 2 sc, dc in next 3 sc, pc in last sc; join to top of beg ch-3.

Rnd 6: Ch 3, dc in next dc, pc in next dc; 2 dc in ch-2 lp, dc in next dc; * ch 2, dc in next dc, ch 2; in third ch of ch-5 lp work dc, ch 5, and dc; ch 2, dc in next dc, ch 2, dc in next dc, 2 dc in ch-2 lp; pc in next dc, ** dc in next 5 st; pc in next st; 2 dc in next ch-2 lp, dc in next dc; rep from * twice more; rep from * to ** once; then dc in last 3 st; join with sl st to top of beg ch-3.

Rnd 7: Ch 3, dc in next 4 dc, pc in next dc; 2 dc in ch-2 lp, dc in next dc; rep bet * of Rnd 6, except work 11 dc bet pc; end dc in last 6 st; join to top of beg ch-3.

Rnd 8: Ch 3, dc in next 7 st, pc in next st, 2 dc in ch-2 lp, dc in next dc; rep bet * of Rnd 6 working 17 dc bet pc; end dc in last 9 st; join to top of beg ch-3.

Rnd 9: Rep as established working 23 dc bet pc.

Rnd 10: Rep as established working 29 dc bet pc.

Rnd 11: Ch 1, sc in each st around, working 2 sc in each corner st; join to beg sc; fasten off.

ASSEMBLY: Using crochet cotton and with right sides facing, whipstitch motifs together into 18 rows, with 13 motifs in each row; whipstitch rows together. Working under both lps, sc evenly spaced around entire spread, working 3 sc in each corner.

DIAMOND POPCORN BEDSPREAD

Shown on page 49.

Bedspread measures approximately 80x100 inches without fringe.

MATERIALS

DMC Cebelia crochet cotton, Size 10 (50-gram ball): 72 balls of ecru or white
Size 8 steel crochet hook
Tapestry needle

Abbreviations: See page 186.
Gauge: Motif measures 5 inches along each side.

INSTRUCTIONS

MOTIF (make 320): Ch 8; join with sl st to form ring.

Rnd 1: **Ch 3, work 4 dc in ring, drop lp from hook, insert hook in top of ch-3 and draw the dropped lp through—beg popcorn (pc) made;** (ch 2, **work 5 dc in ring, drop lp from hook, insert hook in top of first dc of 5-dc grp and draw dropped lp through—pc made**) 7 times; ch 2, join with sl st to top of beg pc.

Rnd 2: Sl st in ch-2 sp, **ch 3, holding back last lp of each dc on hook, work 2 dc in same sp, yo, and draw through 3 lps on hook—beg cluster (cl) made;** ch 3, **holding back last lp of each dc on hook, work 3 dc in same sp, yo, and draw through 4 lps on hook—cl made;** * ch 2, in next sp work 3 dc, ch 2; ** in next sp work cl, ch 3, and cl—corner made; rep from * twice more; then rep from * to ** once; join last ch-2 with sl st to top of beg cl.

Note: In instructions that follow, "work corner" means to work cl, ch 3, and cl in ch-3 sp of corner.

Rnd 3: Sl st into ch-3 corner sp; in same sp work beg cl, ch 3, and cl; * ch 2, 2 dc in next sp, dc in next 3 dc, 2 dc in next sp, ch 2, ** work corner; rep from * twice more; then rep from * to ** once; join last ch-2 to top of beg cl.

Note: For rem 6 rnds, begin each rnd as follows: Sl st into ch-3 corner sp; in same sp work beg cl, ch 3, and cl. These directions will read "Beg rnd."

Rnd 4: Beg rnd, * ch 2, 2 dc in next sp, dc in next 7 dc, 2 dc in next sp, ch 2, ** work corner; rep from * twice more; then rep from * to ** once more; join last ch-2 to top of beg cl.

Rnd 5: Beg rnd, * ch 2, 2 dc in next sp, dc in next 5 dc, pc in next dc, dc in next 5 dc, 2 dc in next sp, ch 2, ** work corner; rep from * twice more; then rep from * to ** once more; join last ch-2 with sl st to top of beg cl.

Rnd 6: Beg rnd, * ch 2, 2 dc in next sp, dc in next 5 dc, pc in next dc, dc in next 3 st, pc in next st, dc in next 5 dc, 2 dc in next sp, ch 2, ** work corner; rep from * twice more; then rep from * to ** once more; join to top of beg cl.

Rnd 7: Beg rnd, * ch 2, 2 dc in next sp, dc in next 5 st, (pc in next st, dc in next 3 st) twice; pc in next st, dc in next 5 dc, 2 dc in next sp, ch 2, ** work corner; rep from * twice more; then rep from * to ** once more; join last ch-2 with sl st to top of beg cl.

Rnd 8: Beg rnd, * ch 2, 2 dc in next sp, dc in next 5 st, (pc in next st, dc in next 3 st) 3 times; pc in next st, dc in next 5 dc, 2 dc in next sp, ch 2, ** work corner; rep from * twice more; then rep from * to ** once more; join last ch-2 to top of beg cl.

Rnd 9: Beg rnd, * ch 2, 2 dc in next sp, dc in next 5 st, (pc in next st, dc in next 3 st) 4 times; pc in next st, dc in next 5 dc, 2 dc in next sp, ch 2, ** work corner; rep

from * twice more; then rep from * to ** once more; join last ch-2 to top of beg cl; fasten off.

ASSEMBLY: Using crochet cotton and with right sides facing, whipstitch motifs together into 20 rows, each row having 16 motifs; then whipstitch rows together.

EDGING: With right side of spread facing up, join thread in any corner st, ch 5, dc in same st; * ch 2, sk 2 st, dc in next st; rep from * to corner; in corner st work dc, ch 3, and dc; rep from first * around sides of spread; join last ch-2 into third ch of beg ch-5; fasten off. *Note:* Work dc in sides of dc-posts along sides of spread.

FRINGE: Wrap thread 8 times around 4-inch-wide cardboard; cut. Working from wrong side, insert hook in ch-2 sp of edging and pull lp of doubled fringe through, then pull ends of fringe through lp and tighten. Attach fringe in each ch-2 sp of two long sides and one short side.

POPCORN STAR BEDSPREAD

Shown on page 48.

Bedspread measures approximately 84x108, excluding fringe.

MATERIALS

DMC Brilliant crochet cotton (50-gram ball): 92 balls of white or ecru
Size 7 steel crochet hook or size to obtain gauge cited below
Tapestry needle

Abbreviations: See page 186.
Gauge: 8 dc = 1 inch; 4 rows = 1 inch; block measures 12 inches along *each* side.

INSTRUCTIONS

BLOCK MOTIF (make 63): Beg at center, ch 4, join with sl st to form ring.

Rnd 1: Ch 3, work 15 dc in ring; join with sl st to top of beg ch-3.

Rnd 2: Ch 3, **work 4 dc in same st as join; drop lp from hook, insert hook in top of ch-3 at beg of rnd, pull dropped lp through—beg popcorn (pc) made;** * ch 2, sk dc, **5 dc in next dc, drop lp from hook, insert hook in top of first dc of 5-dc grp, draw dropped lp through—pc made;** rep from * 6 times more; end ch 2, join with sl st to top of beg pc—8 pc made.

Rnd 3: Sl st into ch-2 sp, ch 3, work beg pc in same sp; (ch 3, pc in next ch-2 sp) 7 times; end ch 3, join with sl st to top of beg pc.

Rnd 4: Sl st into next sp, ch 3, in same sp work 6 dc; (7 dc in next sp) 7 times; join with sl st to top of beg ch-3—56 dc around.

Rnd 5: Ch 5, dc in same st as join; * ch 2, sk 3 dc, dc in next 7 dc, ch 2, ** sk 3 dc, in next dc work dc, ch 2, and dc—corner made; rep from * around; end last rep at **; join last ch-2 to third ch of beg ch-5.

Rnd 6: Sl st into ch-2 sp; ch 3, in same sp work dc, ch 2, and 2 dc; * ch 2, 2 dc in next ch-2 sp, dc in next 7 dc, 2 dc in ch-2 sp, ch 2; ** in corner sp work 2 dc, ch 2, and 2 dc; rep from * around; end last rep at **; join to top of beg ch-3.

Rnd 7: Sl st into next dc and into ch-2 sp; ch 3, in same sp work 2 dc, ch 2, and 3 dc; * ch 2, 2 dc in next ch-2 sp, dc in next 11 dc, 2 dc in ch-2 sp, ch 2, ** in corner ch-2 sp work 3 dc, ch 2, and 3 dc; rep from * around; end last rep at **; join last ch-2 to top of beg ch-3.

Rnd 8: Sl st into next 2 dc and into ch-2 sp; ch 3, in same sp work 3 dc, ch 2, and 4 dc; * ch 2, 2 dc in

continued

next ch-2 sp, dc in next 15 dc, 2 dc in ch-2 sp, ch 2; ** in corner sp work 4 dc, ch 2, and 4 dc; rep from * around; end last rep at **; join last ch-2 to top of beg ch-3.

Rnd 9: Sl st into next 3 dc and into ch-2 sp, ch 3, in same sp work 4 dc, ch 2, and 5 dc; * ch 2, 2 dc in next ch-2 sp, dc in next 8 dc, ch 2, sk 3 dc, dc in next 8 dc, 2 dc in ch-2 sp, ch 2; ** in corner sp work 5 dc, ch 2, and 5 dc; rep from * around; end last rep at **; join last ch-2 to top of beg ch-3.

Rnd 10: Sl st in next 2 dc, ch 3, dc in next 2 dc; in corner sp work 3 dc, ch 2, and 3 dc; * dc in next 3 dc, ch 2, 2 dc in next ch-2 sp, dc in next 8 dc, ch 2, sk 2 dc, pc in ch-2 sp, ch 2, sk 2 dc, dc in next 8 dc, 2 dc in next ch-2 sp, ch 2; ** sk 2 dc, dc in next 3 dc; in corner sp work 3 dc, ch 2, and 3 dc; rep from * around; end last rep at **; join last ch-2 to top of beg ch-3.

Note: In the instructions that follow, "work corner" always means to work 3 dc, ch 2, and 3 dc in the ch-3 corner space.

Rnd 11: Sl st into next 2 dc, ch 3, dc in next 3 dc; * work corner, dc in next 4 dc, ch 2, 2 dc in ch-2 sp, dc in next 8 dc; ch 2, sk 2 dc, (pc in next ch-2 sp, ch 2) twice; sk 2 dc, dc in next 8 dc, 2 dc in ch-2 sp, ch 2; ** sk 2 dc, dc in next 4 dc, rep from * around; end last rep at **; join last ch-2 to top of beg ch-3.

Rnd 12: Sl st into next 2 dc, ch 3, dc in next 4 dc; * work corner, dc in next 5 dc, ch 2, 2 dc in ch-2 lp, dc in next 8 dc, ch 2, (pc in next sp, ch 2) 3 times; sk next 2 dc, dc in next 8 dc, 2 dc in ch-2 lp, ch 2, ** sk 2 dc, dc in next 5 dc; rep from * around; end last rep at **; join to top of beg ch-3.

Rnd 13: Sl st into next 2 dc, ch 3, dc in next 5 dc; * work corner, dc in next 6 dc, ch 2, 2 dc in ch-2 lp, dc in next 8 dc, ch 2, (pc in next ch-2 sp, ch 2) 4 times; sk next

2 dc, dc in next 8 dc, 2 dc in ch-2 lp, ch 2, ** sk 2 dc, dc in next 6 dc; rep from * around; end last rep at **; join to top of beg ch-3.

Rnd 14: Sl st into next 2 dc, ch 3, dc in next 6 dc; * work corner, dc in next 7 dc; ch 2, 4 dc in ch-2 lp, ch 2, sk 2 dc, dc in next 8 dc; 2 dc in ch-2 lp, ch 2, (pc in next sp, ch 2) 3 times; 2 dc in ch-2 sp, dc in next 8 dc; ch 2, 4 dc in ch-2 sp, ch 2, ** sk 2 dc, dc in next 7 dc; rep from * around; end last rep at **; join to top of beg ch-3.

Rnd 15: Sl st into next 2 dc, ch 3, dc in next 7 dc; * in corner work 4 dc, ch 2, and 4 dc; dc in next 8 dc; (ch 2, 2 dc in next ch-2 sp) twice; ch 2, sk 2 dc, dc in next 8 dc, 2 dc in ch-2 lp, ch 2, (pc in next sp, ch 2) twice; 2 dc in ch-2 sp, dc in next 8 dc; (ch 2, 2 dc in next ch-2 sp) twice; ch 2, sk 2 dc, ** dc in next 8 dc; rep from * around; end last rep at **; join to top of beg ch-3.

Rnd 16: Ch 3, dc in next 5 dc, * ch 2, sk 2 dc, dc in next 4 dc; work corner; dc in next 4 dc, ch 2, sk 2 dc, dc in next 6 dc; 2 dc in ch-2 sp, ch 2, 4 dc in next ch-2 sp, ch 5, sk 4 dc, dc in next 8 dc; 2 dc in ch-2 sp, ch 2, pc in next sp, ch 2, 2 dc in ch-2 lp, dc in next 8 dc; ch 5, sk 4 dc, 4 dc in next ch-2 sp, ch 2, 2 dc in next ch-2 sp, ** dc in next 6 dc; rep from * around; end last rep at **; join to top of beg ch-3.

Rnd 17: Ch 3, dc in next 3 dc, ch 5, sc in ch-2 sp, * ch 5, sk 2 dc, dc in next 5 dc, work corner; dc in next 5 dc, ch 5, sc in ch-2 sp, ch 5, sk 2 dc, dc in next 4 dc, ch 2, 4 dc in next ch-2 sp; ch 2, sk 3 dc, dc in next dc, 3 dc in ch-5 lp, ch 5, sk 2 dc, dc in next 8 dc, 2 dc in ch-2 lp, ch 2, 2 dc in next ch-2 lp, dc in 8 dc, ch 5, 3 dc at end of next ch-5 lp, dc in next dc, ch 2, sk 3 dc, 4 dc in next ch-2 sp, ch 2, ** sk 2 dc, dc

in next 4 dc, ch 5, sc in ch-2 lp; rep from * around; end last rep at **; join to top of beg ch-3.

Rnd 18: Sl st into next 3 dc, ch 3, * 3 dc in ch-5 lp, ch 2, 2 dc at end of next ch-5 lp, dc in next 8 dc, in corner work 2 dc, ch 2, and 2 dc; dc in next 8 dc, 2 dc in ch-5 lp, ch 2, 3 dc at end of next ch-5 lp, dc in next dc, ch 2, 2 dc in next ch-2 lp, ch 2; 4 dc in next ch-2 lp; ch 2, 2 dc in next ch-5 lp, ch 5, sk 2 dc, dc in next 8 dc, 3 dc in ch-2 lp, dc in next 8 dc, ch 5, 2 dc at end of next ch-5 lp, ch 2; 2 dc, ch 1, and 2 dc in ch-2 lp; ch 2, 2 dc in next ch-2 lp, ch 2, sk 3 dc, ** dc in next dc; rep from * around; end last rep at **; join to top of beg ch-3.

Rnd 19: Sl st into next 2 dc, ch 3, dc in next dc, 2 dc in ch-2 sp, * dc in next 4 dc, ch 2, sk 2 dc, dc in next 6 dc, work corner, dc in next 6 dc, ch 2, sk 2 dc, dc in next 4 dc, 2 dc in ch-2 lp, dc in next 2 dc, (ch 5, sk 4 dc, 4 dc in next ch-2 lp) twice; ch 5, sk 4 dc, dc in next 15 dc, (ch 5, sk 4 dc, 4 dc in next ch-2 sp) twice; ch 5, sk 4 dc, ** dc in next 2 dc, 2 dc in ch-2 sp; rep from * around; end last rep at **; join to top of beg ch-3.

Rnd 20: Sl st into next 2 dc, ch 3, dc in next 3 dc, * ch 5, sc in ch-2 lp, ch 5, sk 2 dc, dc in next 7 dc; in corner work 2 dc, ch 2, and 2 dc; dc in next 7 dc, ch 5, sc in ch-2 lp, ch 5, sk 2 dc, dc in next 4 dc; (ch 5, 4 dc in next ch-5 lp) 3 times; ch 5, sk 2 dc, dc in next 11 dc; (ch 5, 4 dc in next ch-5 lp) 3 times; ch 5, sk 2 dc, ** dc in next 4 dc; rep from * around; end last rep at **; join to top of beg ch-3.

Rnd 21: Sl st into next 3 dc, ch 3, 3 dc in next ch-5 lp; * ch 2, 2 dc at end of next ch-5 lp, dc in next 9 dc, work corner, dc in next 9 dc, 2 dc in ch-5 lp, ch 2, 3 dc at end of next ch-5 lp, dc in next dc, ch 2, 2 dc at end of next ch-5 lp; (ch 2, in next ch-5 lp work 2 dc, ch 2, and 2 dc) twice; ch 2, 2 dc in next ch-5 lp, ch 2, sk 2 dc, dc in next 7 dc, ch 2, 2 dc in next ch-5 lp; (ch 2, in next ch-5 lp work 2 dc, ch 2, and 2 dc) twice; ch 2, 2 dc in next ch-5 lp, ch 2, sk 3 dc, ** dc in next dc, 3 dc in next ch-5 lp; rep from * around; end last rep at **; join to top of beg ch-3; fasten off.

ASSEMBLY: With right sides facing and using crochet thread, whipstitch motifs together into nine rows, each row with seven motifs; whipstitch rows together. Join thread and work sc in each st across the top of the spread (one short side). Then work as follows around the remaining three sides: * sc in next 3 st, ch 3, sk 3 st; rep from * around; join to beg sc.

FRINGE: Wrap thread around 4-inch-wide strip of cardboard 12 times; cut. Knot fringe in each ch-3 lp along three sides.

SPIDERWEB POPCORN BEDSPREAD

Shown on page 51.

Bedspread measures approximately 70x98 inches, excluding fringe. Any size spread can be made by adjusting number of blocks to fit bed.

MATERIALS

Coats & Clark South Maid crochet cotton, Size 10 (400-yard ball): 38 balls (one ball makes one block)
Size 6 steel crochet hook or size to obtain gauge cited below
Tapestry needle

Abbreviations: See page 186.
Gauge: Each block measures 14 inches square.

INSTRUCTIONS

BLOCK (make 35): Ch 7, join with sl st to form ring.

Rnd 1: Ch 3, 2 dc in ring, (ch 3—for corner; 3 dc in ring) 3 times; ch 3, join with sl st to top of beg ch-3.

Note: Hereafter, work all st in back lps.

Rnd 2: Ch 3, dc in next 2 dc; * in ch-3 corner sp work 2 dc, ch 3, and 2 dc—corner made; ** dc in next 3 dc; rep from * around; end last rep at **; join with sl st to top of beg ch-3.

Rnd 3: Ch 3, dc in next 4 dc, * in ch-3 corner sp work 2 dc, ch 3, and 2 dc, ** dc in next 7 dc; rep from * around; end last rep at **; dc in last 2 dc; join with sl st to top of beg ch-3.

Note: In all subsequent rnds, when instructions read "work corner," work 2 dc, ch 3, and 2 dc in the corner ch-3 sp.

Rnd 4: Ch 3, **work 5 dc in next dc, drop hook from work, insert hook in first dc of 5-dc grp and draw the dropped lp through—popcorn (pc) made;** * dc in next 5 dc, work corner; ** dc in next 5 dc; pc in next dc, rep from * around; end last rep at **; then dc in last 4 dc; join to beg ch-3.

Rnd 5: Ch 3, dc in next 2 st, pc in next st, dc in next 5 dc; * work corner, dc in next 5 dc, pc in next st, ** dc in next 3 st, pc in next st, dc in next 5 dc; rep from * around; end last rep at **; join to top of beg ch-3.

Rnd 6: Ch 3, pc in next st, dc in next 3 st, pc in next st, dc in next 5 dc; * work corner, dc in next 5 dc, ** (pc in next st, dc in next 3 st) twice; pc in next st, dc in next 5 dc; rep from * around; end last rep at **; then pc in next st, dc in next 2 st; join to top of beg ch-3.

Rnd 7: Ch 3, dc in next 2 st, pc in next st, dc in next 3 st, pc in next st, dc in next 5 dc; * work corner, dc in next 5 dc, ** (pc in next st, dc in next 3 st) 3 times, pc in next st, dc in next 5 sts; rep from * around; end last rep at **; then pc in next st, dc in next 3 st, pc in next st; join as before.

Rnd 8: Ch 3, pc in next st, dc in next 3 st, pc in next st, dc in next 7 dc, * ch 13, dc in next 2 dc; work corner, dc in next 2 dc, ch 13, dc in next 7 st, ** (pc in next st, dc in next 3 sts) twice; pc in next st, dc in next 7 st; rep from * around; end last rep at **; then pc in next st, dc in last 2 st; join.

Rnd 9: Ch 3, dc in next 2 st, pc in next st, dc in next 7 dc; * ch 4, sk 5 ch of ch-13 lp, sc in next 3 ch, ch 4, sk 2 dc, dc in next 2 dc; work corner, dc in next 2 dc, ch 4, sk 5 ch of ch-13 lp, sc in next 3 ch, ch 4, sk 2 dc, dc in next 7 st; pc in next st, ** dc in next 3 st, pc in next st, dc in next 7 st; rep from * around; end last rep at **; join.

Rnd 10: Ch 3, pc in next st, dc in next 7 st, * (ch 4, sc in fourth ch of ch-4 lp, sc in next 3 sc, sc in next ch, ch 4, sk 2 dc), dc in next 2 dc; work corner, dc in next 2 dc, rep bet ( )s once; ** dc in next 7 st, pc in next st, dc in next 7 st; rep from * around; end last rep at **; then dc in last 6 st; join.

Rnd 11: Ch 3, dc in next 6 st, * (ch 4, sc in fourth ch of ch-4 sp, sc in next 5 sc, sc in next ch, ch 4, sk 2 dc); dc in next 2 dc, work corner, dc in next 2 dc, rep bet ( )s once; ** dc in next 11 st; rep from * around; end last rep at **; then dc in last 4 dc; join.

Rnd 12: Ch 3, dc in next 4 st, * (ch 4, sc in fourth ch of ch 4 sp, sc in next 7 sc, sc in next ch, ch 4, sk 2 dc), dc in next 2 dc, work corner, dc in next 2 dc, rep bet ( )s once; ** dc in next 7 dc; rep from * around; end last rep at **; then dc in last 2 dc; join.

continued

Rnd 13: Ch 3, dc in next 3 dc, * (ch 5, sc in fourth ch of ch-4, sc in next 9 sc, sc in next ch, ch 5, sk 2 dc); dc in next 2 dc, ** work corner, dc in next 2 dc, rep bet ( )s once; dc in next 4 dc; rep from * around; end last rep at **; join.

Rnd 14: Ch 3, dc in next dc, * ch 13, dc in next 2 dc, dc in next 2 ch, ch 5, sk sc, sc in 9 sc, ch 5, sk next 3 ch, dc in next 2 ch, dc in next 2 dc; ch 13, dc in next 2 dc, work corner; dc in next 2 dc; ch 13, dc in next 2 dc, dc in next 2 ch, ch 5, sk sc, sc in 9 sc, ch 5, sk next 3 ch, dc in next 2 ch, dc in next 2 dc; rep from * around; end dc in last 2 ch; join; fasten off.

Rnd 15: Join thread in any corner sp, ch 3, in same sp work dc, ch 3, and 2 dc; * (dc in next 2 dc, ch 4, sk first 5 ch of ch-13 lp, sc in next 3 ch, ch 4, sk 2 dc, dc in next 2 dc, dc in next 2 ch, ch 5, sk sc, sc in 7 sc, ch 5, sk 3 ch, dc in next 2 ch) twice; dc in next 2 dc, ch 4, sk first 5 ch of ch-13 lp, sc in next 3 ch, ch 4, sk 2 dc, dc in next 2 dc; ** work corner; rep from * around; end last rep at **; join.

Rnd 16: Ch 3, dc in next dc, work corner; * (dc in 2 dc, ch 4, sk 3 ch, sc in next ch, sc in 3 sc, sc in next ch, ch 4, sk 2 dc, dc in next 2 dc, dc in 2 ch, ch 5, sk sc, sc in 5 sc, ch 5, sk 3 ch, dc in next 2 ch) twice; dc in next 2 dc, ch 4, sk 3 ch, sc in next ch, sc in 3 sc, sc in next ch, ch 4, ** sk 2 dc, dc in next 2 dc; work corner; rep from * around; end last rep at **; join.

Rnd 17: Sl st in next 2 dc, ch 3, dc in next dc, work corner; * (dc in 2 dc, ch 4, sk 3 ch, sc in next ch, sc in 5 sc, sc in next ch, ch 4, sk 2 dc, dc in next 2 dc, dc in 2 ch, ch 5, sk sc, sc in 3 sc, ch 5, sk 3 ch, dc in next 2 ch) twice; dc in next 2 dc, ch 4, sk 3 ch, sc in next ch, sc in 5 sc, sc in next ch, ch 4, ** sk 2 dc, dc in next 2 dc; work corner; rep from * around; end last rep at **; join to top of beg ch-3.

Rnd 18: Sl st in next 2 dc, ch 3, dc in next dc, work corner; * (dc in 2 dc, ch 4, sk 3 ch, sc in next ch, sc in 7 sc, sc in next ch, ch 4, sk 2 dc, dc in next 2 dc, dc in 2 ch, dc in last 2 ch of next ch-5 lp) twice; dc in 2 dc, ch 4, sk 3 ch, sc in next ch, sc in 7 sc, sc in next ch, ch 4, ** sk 2 dc, dc in next 2 dc, work corner, rep from * around; end last rep at **; join.

Rnd 19: Sl st in next 2 dc, ch 3, dc in next dc, work corner; dc in 2 dc, * ch 5, sk 3 ch, sc in next ch, sc in 9 sc, sc in next ch, ch 5, sk 2 dc, dc in next 4 dc; ch 5, sk 3 ch, sc in next ch, sc in 9 sc, sc in next ch, ch 5, sk 2 dc, dc in next 4 dc; ch 5, sk 3 ch, sc in next ch, sc in 9 sc, sc in next ch, ch 5, ** sk 2 dc, dc in next 2 dc, work corner; rep from * around; end last rep at **; join.

Rnd 20: Sl st in next 2 dc, ch 3, dc in next dc, work corner; * (dc in 2 dc, ch 13, dc in next 2 dc, dc in 2 ch, ch 5, sk sc, sc in 9 sc, ch 5, sk 3 ch, dc in next 2 ch) 3 times; dc in 2 dc, ch 13, ** dc in next 2 dc; work corner; rep from * around; end last rep at **; join.

Rnd 21: Sl st in next 2 dc, ch 3, dc in next dc, work corner; * (dc in 2 dc, ch 4, sk 5 ch, sc in next 3 ch, ch 4, sk 2 dc, dc in next 2 dc, dc in next 2 ch, ch 5, sk sc, sc in 7 sc, ch 5, sk 3 ch, dc in next 2 ch) three times; dc in next 2 dc, ch 4, sk 5 ch, sc in next 3 ch, ch 4, ** sk 2 dc, dc in next 2 dc; work corner; rep from * around; end last rep at **; join.

Rnds 22–24: Work in spider-web pattern as established (refer to rnds 16–18); fasten off at end of Rnd 24. Always sl st over 2 dc, ch 3, dc in next dc to begin each rnd; end each rnd with ch 4 and join to top of beg ch-3.

ASSEMBLY: With right sides facing, using a single strand of crochet thread, and sewing through the back lps, whipstitch the blocks together into seven rows, each row with five blocks. Whipstitch rows together. Join thread at any corner, ch 5, sc in same st, * ch 5, sk 3 st, sc in next st; rep from * around, working sc, ch 5, and sc in each corner st; fasten off.

FRINGE: Wrap thread around a 5-inch strip of cardboard. In bundles of eight, knot the fringe in the ch-5 lps on three sides (two long and one short).

PILLOWCASE AND SHEET EDGINGS

Shown on page 50.

Both edgings measure 2 inches wide.

MATERIALS

Clark's Big Ball 3-cord mercerized crochet cotton, Size 20 (300-yard ball): 3 balls ecru will make edging for one pair of cases and one sheet
Size 9 steel crochet hook or size to reach gauge cited below

Abbreviations: See page 186.
Gauge: 13 dc = 1 inch; 6 dc rows = 1 inch.

INSTRUCTIONS
For the pillowcase edging
Note: This edging is worked in an 11-row pattern repeat for the desired length. When the length is completed, a second edging is added to the strip only along one side to complete the outside edge.

Row 1: Ch 26, dc in eighth ch from hook and in next 6 ch, ch 4, sk 4 ch, dc in next 3 ch; ch 1, sk ch, dc in last 4 ch; ch 3, turn.

Row 2: Sk first dc, dc in next 3 dc, ch 1, dc in next dc; ch 1, sk dc, dc in next dc, 2 dc in ch-4 lp, ch 5, sk 2 dc, dc in next 5 dc, ch 2, sk next 2 ch; dc in next ch; ch 5, turn.

Row 3: Sk first dc, dc in next 3 dc, ch 5, 2 dc in ch-5 lp, dc in next dc, ch 1, sk dc, dc in next dc; (ch 1, dc in next dc) 2 times; dc in 2 dc and in top of ch-3; ch 3, turn.

Row 4: Sk first dc, dc in next 3 dc; (ch 1, dc in next dc) 3 times; ch 1, sk dc, dc in next dc, 2 dc in ch-5 lp, ch 6, sk 2 dc, dc in next dc; ch 2, sk 2 ch, dc in next ch; ch 5, turn.

Row 5: Sk first dc, dc in next dc, ch 4, 2 dc in ch-6 lp, dc in next dc, ch 1, sk dc, dc in next dc; (ch 1, dc in next dc) 4 times, dc in last 2 dc and in top of ch-3; ch 3, turn.

Row 6: Sk first dc, dc in next 3 dc; (ch 1, dc in next dc) 5 times; dc in next 2 dc, ch 4, dc in next dc, ch 2, sk 2 ch, dc in next ch; ch 5, turn.

Row 7: Sk first dc, dc in next dc, ch 6, sk 2 dc, dc in next dc, dc in ch-1 sp; (dc in next dc, ch 1) 4 times; dc in last 3 dc and in top of ch-3; ch 3, turn.

Row 8: Sk first dc, dc in next 3 dc; (ch 1, dc in next dc) 3 times; dc in sp, dc in next dc, ch 5, 2 dc in ch-6 lp, dc in next dc, ch 2, sk 2 ch, dc in next ch; ch 5, turn.

Row 9: Sk first dc, dc in next 3 dc, 2 dc in ch-5 lp, ch 5, sk 2 dc, dc in next dc, dc in sp; (dc in next dc, ch 1) twice; dc in last 3 dc and in top of ch-3; ch 3, turn.

Row 10: Sk first dc, dc in next 3 dc, ch 1, dc in dc, dc in sp, dc in next dc, ch 4, 2 dc in ch-5 lp, dc in next 5 dc, ch 2, sk 2 ch, dc in next ch; ch 5, turn.

Row 11: Sk first dc, dc in next 7 dc, ch 4, dc in next 3 dc, ch 1, dc in last 3 dc and in top of ch-3; ch 3, turn.

Rep rows 2–11 until work is length of pillowcase edge plus 4 or 5 inches to allow for thread shrinkage; end with Row 10; ch 3, turn at end of Row 10.

EDGING: *Row 1:* Dc in first sp on side, dc in end of row, dc in next sp, dc in end of next row; * ch 3, sk 2 sps, dc in end of next row; (dc in sp, dc in end of next row) twice; ch 3, sk 2 sps, dc in end of next row; (dc in sp, dc in end of next row) 4 times; rep from * along edge to within 4 sps of other end; ch 3, sk 2 sps, (dc in end of next row, dc in sp) twice, dc in center st of end ch-5; ch 3, turn.

Row 2: Sk first dc, dc in next 2 dc; * ch 3, sk 2 dc, 2 dc over ch-3 lp, dc in next dc; (ch 1, sk dc, dc in next dc) twice; 2 dc over ch-3 lp, ch 3, sk 2 dc, dc in next 5 dc; rep from * across, end last rep with dc in last 2 dc and in top of ch-3; ch 6, turn.

Row 3: Sk first 3 dc, * 2 dc over ch-3 lp, dc in next dc, ch 1, sk 2 dc; in next dc work (dc, ch 1) 5 times; sk 2 dc, dc in next dc, 2 dc over ch-3 lp, ch 3, sk 2 dc, dc in next dc, ch 3; rep from * across; end with dc in top of ch-3; ch 4, turn.

Row 4: * Work 2 dc over next ch-3 lp, dc in next dc, sk 2 dc, (ch 2, trc in next dc) 5 times; ch 2, sk 2 dc, dc in next dc, 2 dc over ch-3 lp, ch 3; rep from * across; end last repeat with ch 1, dc in fourth ch of ch-6; ch 3, turn.

Row 5: Dc in ch-1 sp, * dc in next dc, (in next trc make dc; **ch 4, sl st in third ch from hook—picot made,** ch 1, dc in same trc) 5 times; sk 2 dc, dc in next dc; in ch-3 sp make 2 dc, ch 3, sl st in top of last dc made, work 2 dc in same sp; rep from * across; end with dc in last dc and 2 dc in end sp; fasten off.

FINISHING: Whipstitch ends of edging together with double strand of sewing thread, matching pattern. Wash and press edging. Sew to lower edge of pillowcase by hand or machine.

For the sheet edging

Row 1: Ch 34, dc in sixth ch from hook and in next 2 ch, ch 4, sk 4 ch, dc in next 13 ch, ch 4, sk 4 ch, dc in next 3 ch, ch 1, sk ch, dc in last ch; ch 4, turn.

Row 2: Sk first dc, dc in next dc, ch 1, sk dc, dc in next dc, 2 dc over ch-4 lp, ch 5, sk 2 dc, dc in 9 dc, ch 5, sk 2 dc, 2 dc over ch-4 lp, dc in next dc, ch 1, sk dc, dc in next dc, ch 1, sk ch, dc in next ch; ch 4, turn.

Row 3: Sk first dc, (dc in next dc, ch 1) twice; sk dc, dc in next dc, 2 dc over ch-5 lp, ch 5, sk 2 dc, dc in 5 dc, ch 5, sk 2 dc, 2 dc over ch-5 lp, dc in next dc, ch 1, sk dc; (dc in next dc, ch 1) twice; sk ch, dc in next ch; ch 4, turn.

Row 4: (Dc in next dc, ch 1) 3 times; sk dc, dc in next dc, 2 dc over ch-5 lp, ch 6, sk 2 dc, dc in center dc, ch 6, sk 2 dc, 2 dc over ch-5 lp, dc in next dc, ch 1, sk dc; (dc in next dc, ch 1) 3 times; sk ch, dc in next ch; ch 4, turn.

Row 5: (Dc in next dc, ch 1) 4 times; sk dc, dc in next dc, 2 dc over ch-6 lp, ch 4, dc in next dc, ch 4, 2 dc over next ch-6 lp, dc in next dc, ch 1, sk dc; (dc in next dc, ch 1) 4 times; sk ch, dc in next ch; ch 4, turn.

Row 6: (Dc in next dc, ch 1) 4 times; dc in next 3 dc, ch 4, dc in next dc, ch 4, dc in next 3 dc; (ch 1, dc in next dc) 4 times; ch 1, sk ch, dc in next ch; ch 4, turn.

Row 7: (Dc in next dc, ch 1) 3 times, dc in next dc, dc in ch-1 sp, dc in next dc, ch 6, sk 2 dc, dc in next dc, ch 6, sk 2 dc, dc in next dc, dc in ch-1 sp; (dc in next dc, ch 1) 4 times; sk ch, dc in next ch; ch 4, turn.

Row 8: (Dc in next dc, ch 1) twice, dc in next dc, dc in ch-1 sp, dc in next dc, ch 5, sk 2 dc, 2 dc over ch-6 lp, dc in next dc, 2 dc over next ch-6 lp, ch 5, sk 2 dc, dc in dc, dc in ch-1 sp; (dc in next dc,
continued

ch 1) 3 times; sk ch, dc in next ch; ch 4, turn.

Row 9: Dc in next dc, ch 1, dc in next dc, dc in ch-1 sp, dc in next dc, ch 5, 2 dc over ch-5 lp, dc in 5 dc, 2 dc over next ch-5 lp, ch 5, sk 2 dc, dc in next dc, dc in ch-1 sp; (dc in next dc, ch 1) twice; sk ch, dc in next ch; ch 4, turn.

Row 10: Dc in next dc, dc in ch-1 sp, dc in next dc, ch 4, 2 dc over ch-5 lp, dc in 9 dc, 2 dc over ch-5 lp, ch 4, sk 2 dc, dc in next dc, dc in ch-1 sp, dc in next dc, ch 1, sk ch, dc in next ch; ch 4, turn.

Row 11: Dc in next 3 dc, ch 4, dc in 13 dc, ch 4, dc in 3 dc, ch 1, sk ch, dc in next ch; ch 4, turn.

Rep rows 2–11 until work is required length, ending with Row 10. Do not make ch-4 at end of last row, but turn and work along length of trim as follows: Make sc in corner of last row just made. Working in sps along side; * work hdc and dc in first sp, dc in end of row, make dc and hdc in next sp, sc in end of next row; rep from * along side, making sc in corner at other end. Work sc evenly across short side, sc in next corner and work in sps along opposite long side in same way as before; fasten off. Wash and press crochet. Sew edging across top hem of sheet by hand or machine.

FIVE–PANEL FILET BEDSPREAD

Shown on pages 52 and 53.

Bedspread measures approximately 80x84 inches.

MATERIALS

DMC Brilliant knitting and crochet cotton (50-gram ball): 68 balls of ecru or white
Size 8 steel crochet hook
Tapestry needle

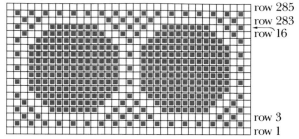

Center Panel (make 1)

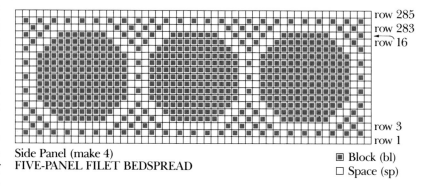

Side Panel (make 4)
FIVE-PANEL FILET BEDSPREAD

■ Block (bl)
□ Space (sp)

Abbreviations: See page 186.
Gauge: 8 dc = 1 inch; 5 rows = 1 inch.

INSTRUCTIONS

SIDE PANEL (make 4): Beg along bottom edge, ch 158.

Row 1: Dc in eighth ch from hook; * ch 2, sk 2 ch, dc in next ch; rep from * across—51 sps made; ch 5, turn.

Row 2: Sk first dc, dc in next dc, *** 2 dc in ch-2 sp, dc in next dc— bl made;** ch 2, dc in next dc; rep from * across; end ch 2, sk next 2 ch, dc in next ch—26 sps and 25 bls made; ch 5, turn.

Row 3: Sk first dc, dc in next dc; (ch 2, sk 2 dc, dc in next dc; 2 dc in ch-2 sp, dc in next dc) twice; * (ch 2, sk 2 dc, dc in next dc, ch 2, dc in next dc) 4 times; (ch 2, sk 2 dc, dc in next dc, 2 dc in ch-2 sp, dc in next dc) 4 times; rep from * 3 times more; at end of third rep work between the last set of ( )s twice instead of 4 times; then ch 2, sk 2 dc, dc in next dc, ch 2, sk 2 ch of turning ch, dc in next ch; ch 5, turn.

Rows 4–16: Work from Side Panel chart, *above.* Then rep rows 3–16 nineteen times more—282 rows completed. Work rows 283–285; fasten off.

CENTER PANEL (make 1): Ch 110.

Row 1: Dc in eighth ch from hook; * ch 2, sk 2 ch, dc in next ch; rep from * across—35 sps made.

Rows 2–16: Work from Center Panel chart, *above.* Then rep rows 3–16 nineteen times more. Work rows 283–285; fasten off.

ASSEMBLY: With right sides facing and using crochet thread, whipstitch two side panels together; repeat for the other two panels. Sew center panel between the large side panels.

EDGING: *Rnd 1:* Join thread in any corner sp, ch 3, in same sp work 6 dc; * in next sp work 2 dc, dc in next dc; rep from * around working 7 dc in each corner; join to top of beg ch-3.

Rnd 2: Sc to center st of corner, **ch 5, sl st in fifth ch from hook—picot made;** sc in next 3 st, work picot; * sc in next 6 st, work picot; rep from * around, working picot in center of each corner; fasten off.

DUST RUFFLE EDGING

Shown on pages 52 and 53.

Edging measures approximately 4¼ inches wide.

MATERIALS

Clark's Big Ball crochet thread, Size 30 (350-yard ball): 1 ball makes 21 inches of edging
Size 12 steel crochet hook or size to obtain gauge cited below

Abbreviations: See page 186.
Gauge: 5 dc spaces = 1 inch; 5 dc rows = 1 inch.

INSTRUCTIONS

Beg along narrow edge, ch 70.

Row 1: Dc in eighth ch from hook, (ch 2, sk 2 ch, dc in next ch) 6 times; dc in next 3 ch, ch 6, sk 3 ch, sc in next 28 ch, ch 6, sk 3 ch, dc in next 4 ch, ch 2, sk 2 ch, dc in next ch; ch 5, turn.

Row 2: Sk first dc, dc in next dc, ch 2, sk 2 dc, dc in next dc, 3 dc in ch-6 lp, ch 6, sk 3 sc, sc in next 22 sc, ch 6, 3 dc in ch-6 lp, dc in next dc, ch 13, sk 2 dc, dc in next dc, 2 dc in ch-2 lp, dc in next dc, (ch 2, dc in next dc) 5 times; ch 2, sk 2 ch, dc in next ch; ch 5, turn.

Row 3: Sk first dc, dc in next dc; (ch 2, dc in next dc) 4 times; 2 dc in ch-2 sp, dc in next dc, ch 6, 4 sc in ch-13 lp, ch 6, sk 3 dc, dc in next dc, 3 dc in ch-6 lp, ch 6, sk 3 sc, sc in 16 sc, ch 6, 3 dc in ch-6 lp, dc in next dc, ch 2, sk 2 dc, dc in next dc, ch 2, dc in next dc, ch 2, sk 2 ch, dc in next ch; ch 5, turn.

Note: Hereafter, end all rows with "ch 2, sk 2 ch, dc in next ch; ch 5, turn."

Row 4: Sk first dc, dc in next dc; (ch 2, dc in next dc) twice; ch 2, sk 2 dc, dc in next dc, 3 dc in ch-6 lp, ch 6, sk 3 sc, sc in next 10 sc, ch 6, 3 dc in next ch-6 lp, dc in next dc, ch 6, 3 sc in ch-6 lp, sc in 4 sc, 3 sc in ch-6 lp, ch 6, sk 3 dc, dc in next dc, 2 dc in ch-lp, dc in next dc; (ch 2, dc in next dc) 3 times; end row.

Row 5: Sk first dc, dc in next dc; (ch 2, dc in next dc) twice; 2 dc in ch-lp, dc in next dc, ch 6, 3 sc in ch-6 lp, sc in next 10 sc, 3 sc over ch-6 lp, ch 6, sk 3 dc, dc in next dc, 3 dc in ch-6 lp, ch 6, sk 3 sc, sc in 4 sc, ch 6, 3 dc in ch-6 lp, dc in next dc, ch 2, sk 2 dc, dc in next dc; (ch 2, dc in next dc) 3 times; end row.

Row 6: Sk first dc, dc in next dc, (ch 2, dc in next dc) 4 times; ch 2, sk 2 dc, dc in next dc, 3 dc in ch-6 lp, ch 2, 3 dc in next ch-6 lp, dc in next dc, ch 6, 3 sc over ch-6 lp, sc in next 16 sc, 3 sc in ch-6 lp, ch 6, sk 3 dc, dc in next dc, 2 dc in ch-2 lp, dc in next dc, ch 2, dc in next dc; end row.

Row 7: Sk first dc, dc in next dc, 2 dc in ch-lp, dc in next dc, ch 6, 3 sc in ch-6 lp, sc in 22 sc, 3 sc in ch-6 lp, ch 6, sk 3 dc, dc in next dc, 2 dc in ch-lp, dc in next dc, ch 2, sk 2 dc, dc in next dc; (ch 2, dc in next dc) 5 times; end row.

Row 8: Sk first dc, dc in next dc; (ch 2, dc in next dc) 5 times; 2 dc in ch-lp; dc in next dc; ch 13, sk 2 dc, dc in next dc, 3 dc in ch-6 lp, ch 6, sk 3 sc, sc in 22 sc, ch 6, 3 dc in ch-6 lp, dc in next dc, ch 2, sk 2 dc, dc in next dc; end row.

Row 9: Sk first dc, dc in next dc, ch 2, dc in next dc, ch 2, sk 2 dc, dc in next dc, 3 dc in ch-6 lp, ch 6, sk 3 sc, sc in 16 sc, ch 6, 3 dc in ch-6 lp, dc in next dc, ch 6, 4 sc in ch-13 lp, ch 6, sk 3 dc, dc in next dc, 2 dc in ch-lp, dc in next dc; (ch 2, dc in next dc) 4 times; end row.

Row 10: Sk first dc, dc in next dc, (ch 2, dc in next dc) 3 times; 2 dc in ch-lp, dc in next dc, ch 6, 3 sc in ch-6 lp, sc in 4 sc, 3 sc in ch-6 lp, ch 6, sk 3 dc, dc in next dc, 3 dc in ch-6 lp, ch 6, sk 3 sc, sc in 10 sc, ch 6, 3 dc in ch-6 lp, dc in next dc, ch 2, sk 2 dc, dc in next dc; (ch 2, dc in next dc) twice; end row.

Row 11: Sk first dc, dc in next dc, (ch 2, dc in next dc) 3 times; ch 2, sk 2 dc, dc in next dc, 3 dc in ch-6 lp, ch 6, sk 3 sc, sc in 4 sc, ch 6, 3 dc in ch-6 lp, dc in next dc, ch 6, 3 sc in ch-6 lp, sc in 10 sc, 3 sc in ch-6 lp, ch 6, sk 3 dc, dc in next dc, 2 dc in ch-lp, dc in next dc; (ch 2, dc in next dc) twice; end row.

Row 12: Sk first dc, dc in next dc, ch 2, dc in next dc, 2 dc in ch-lp, dc in next dc, ch 6, 3 sc in ch-6 lp, sc in 16 sc, 3 sc in ch-6 lp, ch 6, sk 3 dc, dc in next dc, 3 dc in ch-6 lp, ch 2, 3 dc in next ch-6 lp, dc in next dc; ch 2, sk 2 dc, dc in next dc, (ch 2, dc in next dc) 4 times; end row.

Row 13: Sk first dc, dc in next dc; (ch 2, dc in next dc) 5 times; ch 2, sk 2 dc, dc in next dc, 2 dc in ch-lp, dc in next dc, ch 6, 3 sc in ch-6 lp, sc in 22 sc, 3 sc in ch-6 lp, ch 6, sk 3 dc, dc in next dc, 2 dc in ch-lp, dc in next dc; end row.

Rep rows 2–13 for pattern for desired length; fasten off. Wash edging in hot water prior to inserting it into dust ruffle fabric. Hand- or machine-sew edging to fabric 3 inches from finished hemline. Then cut away fabric from behind the lace, leaving sufficient fabric (½ inch) along cut ends to turn back and hem in place.

Tabletop Treasures

A FEAST
OF ELEGANCE

❦

Lace-adorned tables abounded in the Victorian home, and—large or small—they offered the mistress of the house places to display her artistry. Atop cloths and doilies of intricate design, she arranged ever-changing still lifes out of the materials at hand, whether they were the ephemeral elements of an afternoon tea or an heirloom collection of objets d'art.

Like many favorite 19th-century crochet designs, the pattern block for the lovely Star Snowflake Runner at *left* was adapted from a traditional patchwork motif, the eight-pointed LeMoyne Star. The border is worked in filet crochet.

Expressions of unabashed sentimentality filled the Valentine's Day greetings of Victorian gentlemen and were often accompanied by flowers or candy.

Treasured mementos deserve a proper setting, and the delightful hearts and flowers runner, *above*, offers a perfect backdrop for a collection of valentines. Worked in filet crochet with a sprinkling of the spiderweb pattern, this lovely diamond-shaped doily has a romantic aura all its own.

For Valentine's Day or any special occasion, set your table with the graceful pineapple pattern place mats and matching coasters pictured *opposite*. This handsome set provides a sumptuous background for any meal—from high tea to an elegant champagne supper. To show off the lovely patterns, use clear or tinted glass dishes that allow the lacy designs to show through.

Instructions for these table toppers are on pages 72–74.

A tableau of white gloves, opera glasses, beaded bag, and souvenir program arranged atop a splendid pineapple doily, *opposite*, recalls a music lover's return from a grand operatic event.

A rose-bedecked runner, *above*, complements an arrangement of rose pattern china pieces—cherished one-of-a-kind collectibles even in grandmother's day.

Instructions for the doily and runner are on pages 74–78.

Whether one thrilled to a formal night at the opera or spent happy evenings at home singing parlor songs with family and friends, music was an integral part of family life throughout the 19th and early 20th centuries. A piano, like the one pictured in the parlor, opposite, was considered indispensable to a proper middle-class home.

Parlor games were an important facet of Victorian family life. Here, two handsome crocheted tablecloths offer artful backdrops for popular family activities of the day. The stereoscope on the wheel-motif cloth, *above,* was used for looking at three-dimensional views of distant and exotic places—a favorite Victorian pastime for youngsters and adults.

One can imagine children sipping hot cider and playing a leisurely game of checkers on the pineapple cloth, *opposite,* while the entire family listened in delight to the glorious sounds emanating from Mr. Edison's marvelous talking machine.

Make either of these cloths to fit a table of any shape, following the instructions on pages 78 and 79.

STAR SNOWFLAKE TABLE RUNNER

Shown on pages 62 and 63.

Runner measures approximately 32x76 inches, including border.

MATERIALS

Bucilla Blue Label crochet and knitting cotton (400-yard skein): 9 skeins ecru
Size 6 steel crochet hook or size to obtain gauge cited below

Abbreviations: See page 186.
Gauge: 9 dc = 1 inch; 4 rows = 1 inch.

INSTRUCTIONS

Note: Runner is made of 12 motifs that are sewn together. A filet crochet border is made separately and sewn to the assembled squares.

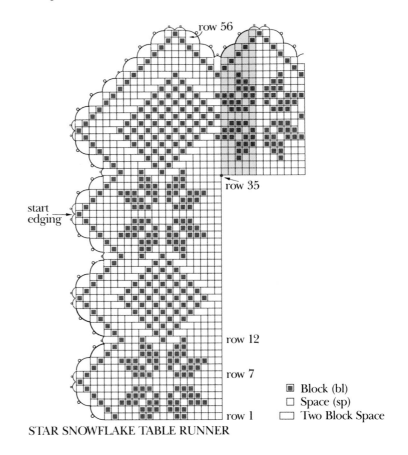

STAR SNOWFLAKE TABLE RUNNER

■ Block (bl)
□ Space (sp)
▭ Two Block Space

MOTIF (make 12): Beg at center, ch 8; join with sl st to form ring.

Rnd 1: Ch 7, (dc in ring, ch 2, dc in ring, ch 4) 3 times; end dc in ring, ch 2; join with sl st to third ch of beg ch-7.

Rnd 2: Ch 3, * 3 dc, ch 5, and 3 dc in ch-4 corner lp; dc in next dc, ch 2, ** dc in next dc; rep from * around; end last rep at **; join with sl st to top of beg ch-3.

Rnd 3: Ch 3, dc in next 3 dc; * 3 dc, ch 5, and 3 dc in corner ch-5 lp; dc in next 4 dc, ch 2, ** dc in next 4 dc; rep from * around; end last rep at **; join with sl st to top of beg ch-3.

Rnd 4: Ch 3, dc in next 6 dc; * 3 dc, ch 5, and 3 dc in corner ch-5 lp; dc in next 7 dc, ch 2, ** dc in next 7 dc; rep from * around; end last rep at **; join with sl st to top of beg ch-3.

Rnd 5: Ch 3, dc in next 9 dc; * 3 dc, ch 5, and 3 dc in corner ch-5 lp; dc in next 10 dc, ch 2, ** dc in next 10 dc; rep from * around; end last rep at **; join with sl st to top of beg ch-3.

Rnd 6: Ch 3, dc in next 12 dc; * 3 dc, ch 5, and 3 dc in corner ch-5 lp; dc in next 13 dc, ch 2, ** dc in next 13 dc; rep from * around; end last rep at **; join with sl st to top of beg ch-3.

Rnd 7: Ch 3, dc in next 15 dc; * 3 dc, ch 5, and 3 dc in corner ch-5 lp; dc in next 16 dc, ch 2, ** dc in next 16 dc; rep from * around; end last rep at **; join with sl st to top of beg ch-3.

Rnd 8: Ch 3, dc in next 18 dc; * 3 dc, ch 5, and 3 dc in corner ch-5 lp; dc in next 19 dc, ch 2, ** dc in next 19 dc; rep from * around; end last rep at **; join with sl st to top of beg ch-3.

Rnd 9: Ch 5; * sk 2 dc, dc in next 19 dc, ch 2, dc in third ch of corner ch-5 lp, ch 5, dc in same ch, ch 2, dc in next 19 dc; ch 2, sk 2 dc, dc in next dc, ch 2, ** dc in next dc, ch 2, rep from * around; end last rep at **; join with sl st to third ch of beg ch-5.

Rnd 10: Ch 5, dc in next dc; * ch 2, sk 2 dc, dc in next 16 dc, ch 2, dc in next dc, ch 2, dc in third ch of corner ch-5 lp, ch 5, dc in same ch, ch 2, dc in next dc, ch 2, dc in next 16 dc, ch 2, sk 2 dc, dc in next dc, ch 2, dc in next dc, 2 dc in next ch-2 sp, ** dc in next dc; ch 2, dc in next dc; rep from * around; end last rep at **; join with sl st to third ch of beg ch-5.

Rnd 11: Ch 3, 2 dc in ch-2 sp, dc in next dc; * ch 2, dc in next dc, ch 2, sk 2 dc, dc in next 13 dc; (ch 2, dc in next dc) twice; ch 2, dc in third ch of corner ch-5 lp, ch 5, dc in same ch; rep bet ( )s twice; ch 2, dc in next 13 dc, ch 2, sk 2 dc, dc in next dc, ch 2, dc in next dc, 2 dc in ch-2 sp, dc in next dc, ch 2, sk 2 dc, ** dc in next dc, 2 dc in ch-2 sp, dc in next dc; rep from * around; end last rep at **; join with sl st to top of beg ch-3.

Rnd 12: Ch 5; * sk 2 dc, dc in next dc, 2 dc in ch-2 sp, dc in next dc, ch 2, dc in next dc, ch 2, sk 2 dc, dc in next 10 dc, (ch 2, dc in next dc) 3 times; ch 2, dc in third ch of corner ch-5 lp, ch 5, dc in same ch; rep bet ( )s 3 times; ch 2, dc in next 10 dc, ch 2, sk 2 dc, dc in next dc, ch 2, dc in next dc, 2 dc in ch-2 sp, dc in next dc, ch 2, sk 2 dc, dc in next dc, 2 dc in ch-2 sp, ** dc in next dc, ch 2; rep from * around; end last rep at **; join to third ch of beg ch-5.

Rnd 13: Ch 3, 2 dc in ch-2 sp, dc in next dc; * ch 2, sk 2 dc, dc in next dc, 2 dc in ch-2 sp, dc in next dc, ch 2, dc in next dc, ch 2, sk 2 dc, dc in next 7 dc; (ch 2, dc in next dc) 4 times; ch 2, dc in third ch of corner ch-5 lp, ch 5, dc in same ch; rep bet ( )s 4 times; ch 2, dc in next 7 dc, ch 2, sk 2 dc, dc in next dc, ch 2, dc in next dc, ** (2 dc in ch-2 sp, dc in next dc, ch 2, sk 2 dc, dc in next dc) twice; 2 dc in next ch-2 sp, dc in next dc, rep from * around; end last rep at **; then work 2 dc in next ch-2 sp, dc in next dc, ch 2, sk 2 dc, dc in next dc, 2 dc in ch-2 sp, dc in next dc, ch 2; join to top of beg ch-3.

Rnd 14: Ch 5, sk 2 dc, dc in next dc; * 2 dc in ch-2 sp, dc in next dc, ch 2, sk 2 dc, dc in next dc, 2 dc in ch-2 sp, dc in next dc, ch 2, dc in next dc, ch 2, sk 2 dc, dc in next 4 dc; (ch 2, dc in next dc) 5 times; ch 2, dc in third ch of corner ch-5 lp, ch 5, dc in same ch; rep bet ( )s 5 times; ch 2, dc in next 4 dc, ch 2, sk 2 dc, dc in next dc, ch 2, dc in next dc; (2 dc in ch-2 sp, dc in next dc, ch 2, sk 2 dc, dc in next dc) 3 times; rep from * around;

work bet last set of ( )s 2 times instead of 3 on last rep; then work 2 dc in last ch-2 sp; join with sl st to third ch of beg ch-5.

Rnd 15: Ch 3, 2 dc in ch-2 sp, dc in next dc, ch 2, sk 2 dc, dc in next dc; * 2 dc in ch-2 sp, dc in next dc, ch 2, sk 2 dc, dc in next dc, 2 dc in ch-2 sp, dc in next dc, ch 2, dc in next dc, ch 2, sk 2 dc, dc in next dc; (ch 2, dc in next dc) 6 times; ch 2, dc in third ch of corner ch-5 lp, ch 5, dc in same ch; (ch 2, dc in next dc) 7 times; ch 2, sk 2 dc, dc in next dc, ch 2, dc in next dc; ** (2 dc in ch-2 sp, dc in next dc, ch 2, sk 2 dc, dc in next dc) 4 times; rep from * around; end last rep at **; then work (2 dc in ch-2 sp, dc in next dc, ch 2, sk 2 dc) twice; 2 dc in ch-2 sp, dc in next dc, ch 2; join with sl st to top of beg ch-3.

Rnd 16: Ch 5, sk 2 dc, dc in next dc; * (2 dc in ch-2 sp, dc in next dc, ch 2, sk 2 dc, dc in next dc) twice; 2 dc in ch-2 sp, dc in next dc; (ch 2, dc in next dc) 8 times; ch 2, dc in third ch of corner ch-5 lp, ch 5, dc in same ch; (ch 2, dc in next dc) 9 times; ** (2 dc in ch-2 sp, dc in next dc, ch 2, sk 2 dc, dc in next dc) 4 times; rep from * around; end last rep at **; then work (2 dc in ch-2 sp, dc in next dc, ch 2, sk 2 dc, dc in next dc) 3 times; 2 dc in ch-2 sp, join to third ch of beg ch-5; fasten off.

Lay the motifs out into a rectangle made up of two rows of six motifs each; using crochet cotton, whipstitch the motifs together.

BORDER: When working from the border chart, *opposite*, work odd-numbered rows from right to left; work even-numbered rows from left to right. The *curved* line on the chart represents the edging around the border of the assembled runner. Disregard this line when working the instructions for the border that follow.

Beg at narrow edge, ch 56.

Row 1: Dc in eighth ch from hook, * **ch 2, sk 2 ch, dc in next ch—sp made;** rep from * 3 times more; **dc in next 6 ch—2 bls made;** 3 sp, 2 bl, 3 sp, **dc in next 3 ch—bl made;** ch 2, sk 2 ch, dc in last ch; ch 3, turn.

Row 2: **2 dc in ch-2 sp, dc in next dc—bl over sp made; ch 2, sk 2 dc, dc in next dc—sp over bl made;** * **ch 2, dc in next dc— sp over sp made;** rep from * 2 times more; dc in next 6 dc, 2 dc in ch-2 sp, dc in next dc; **ch 2, dc in next dc—sp over sp made,** bl over sp, 2 bls over 2 bls; (sp over sp) 4 times; end ch 2, sk next 2 ch, dc in next ch; ch 5, turn.

Row 3: Sk first dc, dc in next dc, sp over sp; (bl over sp) 3 times; sp over bl, 2 bls over 2 bls, sp over sp, 2 bls over 2 bls, sp over bl; (bl over sp) 3 times; sp over sp, sp over bl; * **yo, draw up lp in base of last dc made, yo, draw through 1 lp on hook—base for next st; (yo, draw through 2 lps on hook) twice, rep from * two times more—bl inc made; ch 2, trc in base of last dc made—sp inc made;** ch 3, turn.

Rows 4–7: Follow chart; do not ch 3 to turn at end of Row 7, turn.

Row 8: Sl st across to fourth dc; ch 3, 2 dc in ch-2 sp, dc in next dc; follow chart across row.

Rows 9–11: Work from chart.

Rows 12–35: Following the chart, rep rows 12–35 two times for one short side of the runner.

CORNER: *Rows 36–56:* Follow the chart to work the corner motif; do not work the shaded portion at this time; fasten off at end of Row 56.

Referring to the shaded portion of the chart, rejoin the thread at the dot marked on the inside edge of Row 35 to begin the next side. Work Row 1 of the chart.

continued

Rep rows 2–35 of chart; then repeat rows 12–35 eight times for the long side of the runner. Complete rem two sides as established. Fasten off at end of Row 56 on fourth corner.

Use crochet cotton to whipstitch the first row of the border to the edge of the last corner. Whipstitch the border to the assembled rectangle.

EDGING: Referring to the heavy black line on the chart, join thread bet 2 dc on the edge of a dc-bl of any border point as marked on the chart. * **(Ch 8, sl st in fourth ch from hook—picot made,** ch 4, sc in next turning ch) 6 times, picot, ch 4, sc bet 2 dc of dc-bl, rep from * around; join with sl st to joining st; fasten off.

PINEAPPLE LUNCHEON SET

Shown on page 65.

Place mat measures 15 inches in diameter. Coaster measures 8 inches in diameter.

MATERIALS

For one place mat and coaster
Clark's Big Ball 3-cord crochet cotton, Size 20 (300-yard ball): 2 balls of white
Size 8 steel crochet hook

Abbreviations: See page 186.

INSTRUCTIONS

For the place mat
Beg in center, ch 10, join with sl st to form ring.

Rnd 1: Ch 3, work 32 dc in ring; join with sl st to top of beg ch-3.

Rnd 2: Ch 3, dc in each dc around; join to top of beg ch-3.

Rnd 3: Ch 3, dc in same st as join; 2 dc in each dc around; join to top of beg ch-3—66 dc around.

Rnd 4: Rep Rnd 2.

Rnd 5: Ch 3, dc in same st as join; * ch 3, sk 2 dc, 2 dc in next dc; rep from * around; end ch 3, join to top of beg ch-3.

Rnd 6: Sl st into next dc and into next sp, ch 3, in same sp make dc, ch 2, and 2 dc; in each ch-3 sp around **make 2 dc, ch 2, and 2 dc—shell made;** join with sl st to top of beg ch-3—22 shells made.

Rnd 7: Sl st into next dc and into next ch-2 sp, ch 3, in same sp make dc, ch 2, and 2 dc; * ch 1, **in next ch-2 sp make 2 dc, ch 2, and 2 dc—shell over shell made;** rep from * 20 times more; end ch 1, join to top of beg ch-3.

Rnds 8–12: Rep Rnd 7, adding 1 ch between each shell in each round—at end of Rnd 12 there are 6 ch bet each shell.

Rnd 13: Sl st into next dc and into next sp, ch 3, in same sp make dc, ch 5, and 2 dc; * ch 6, shell over shell, ch 6 **; in next ch-2 sp make 2 dc, ch 5, and 2 dc; rep from * around; end last rep at **; join to top of beg ch-3.

Rnd 14: Sl st into next dc and into next sp, ch 4, in same sp work 12 trc; * ch 5, shell over shell; ch 5, ** 13 trc in next ch-5 sp; rep from * around; end last rep at **; join to top of beg ch-4.

Rnd 15: Ch 5 (counts as trc and ch-1), trc in next trc; (ch 1, trc in next trc) 11 times; * ch 3, shell over shell, ch 3 **; trc in next trc, (ch 1, trc in next trc) 12 times; rep from * around; end last rep at **; join to fourth ch of beg ch-5.

Rnd 16: Sl st into next ch, sc in same sp; * (ch 3, sc into next ch-1 sp) 11 times, ch 3, shell over shell, ch 3 **; sc in next ch-1 sp, rep from * around; end last rep at **; sc in first ch-3 pineapple lp.

Note: Hereafter all rnds end with ch 3, sc in first pineapple lp.

Rnd 17: (Ch 3, sc in next lp) 10 times; * ch 3, shell over shell; (ch 3, sc in next lp) 11 times; rep from * around.

Rnd 18: (Ch 3, sc in next lp) 9 times; * ch 3, in ch-2 sp of next shell make 2 dc, ch 2, 2 dc, ch 2, and 2 dc; (ch 3, sc in next lp) 10 times; rep from * around.

Rnd 19: (Ch 3, sc in next lp) 8 times; * ch 3, in next ch-2 sp make shell; ch 2, shell in next ch-2 sp; (ch 3, sc in next lp) 9 times; rep from * around.

Rnd 20: (Ch 3, sc in next lp) 7 times; * ch 3, shell over shell, ch 1, shell in next ch-2 sp, ch 1, shell over shell; (ch 3, sc in next lp) 8 times; rep from * around.

Rnd 21: (Ch 3, sc in next lp) 6 times; * (ch 3, shell over shell) 3 times; (ch 3, sc in next lp) 7 times; rep from * around.

Rnd 22: (Ch 3, sc in next lp) 5 times; * ch 3, shell over shell; (ch 4, shell over shell) twice; (ch 3, sc in next lp) 6 times; rep from * around.

Rnd 23: (Ch 3, sc in next lp) 4 times; * ch 3, shell over shell, ch 5; in next shell make 2 dc, ch 5, and 2 dc; ch 5, shell over shell; (ch 3, sc in next lp) 5 times; rep from * around.

Rnd 24: (Ch 3, sc in next lp) 3 times; * ch 3, shell over shell, ch 3, 14 trc in next ch-5 lp of shell, ch 3, shell over shell; (ch 3, sc in next lp) 4 times; rep from * around.

Rnd 25: (Ch 3, sc in next lp) twice; * ch 3, shell over shell, ch 3, trc in next trc; (ch 1, trc in next trc) 13 times; ch 3, shell over shell; (ch 3, sc in next lp) 3 times; rep from * around.

Rnd 26: Ch 3, sc in next lp; * ch 3, shell over shell; (ch 3, sc in next ch-1 sp) 13 times; ch 3, shell over shell; (ch 3, sc in next lp) twice; rep from * around.

Rnd 27: * Ch 4, shell over shell; (ch 3, sc in next lp) 12 times; ch 3, shell over shell; ch 4, sc in next lp; rep from * around, end with ch 4, sl st in first sc; fasten off.

TIPS OF PINEAPPLE: *Note:* Work is now done in rows.

Row 28: Attach thread in ch-2 sp of next shell of previous rnd; ch 3, in same sp make dc, ch 2, and 2 dc; (ch 3, sc in next lp) 11 times; ch 3, shell over shell; ch 3, turn.

Rows 29–36: Shell over shell; (ch 3, sc in next lp) 10 times; ch 3, shell over shell; ch 3, turn. Continue in this manner, having 1 less ch-3 pineapple lp on each row until Row 36 is completed.

Row 37: Shell over shell; (ch 3, sc in next lp) twice; ch 3, shell over shell—1 lp remaining at point; ch 3, turn. Make shell over shell, ch 4, sc in next lp, ch 4, 2 dc in next shell, ch 1, sl st back in ch-2 sp of last shell; ch 1, 2 dc where last 2 dc were made; fasten off.

Attach thread in ch-2 sp of next shell of Rnd 27 and complete the next pineapple tip in the same manner. Work rem 11 tips in the same manner.

EDGING: *Rnd 1:* Attach thread to tip of any pineapple where shells are joined; ch 3, in same place make dc, ch 2, and 2 dc; * (ch 3, shell into turning ch-3 between 2 rows) 5 times; ch 2, holding back last lp of next 2 dc, work dc in ch-2 sp of shell preceding ch-4 (on Rnd 27), then dc in ch-2 sp of next shell (where thread was attached to work the pineapple tip), yo and draw through all lps on hook; (ch 3, shell in turning ch-3 between next 2 rows) 5 times; ch 3, shell at point of next tip where shells were joined, rep from * around; end ch 3, join.

Rnd 2: Sl st into next dc and into next sp, ch 8, sc in fifth ch from hook; dc in same place as sl st; * ch 3, sc into next ch-3 lp, ch

3; in next shell make dc, **ch 5, sc in fifth ch from hook—picot made,** and dc; rep from * 4 times more; ch 3, sc in next dc, ch 3; in next shell make dc, picot, dc; ch 3, sc into next ch-3 lp. Continue around in this manner; fasten off.

For the coaster

Ch 10, join with sl st to form ring.

Rnd 1: Ch 3, make 20 dc in ring; join to top of beg ch-3.

Rnd 2: Ch 3, dc in same st as join; work 2 dc in each dc around; join to top of beg ch-3—42 dc.

Rnds 3–5: Work same as rnds 5–7 of place mat—14 dc grp.

Rnd 6: Rep Rnd 5 except work ch-2 between shells.

Rnd 7: Sl st into next dc and into next sp, ch 3, in same sp make dc, ch 5, and 2 dc; * ch 4, shell over shell, ch 4 **; in sp of next shell make 2 dc, ch 5, and 2 dc; rep from * around; end last rep at **; join to top of beg ch-3.

Rnd 8: Sl st in next dc and in next sp, ch 4 (counts as trc), 10 trc in ch-5 sp, * ch 3, shell over shell, ch 3 **, 11 trc in next ch-5 sp; rep from * around, end last rep at **; join to top of beg ch-4.

Rnd 9: Ch 5 (counts as trc and ch-1), trc in next trc; (ch 1, trc in next trc) 9 times; * ch 3, shell over shell, ch 3, ** trc in next trc; (ch 1, trc in next trc) 10 times; rep from * around; end last rep at **; join to fourth ch of beg ch-5.

Rnd 10: Sl st into next ch, sc in same sp; * (ch 3, sc into next ch-1 sp) 9 times, ch 3, shell over shell, ch 3, sc in next ch-1 sp, rep from * around; end ch 3, sc in first ch-3 pineapple lp.

Rnd 11: (Ch 3, sc in next lp) 8 times, * ch 3, shell over next shell; (ch 3, sc in next lp) 9 times; rep from * around; end with sl st in sc at beg of rnd; fasten off.

TIPS OF PINEAPPLES: *Note:*

Work is now done in rows.

Row 12: Join thread in ch-2 sp of next shell of previous rnd; ch 3, in same sp make dc, ch 2, and 2 dc; (ch 3, sc in next loop) 8 times; ch 3, shell in shell; ch 3, turn.

Rows 13–17: Shell over shell; (ch 3, sc in next loop) 7 times; ch 3, shell over next shell; ch 3, turn. Continue in this manner, having 1 less ch-3 lp in each pineapple until Row 17 is completed.

Row 18: Shell over shell; (ch 3, sc in next lp) twice; ch 3, shell over shell—1 lp remaining at point; ch 3, turn. Make shell over shell, ch 4, sc in next lp, ch 4, 2 dc in next shell, ch 1, sl st back in ch-2 sp of last shell; ch 1, 2 dc where last 2 dc were made; fasten off.

Join thread in ch-2 sp of the same shell used for end of Rnd 12 on previous pineapple tip, and complete the next tip in the same way. Continue in this manner until all seven tips are worked.

EDGING: *Rnd 1:* Attach thread to point of any pineapple tip where shells were joined, ch 3; in same place make dc, ch 2, and 2 dc; * (ch 3, shell in next turning ch) 3 times, ch 2, **holding back last lp of next 2 dc, dc in turning ch before next shell, dc around side of dc of next shell, yo, draw through all lps on hook—dc-dec made;** (ch 3, shell in next turning ch) 3 times, ch 3, shell in point of tip where shells meet; rep from * around; join.

Rnd 2: Sl st in next dc and in next sp, ch 8 (to count as dc and ch-5 for a picot), sc in fifth ch from hook; dc in same place as sl st, * ch 3, sc in next ch-3, ch 3; in next shell make dc, **ch 5, sc in fifth ch from hook—picot made,** and dc, rep from * 2 times more; ch 3, dc in top of dc-dec, ch 3; in next shell make dc, picot and dc; ch 3, sc in next ch-3. Continue around in this manner; join and fasten off; block.

HEART RUNNER

Shown on page 64.

Runner measures 12x32 inches.

MATERIALS
DMC Cordonnet Special crochet
cotton, Size 10 (124-yard ball):
3 balls white
Size 9 steel crochet hook or size
to obtain gauge cited below

Abbreviations: See page 186.
Gauge: 12 trc = 1 inch; 3 rows of
trc = 1 inch.

INSTRUCTIONS
Note: The first half of the runner is
worked from the center out to the
tip and then fastened off. The second half is worked by turning the
work over and joining to the starting ch. Begin to work the second
half at Row 2 (skipping Row 1) of
chart, *above right,* and work to Row
44 to complete the opposite side.

FIRST HALF OF RUNNER:
Beginning at center of runner, ch
136.
Row 1: Trc in ninth ch from
hook; (ch 2, sk 2 ch, trc in next ch)
16 times; trc in next 3 ch, ch 8, sk
8 ch, sc in next 5 ch, ch 8, sk 8 ch,
trc in next 4 ch; (ch 2, sk 2 ch, trc
in next ch) 17 times; ch 6, turn.
Row 2: Sk first trc, trc in next
trc; (ch 2, trc in next trc) 16 times;
ch 2, sk 2 trc, trc in next trc, 3 trc
in ch-8 lp, ch 8, sk sc, sc in next 3
sc; ch 8, 3 trc in next ch-8 lp, trc in
next trc, ch 2, sk 2 trc, trc in next
trc; (ch 2, trc in next trc) 16 times;
ch 2, sk 2 ch, trc in next ch; ch 6,
turn.
Rows 3–44: Work following the
chart and spiderweb detail, *top
right.* On Row 22 and all dec rows,

dec at each edge as follows: At
end of previous row, do not ch 6;
turn work, sl st across to next trc,
then ch 6; trc in next trc, continue
across row following chart; ch 6,
turn; fasten off at end of Row 44.

SECOND HALF OF RUN-
NER: Turn work with starting ch
running across top of work; join
thread and work across Row 2.
Continue to work rem 42 rows
following the chart as for first half
of the runner; fasten off.

EDGING: Join thread with sl st
in center ch-2 sp at one end of
runner (see arrow on chart).
Rnd 1: In same ch-2 sp work ch
4, trc, ch 3, and 2 trc; ch 3, sc in
next ch-2 sp; ch 3, in next turning
ch work **2 trc, ch 3, 2 trc—shell
made,** * ch 3, sc in next turning
ch; ch 3, shell in next turning ch,
rep from * around; end ch 3, sc in
rem ch-2 sp; ch 3, join with sl st to
top of beg ch-4.
Rnd 2: Sl st into next trc and
into first ch of ch-3 sp; ch 3, **holding back last lp of each dc on
hook, work 2 dc in next ch, yo,
draw through all lps on hook—
cluster (cl) made;** ch 3, sl st into
next ch; * ch 7, sl st in first ch of
next ch-3 lp of shell, work cl, ch 3,
sl st in next ch; rep from *
around; end ch 7, join to base of
first ch-3; fasten off.

ROSE GARDEN TABLE RUNNER

Shown on page 67.

Finished table runner measures
approximately 15x35½ inches.

MATERIALS
Clark's Big Ball 3-cord crochet
cotton, Size 20 (300-yard ball):
5 balls of ecru
Size 11 steel crochet hook or
size to obtain gauge cited
below

Abbreviations: See page 186.
Gauge: 5 sps = 1 inch; 6 rows =
1 inch.

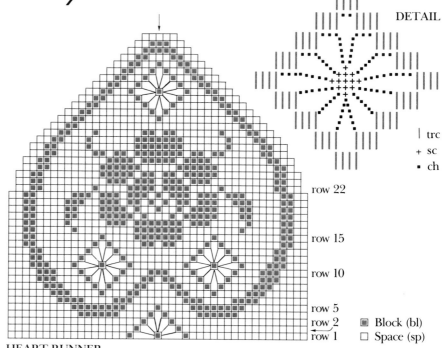

DETAIL

| trc
+ sc
• ch

row 22
row 15
row 10
row 5
row 2
row 1

■ Block (bl)
□ Space (sp)

HEART RUNNER

INSTRUCTIONS

Note: Lacets take up the space equivalent to two blocks, two spaces, or one block and one space. There is always a ch-5 lp (bar) over the top of each lacet stitch of the previous row. When working lacet stitches between the rose and scroll designs, refer to the chart at *right* and on page 76 for their placement.

Beginning at the bottom of the chart, *right*, ch 225.

Row 1: Dc in fourth ch from hook and each ch across; ch 3, turn—223 dc counting beg turning ch as dc.

Row 2: **Dc in next 3 dc—beg bl made; ch 2, sk 2 dc, dc in next dc—sp made;** make 3 more sps, **dc in next 3 dc—bl made,** make 5 more bls; (sp, bl) twice; sp, 6 bls, 6 sps, 6 bls, sp, bl, 2 sps, bl, sp, 6 bls, 6 sps, 6 bls, (sp, bl) twice; sp, 6 bls, 4 sps; then work **dc in next 2 dc, dc in top of turning ch—end bl made;** ch 3, turn.

Continue to work following chart until Row 28 is completed, ending each row with ch 3, turn.

Row 29: Beg bl, bl, sp, bl, 18 sps, bl, sp, 2 bls; then **ch 3, sk 2 dc, sc in next dc, ch 3, dc in next dc—lacet made;** sp, 3 bls, sp, bl, 6 sps, bl, sp, 3 bls, sp, then **ch 3, sc in next dc, ch 3, sk 2 dc, dc in next dc—another lacet made;** make 2 bls, sp, bl, 18 sps, bl, sp, bl, end bl; ch 3, turn.

Row 30: Beg bl, bl, sp, bl, 18 sps, 3 bls, sp, then **ch 5, dc in next dc—bar over lacet made;** ch 3, lacet, 3 bls, sp, 6 bls, sp, 3 bls, lacet, bar over lacet, sp, 3 bls, 18 sps, bl, sp, bl; end bl; ch 3, turn.

Row 31: Beg bl, bl, sp, 2 bls, 17 sps, bl, sp; then **ch 5, sk 3 dc and ch-2, dc in next dc, ch 3, sk 2 ch, sc in next ch, ch 3, dc in next dc—bar and lacet made;** work bar, lacet, sp, bl, 6 sps, bl, sp, (la-

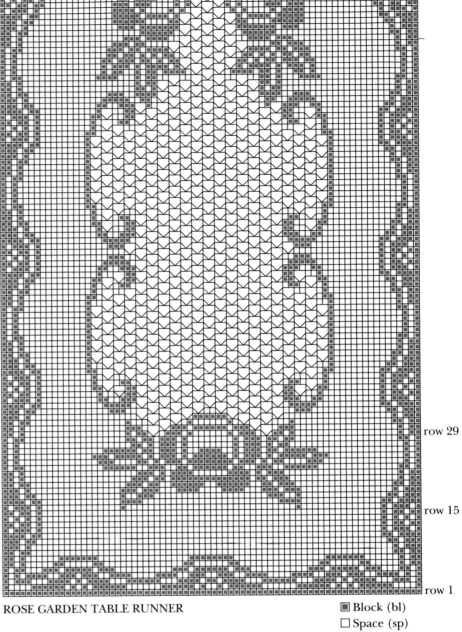

ROSE GARDEN TABLE RUNNER

row 29

row 15

row 1

■ Block (bl)
□ Space (sp)
⌐ Chain 5 loop
◁▷ Lacet stitch

cet, bar) twice; sp, bl, 17 sps, 2 bls, sp, bl, end bl; ch 3, turn.

Row 32: Beg bl, 2 bls, sp, bl, 17 sps, (bar, lacet) 3 times; 6 bls, (lacet, bar) 3 times; 17 sps, bl, sp, 2 bls, end bl; ch 3, turn.

Row 33: Beg bl, 2 bls, sp, 2 bls, 13 sps, 3 bls, **ch 2, sk 2 ch, dc in next ch—sp over bar made;** sp, (bar, lacet) 6 times; bar, 2 sps, 3 bls, 13 sps, 2 bls, sp, 2 bls, end bl; ch 3, turn.

Rows 34–37: Follow chart, *above.* End each row with ch 3, turn.

Row 38: Beg bl, bl, sp, 2 bls, sp, bl; 9 sps, bl, sp, bar; **ch 2, sk 2 ch, dc in next 3 ch, dc in next dc—sp and bl over bar made;** bl, sp, (lacet, bar) 6 times; lacet, sp, bl; **dc in next 3 ch, ch 2, dc in next dc—bl and sp over bar made;** bar, sp, bl, 9 sps, bl, sp, 2 bls, sp, bl, end bl; ch 3, turn.

Starting with Row 39, follow chart to opposite end of runner. See page 76 for second half of chart. Fasten off.

PINEAPPLE DOILY

Shown on page 66.

Doily measures approximately 19½ inches in diameter.

MATERIALS

Clark's Big Ball 3-cord crochet cotton, Size 20 (300-yard ball): 2 balls ecru

Size 11 steel crochet hook or size to obtain gauge cited below

Abbreviations: See page 186.
Gauge: 7 dc = 1 inch; 4 shell rows = 1 inch.

INSTRUCTIONS

Beg at center, ch 8, join with sl st to form ring.

Rnd 1: Ch 3, 19 dc in ring, join with sl st to top of beg ch-3.

Rnd 2: Ch 7, sk dc, dc in next dc; * ch 4, sk dc, dc in next dc, rep from * around; end ch 4, join to third ch of beg ch-7.

Rnd 3: Ch 3; * 5 dc in next lp, dc in next dc, rep from * around; end with 5 dc in last lp, join to top of beg ch-3—60 dc.

Rnd 4: Ch 3; dc in each dc around, working 2 dc in every 14th st; join to top of beg ch-3.

Rnd 5: **Ch 3, 2 dc in same st, ch 3, 3 dc in same st—beg shell made;** * ch 6, sk 7 dc, 5 trc in next dc, ch 6, ** sk 7 dc, **3 dc, ch 3, 3 dc in next dc—shell made,** rep from * around; end last rep at **; join to top of beg ch-3.

Rnd 6: Sl st to center ch-3 sp of beg shell, make beg shell in same sp; * ch 6, 2 trc in each of the next 5 trc, ch 6, ** shell in next shell, rep from * around; end last rep at **; join to top of beg ch-3.

Rnd 7: Sl st to ch-3 sp of beg shell, make beg shell in same sp; * ch 6, (2 trc in next trc, trc in next trc) twice, 2 trc in next trc, ch 1, (2 trc in next trc, trc in next trc) twice, 2 trc in next trc, ch 6, ** shell in next shell, rep from * around; end last rep at **; join to top of beg ch-3.

Note: Hereafter, all rnds are joined with sl st to top of beg ch-3 unless specified otherwise.

Rnd 8: Sl st to ch-3 sp of beg shell, make beg shell in same sp; * ch 5, sk trc; 2 dc, ch 2, and 2 dc in next trc; ch 5, sk 6 trc, shell in next ch-1 sp; ch 5, sk 6 trc; 2 dc, ch 2, and 2 dc in next trc; ch 5, ** shell in next shell, rep from *; end last rep at **; join.

Rnd 9: Sl st to ch-3 sp of beg shell, make beg shell in same sp; * ch 4, dc over end of next ch-5 lp, dc in next 2 dc, ch 3, dc in next 2 dc, dc over beg of next ch-5 lp, ch 4, ** shell in next shell, rep from * around; end last rep at **; join.

Rnd 10: Sl st to ch-3 sp of beg shell, make beg shell in same sp; * ch 4, dc over end of next ch-4 lp, dc in next 3 dc, dc in next ch-3 sp, ch 3, dc in same sp, dc in next 3 dc, dc over beg of next ch-4 lp, ch 4, ** shell in next shell, rep from * around; end last rep at **; join.

Rnd 11: Sl st to ch-3 sp of beg shell, ch 3, 2 dc, ch 3, 3 dc, ch 3, 3

dc in same sp; * ch 2, dc over end of next ch-4 lp, dc in next 5 dc, dc in next ch-3 sp, ch 5, dc in same sp, dc in next 5 dc, dc over beg of next ch-4 lp, ch 2 **; 3 dc, ch 3, 3 dc, ch 3, and 3 dc in ch-3 sp of next shell; rep from * around; end last rep at **; join.

Rnd 12: Sl st to next ch-3 sp, make beg shell in same sp, shell in next ch-3 sp; * ch 2, sk first dc of 7-dc grp, dc in 5 dc, ch 2, 7 trc in next ch-5 lp, ch 2, sk dc, dc in next 5 dc, ch 2, ** sk ch-2 lp; (shell in next ch-3 sp) twice; rep from * around; end last rep at **; join.

Rnd 13: Sl st to ch-3 sp of beg shell, make beg shell in same sp, * ch 1, shell in next shell, ch 2, sk first dc of 5-dc grp, dc in next 3 dc, ch 2; (trc in next trc, ch 1) 6 times, trc in next trc; ch 2, sk dc, dc in next 3 dc, ch 2, ** shell in next shell, rep from * around; end last rep at **; join.

Rnd 14: Sl st to ch-3 sp of beg shell, make beg shell in same sp; * ch 2, shell in next shell, ch 1, dc in first 2 dc of 3-dc grp, ch 2, sc in ch-1 sp between first 2 trc; (ch 3, sc in next ch-1 sp) 5 times; ch 2, sk dc, dc in next 2 dc, ch 1, ** shell in next shell, rep from * around; end last rep at **; join.

Rnd 15: Sl st to ch-3 sp of beg shell, make beg shell in same sp; * ch 4, shell in next shell, ch 1, dc in first dc of 2-dc grp, ch 3, sk next ch-2 lp, sc in first ch-3 lp of pineapple; (ch 3, sc in next lp) 4 times; ch 3, sk dc, dc in next dc, ch 1, ** shell in next shell, rep from * around; end last rep at **; join.

Rnd 16: Sl st to ch-3 sp of shell, make beg shell in same sp; * ch 5, sc in next ch-4 lp, ch 5, shell in next shell, ch 5, sk 2 lps, sc in first ch-3 lp of pineapple; (ch 3, sc in next lp) 3 times; ch 5, sk 2 lps, ** shell in next shell, rep from * around; end last rep at **; join.

Rnd 17: Sl st to ch-3 sp of beg shell, make beg shell in same sp; *

ch 5, sc in next ch-5 lp, ch 5, sc in next ch-5 lp, ch 5, shell in next shell, ch 5, sk next ch-5 lp, sc in first ch-3 lp of pineapple; (ch 3, sc in next lp) twice; ch 5, ** shell in next shell, rep from * around; end last rep at **; join.

Rnd 18: Sl st to ch-3 sp of beg shell, make beg shell in same sp; * (ch 5, sc in next ch-5 lp) three times, ch 5, shell in next shell; ch 5, sc in first ch-3 lp of pineapple, ch 3, sc in next ch-3 lp, ch 5, ** shell in next shell, rep from * around; end last rep at **; join.

Rnd 19: Sl st to ch-3 sp of beg shell, make beg shell in same sp; * (ch 5, sc in next ch-5 lp) 4 times, ch 5, shell in next shell, ch 5, sc in rem ch-3 lp of pineapple, ch 5, ** shell in next shell, rep from * around; end last rep at **; join.

Rnd 20: Sl st to ch-3 sp of beg shell, make beg shell in same sp; * (ch 6, sc in next lp) 5 times, ch 6, shell in next shell, ch 5, sc in sc at top of pineapple, ch 5, ** shell in next shell, rep from * around; end last rep at **; join.

Rnd 21: Sl st to ch-3 sp of beg shell, make beg shell in same sp; * (ch 7, sc in next ch-6 lp) 6 times, ch 7, ** (shell in next shell) twice, repeat from * around; end last rep at **, then shell in next shell; join.

Rnd 22: Sl st to ch-3 sp of shell; * (ch 7, sc in next lp) 7 times, ch 7, sc in center of next shell **, ch 7, sc in center of next shell, rep from * around; end last rep at **, then ch 3, trc in beg sl st.

Rnd 23: * Ch 7, sc in next ch-7 lp, rep from * around; end ch 3, trc in trc.

Rnds 24–26: * Ch 8, sc in next lp, rep from * around, end ch 4, trc in trc.

Rnd 27: * Ch 9, sc in next lp, rep from * around; end ch 4, dtr (yo hook 3 times) in trc.

Rnd 28: Same as Rnd 27 except end with ch 9, sl st in dtr.

Rnd 29: Sl st to fifth ch of next ch-9 lp, make beg shell in same sp; * ch 5, sc in next lp, ch 5; 2 dc, ch 2, and 2 dc in fifth ch of next ch-9 lp, ch 5, sc in next lp, ch 5, ** shell in fifth ch of next lp, rep from * around; end last rep at **; join.

Rnd 30: Sl st to ch-3 sp of beg shell, make beg shell in same sp, * ch 8, sk next ch-5 lp, dc over end of next ch-5 lp, dc in next 2 dc, ch 4, dc in next 2 dc, dc over beg of next ch-5 lp, ch 8, ** shell in next shell, rep from * around; end last rep at **; join.

Rnd 31: Sl st to ch-3 sp of beg shell, make beg shell in same sp; * ch 8, dc over end of next ch-8 lp, dc in next 3 dc, dc over beg of next ch-4 lp, ch 4, dc in same lp, dc in next 3 dc, dc over beg of next ch-8 lp, ch 8, ** shell in next shell, rep from * around; end last rep at **; join.

Rnd 32: Sl st to ch-3 sp of beg shell, make beg shell in same sp, * ch 7, dc over end of next ch-8 lp, dc in next 5 dc, dc over beg of next ch-4 lp, ch 4, dc in same lp, dc in next 5 dc, dc over beg of next ch-8 lp, ch 7, ** shell in next shell, rep from * around; end last rep at **; join.

Rnd 33: Sl st to ch-3 sp of beg shell, ch 3, 2 dc, ch 3, 3 dc, ch 3, and 3 dc in same sp; * ch 6, sk first dc of 7-dc grp, dc in next 5 dc, ch 2, 9 trc in next ch-4 lp, ch 2, sk dc, dc in next 5 dc, ch 6, ** 3 dc, ch 3, 3 dc, ch 3, and 3 dc in ch-3 sp of next shell; rep from * around; end last rep at **; join.

Rnd 34: Sl st to first ch-3 sp, make beg shell in same sp, * shell in next ch-3 sp, ch 4, dc in first 4 dc of 5 dc grp, ch 2; (trc in next trc, ch 1) 8 times, trc in next trc; ch 2, sk dc, dc in next 4 dc, ch 4, ** shell in next ch-3 sp, rep from * around; end last rep at **; join.

continued

Note: When instructions read "work beg shell," sl st to ch-3 sp of first shell and work a beg shell.

Rnd 35: Work beg shell; * ch 3, shell in next shell, ch 2, dc in first 3 dc of 4-dc grp; ch 3, sc in first ch-1 sp bet 2 trc; (ch 3, sc in next ch-1 sp) 7 times, ch 3, sk dc, dc in next 3 dc, ch 2, ** shell in next shell, rep from * around; end last rep at **; join.

Rnd 36: Work beg shell; * ch 3, sc in next lp, ch 3, shell in next shell, ch 1, dc in first 2 dc of 3-dc grp; ch 3, sk next ch-3 lp, sc in first lp of pineapple; (ch 3, sc in next lp) 6 times, ch 3, sk dc, dc in next 2 dc, ch 1, ** shell in next shell, rep from * around; end last rep at **; join.

Rnd 37: Work beg shell; * ch 3, sc in next ch-3 lp, ch 3, sc in next ch-3 lp, ch 3, shell in next shell, ch 1, sk first dc of 2-dc grp, dc in next dc, ch 2, sk next ch-3 lp, sc in first lp of pineapple; (ch 3, sc in next lp) 5 times, ch 2, dc in next dc, ch 1, ** shell in next shell, rep from * around; end last rep at **; join.

Rnd 38: Work beg shell; * (ch 4, sc in next ch-3 lp) three times, ch 4, shell in next shell, ch 3, sk next dc and next ch-2 lp, sc in first ch-3 lp of pineapple; (ch 3, sc in next lp) 4 times, ch 3, ** shell in next shell, rep from * around; end last rep at **; join.

Rnds 39 and 40: Same as last round but having 1 more ch-4 lp bet shells and 1 less ch-3 lp across each pineapple in each rnd.

Rnd 41: Work beg shell; * (ch 5, sc in next ch-4 lp) 6 times, ch 5, shell in next shell, ch 3, sc in first ch-3 lp of pineapple, ch 3, sc in next lp, ch 3, ** shell in next shell, rep from * around; end last rep at **; join.

Rnd 42: Work beg shell; * (ch 5, sc in next lp) 7 times, ch 5, shell in next shell, ch 3, sc in rem lp of pineapple, ch 3, ** shell in next shell, rep from * around; end last rep at **; join.

Rnd 43: Work beg shell; * (ch 5, sc in next lp) 8 times, ch 5, shell in next shell, ** shell in next shell, rep from * around; end last rep at **; join.

Rnd 44: Sl st to ch-3 sp of next shell; * (ch 6, sc in next ch-5 lp) 4 times; ch 1, trc in third ch of next ch-5 lp; (ch 4, sl st in top of trc for picot, trc in same sp) 4 times, ch 1, sc in next ch-5 lp; (ch 6, sc in next ch-5 lp) 3 times; ch 6, sc in center of next shell, ch 4, sc in last sc for picot, ** sc in center of next shell, rep from * around; end last rep at **; join with sl st to beg sl st; fasten off. Block to finished size.

WHEEL-MOTIF TABLECLOTH

Shown on page 68.

Tablecloth measures approximately 60x74 inches.

MATERIALS

Clark's Big Ball crochet cotton, Size 10 (200-yard ball): 32 balls ecru
Size 11 steel crochet hook

Abbreviations: See page 186.
Gauge: One motif measures 3½ inches across the center.

INSTRUCTIONS

Motif (make 348): Ch 6, join with sl st to form ring.

Rnd 1: Ch 3, work 23 dc in ring; join with sl st to top of beg ch-3.

Note: Work in back lp of sts unless otherwise specified.

Rnd 2: Ch 5, (sk dc, dc in next dc, ch 2) 11 times; join with sl st in third ch of beg ch-5.

Rnd 3: Sl st in ch-2 sp, ch 4, 3 trc in same sp, ch 3; (4 trc in next sp, ch 3) 11 times; join with sl st in top of beg ch-4.

Rnd 4: Ch 4, trc in next 3 trc, ch 5; (trc in next 4 trc, ch 5) 11 times; join with sl st in top of beg ch-4.

Rnd 5: Ch 4, trc in next 3 trc, ch 7; (trc in next 4 trc, ch 7) 11 times; join with sl st in top of beg ch-4.

Rnd 6: Ch 4, trc in next 3 trc; * ch 4, sc in fourth ch of next ch-7 lp, ch 4, trc in next 4 trc, ch 9, ** trc in next 4 trc, rep from * around, end last rep at **; join in top of beg ch-4; fasten off.

With right sides together and working through back lps, whip-stitch 2 motifs together at 4-trc, ch-9, and 4-trc grp. Assemble cloth into 17 rows, having 9 odd-numbered rows with 20 motifs and 8 even-numbered rows with 21 motifs. Sew alternating rows together.

EDGING: Join thread in the joining bet any 2 motifs; * sc in next 4 ch, sc in sc, sc in next 4 ch, ** sc in next 2 trc, **ch 3, sc in third ch from hook—picot made,** sc in next 2 trc, sc in next 9 ch, sc in next 2 trc, picot, sc in next 2 trc, rep from * around, end last rep at **; join to first sc; fasten off.

PINEAPPLE-MOTIF TABLECLOTH

Shown on page 69.

Cloth measures approximately 56x79 inches.

MATERIALS

Clark's Big Ball 3-cord crochet cotton, Size 20 (300-yard ball): 25 balls of ecru No. 61
Size 12 steel crochet hook or size to obtain gauge

Abbreviations: See page 186.
Gauge: One motif measures 4½ inches across the center.

INSTRUCTIONS

Note: This tablecloth consists of 204 motifs joined in 12 rows of 17 motifs each. Work the first motif through Rnd 13. Work all other motifs through Rnd 12, then join to the previous motif on Rnd 13. When all of the motifs are made and assembled, add the edging.

FIRST MOTIF: Ch 6, join with sl st to form ring.

Rnd 1: Ch 3, work 6 dc in ring; (ch 1, work 7 dc in ring) 3 times; end ch 1; join with sl st to top of beg ch-3—28 dc.

Rnd 2: (Ch 7, sc in next ch-1 sp) 3 times; end ch 7.

Rnd 3: Sl st into first ch of ch-7 lp, ch 4, 9 trc in same lp; * ch 3, 10 trc in next ch-7 lp; rep from * around; end ch 3, join with sl st to top of beg ch-4.

Rnd 4: Ch 5, trc in next trc; (ch 1, trc in next trc) 8 times; * ch 3, sc in center ch of next ch-3 lp, ch 3, ** trc in next trc; (ch 1, trc in next trc) 9 times; rep from * around; end last rep at **; sl st to fourth ch of beg ch-5.

Rnd 5: Ch 1, * sc in next ch-1 sp; (ch 3, sc in next ch-1 sp) 8 times; ch 5; rep from * around; end sl st in first sc.

Rnd 6: Sl st to center ch of first ch-3 lp, ch 1; sc in same lp; * (ch 3, sc in next ch-3 lp) 7 times; ch 3, 3 dc in next ch-5 lp, ch 3; ** sc in next ch-3 lp; rep from * around; end last rep at **; sl st in first sc.

Rnd 7: Sl st to center ch of first ch-3 lp, ch 1, sc in same lp; * (ch 3, sc in next ch-3 lp) 6 times; ch 3, 3 dc in next ch-3 lp, ch 4, 3 dc in next ch-3 lp, ch 3, ** sc in next ch-3 lp; rep from * around; end last rep at **; sl st in first sc.

Rnd 8: Sl st to center ch of first ch-3 lp, ch 1, sc in same lp; * (ch 3,

sc in next ch-3 lp) 5 times; ch 3, 3 dc in next ch-3 lp, ch 5, sc in center of next ch-4 lp, ch 5, 3 dc in next ch-3 lp, ch 3, ** sc in next ch-3 lp; rep from * around; end last rep at **; sl st in first sc.

Rnd 9: Sl st to center ch of first ch-3 lp, ch 1, sc in same lp; * (ch 3, sc in next ch-3 lp) 4 times; ch 3, 3 dc in next ch-3 lp; (ch 5, sc in next ch-5 lp) twice; ch 5, 3 dc in next ch-3 lp, ch 3, ** sc in next ch-3 lp; rep from * around; end last rep at **; sl st in first sc.

Rnd 10: Sl st to center ch of first ch-3 lp, ch 1, sc in same lp; * (ch 3, sc in next ch-3 lp) 3 times; ch 3, 3 dc in next ch-3 lp, ch 5, sc in next ch-5 lp, ch 5; **holding back last lp of each trc on hook, work 3 trc in next ch-5 lp, yo and draw through all 4 lps on hook—trc-cl made;** ch 5, in same ch-5 lp work trc-cl, ch 5, and trc-cl; ch 5, sc in next ch-5 lp, ch 5, 3 dc in next ch-3 lp, ch 3; ** sc in next ch-3 lp; rep from * around; end last rep at **; sl st in first sc.

Rnd 11: Sl st to center ch of first ch-3 lp, ch 1, sc in same lp; * (ch 3, sc in next ch-3 lp) twice; ch 3, 3 dc in next ch-3 lp; (ch 5, sc in next ch-5 lp) 3 times; ch 9; (sc in next ch-5 lp, ch 5) 3 times; 3 dc in next ch-3 lp, ch 3; ** sc in next ch-3 lp; rep from * around; end last rep at **; sl st in first sc.

Rnd 12: Sl st to center ch of first ch-3 lp, ch 1, sc in same lp, ch 3, sc in next ch-3 lp; * ch 3, 3 dc in next ch-3 lp; (ch 5, sc in next ch-5 lp) twice; ch 5, 3 sc at end of ch-5 lp; 4 sc, ch 3, 4 sc, ch 5, 4 sc, ch 3, and 4 sc over ch-9 lp; 3 sc in next ch-5 lp; (ch 5, sc in next ch-5 lp) twice; ch 5, 3 dc in next ch-3 sp, ch 3; ** sc in pineapple ch-3 lp, ch 3, sc in next ch-3 lp; rep from * around; end last rep at **; sl st in first sc.

Rnd 13: Turn; sl st to center of last ch-3 lp of Rnd 12; turn, ch 1, sc in same lp, * ch 5, sk next ch-3

lp, sc in next ch-3 lp; (ch 5, sc in next ch-5 lp) 3 times; ch 5, sc in next ch-3 lp, ch 7, sc in corner ch-5 lp, ch 7, sc in next ch-3 lp; (ch 5, sc in next ch-5 lp) 3 times; ch 5, sc in next ch-3 lp; rep from * around; sl st in first sc; fasten off.

SECOND MOTIF: Work as for First Motif through Rnd 12.

Rnd 13 (joining rnd): Turn, sl st to center of last ch-3 sp of Rnd 12; turn, ch 1, sc in same sp; ch 5, sk ch-3 lp, sc in next ch-3 sp; (ch 5, sc in next ch-5 lp) 3 times; ch 5, sc in next ch-3 lp, ch 7, sc in corner ch-5 lp, sc in corner sc of First Motif, ch 7, sc in ch-3 lp of Second Motif, sc in corresponding sc of First Motif; (ch 2, sc in next sp of Second Motif, ch 2, sc in corresponding sp of First Motif) 8 times; ch 2, sc in ch-3 lp of Second Motif, sc in corresponding sc of First Motif, ch 7, sc in corner lp of Second Motif, sc in corner sc of First Motif. Complete as for Rnd 13 of First Motif. Fasten off.

Repeat Second Motif until 204 motifs are completed and joined in a rectangle of 12 rows of 17 motifs each.

EDGING: *Rnd 1:* Join thread in next to last ch-5 lp after corner; ch 4, trc in same lp; * (ch 5, 2 trc in next lp) to next corner, ch 5; 2 trc, ch 5, and 2 trc in lp before corner sc; rep from * around; end ch 5; join to top of beg ch-4.

Rnd 2: Sl st in next trc and next sp, ch 4; work trc-cl, ch 3, trc-cl, ch 3, and trc-cl in same sp; * (ch 5, sc in next lp) twice; ch 5, ** trc-cl, ch 3, trc-cl, ch 3, and trc-cl in next sp; rep from * to within 2 lps of beg; rep from * to **; join as before.

Rnd 3: Sl st in first trc-cl and next sp, ch 1, sc in same sp, * ch 5, sc in next sp; rep from * around; end ch 5, sl st in first sc; fasten off.

Lacy Meadows

NATURE'S WONDERS IN FILET CROCHET

Victorians were mad for Mother Nature in all her many guises, and many a talented designer sought to capture her exquisite patterns in nets of filet crochet. The poet Elizabeth Barrett Browning might have had this collection of lacy confections in mind when she wrote: "I have been in the meadows all day, and gathered there the nosegay that you see."

The sumptuous spread of rose-patterned filet crochet, *opposite,* features a formal repeat pattern of rose blocks framed in a scalloped border of single blossoms. A dainty 20x22-inch doily with rose bouquet corners fronts the matching ruffled pillow.

*lowers of the field, with
their uncluttered shapes and hearty demeanor, held a
special appeal for early 20th-century needle
artists—many of whom were creative gardeners
as well. The poppy border, opposite, is a case in point.
Each flower appears to be a distinct individual, yet all
seem to bend and sway in the wind with a collective
symphonic exuberance.*

The deep filet border of wind-blown poppies that edges the luncheon cloth, *opposite*, is a magnificent example of Victorian design. Measuring a generous 12 inches deep, this lyrical pattern is adapted to fit a 44½x46-inch cloth.

A bouquet of daisies bedecks the filet insert and luxurious scalloped edging on an old-fashioned linen pillow slip, *right.* The center of each blossom is embellished with a circlet of popcorn stitches, adding depth and texture to this simple pattern. Both insert and edging are easily extended to any length you choose.

See pages 92–95 for instructions and charts for working the cloth edging and page 96 for the pillow edgings.

Cabinets full of birds' nests and baskets of speckled eggs, carefully mounted butterfly specimens, and stacks of sketchbooks filled with pictures of local flora and fauna were cherished treasures in almost every 19th-century American household.

Adventuresome young ladies and their gentlemen companions spent many leisure moments in fields and forests or strolling along the seashore, diligently collecting humble examples of Mother Nature's bounty.

For stay-at-home sisters—and their mothers and aunts—this popular passion for natural history was fueled with a flood of commercially produced patterns. Published in magazines and booklets or offered as sheet handouts, these splendid designs celebrated the incredible beauty and grace to be found in the world of nature.

An enchanting bird and bush motif that resembles the folk art of the Pennsylvania Dutch parades across the filet flounce on the chaise longue, *left.* Used here as a dust ruffle, the same design would serve equally well as a window valance or an elegant edging for sheets or window shades.

A bevy of butterflies trims a small cloth draped across the bedside table, *opposite.* Accented with triangular motifs and edged with a delicate border, this design reflects the airiness of a quiet summer day.

See pages 97 and 98 for instructions for these projects.

Here are two more examples of the Victorians' boundless enthusiasm for botanical designs. The fanciful vineyard motif of grape clusters and vine leaves, *above,* embellishes the insertion panel on an oversize pillow sham. Crochet this strip or any of the other patterns in the book to make a pillow like this one. A few tucks or rows of drawn threadwork or faggoting help integrate the panel into the overall design.

A luncheon cloth, *opposite,* strewn with a thicket of thistles features triangular crocheted inserts on the center square and a garden of thistles "all in a row" on the 7⅛-inch-deep patterned border. Notice the stitched mitered corner that makes this edging a masterful and challenging design.

The instructions for the thistle cloth edging and inserts begin on page 100; the pillow sham panel instructions are on page 103.

WORKING FILET CROCHET DESIGNS

Perhaps the easiest crochet patterns to stitch are filet crochet designs. These exquisite and often intricate designs are worked from charts that are filled with blocks and spaces that create the pattern and allow the crocheter to turn thread into lovely lacy fabric. These designs are used for edgings and insertions in bed linens (see pages 36 and 52), for tablecloths and runners (see pages 9, 64, and 67), for chair antimacassars (see page 10), and for all the projects in this chapter.

Stitching the designs

Filet patterns are worked in rows and produced by stitching an open "net" background where filled-in spaces, called blocks, form the design. These spaces are made by working a chain-2 loop between 2 double crochets. When you build a pattern of blocks within these spaces, you create the design.

To begin a filet pattern, you crochet a foundation chain upon which the first row of the design begins. For ease in remembering the block and space sequence, keep in mind that each block or space is equal to 3 stitches, *plus 1 more stitch.* For example, 1 block is 4 double crochets (1x3, plus 1); 2 side-by-side blocks are 7 double crochets (2x3, plus 1); 3 side-by-side blocks are 10 double crochets (3x3, plus 1).

The patterns are worked from charts in which 1 square equals 1 filet space or 1 filet block.

When working from a chart, read the odd-numbered rows from right to left and the even-numbered rows from left to right, unless the instructions specify otherwise.

Working a space over a space

Double crochet in the double crochet in the row below, work 2 chains, then double crochet in the next double crochet in the row below.

Working a space over a block

Double crochet in the first stitch of the block of the previous row, work 2 chains, skip 2 double crochets, then double crochet in the next double crochet.

Working a block over a space

Double crochet in the double crochet before the space in the row below, work 2 double crochets in the chain-2 space; work a double crochet in the next double crochet.

Working a block over a block

Double crochet in each of the 4 double crochets of the previous row.

Working scalloped edges

Many patterns have scalloped edges that require you to increase or decrease the number of blocks or spaces at the beginning or end of a row. Patterns in this book cite the directions for making increases and decreases at the ends of the rows when called for in the design.

Working turning chains

When working along the straight edges at the ends of rows, you'll need to chain to turn the work and begin the next row. When the pattern begins with a block, chain 3 to turn and to count as the first double crochet.

When the pattern begins with a space, chain 5 to turn and to count as the first double crochet and the first chain-2 space.

Using other stitch patterns in filet crochet

Many patterns use other combinations of stitches to form interesting backgrounds for filet designs. For example, the thistle edging on page 87 is framed by the combination of lacet stitches and chain-5 loops. The directions for this "netting" and any other open background follow the same mathematical sequence (3, plus 1) as the basic filet crochet technique. Unusual background stitches are given with each project in this book.

Working mitered corners

We recommend that only the advanced crocheter attempt the filet designs that incorporate the design in a mitered corner. The corner areas are shaded in our patterns for ease in working. To keep the work lying flat and to maintain the design, it is necessary to work short rows and join these rows to the existing work with either slip stitches, double crochets, or chain stitches. The crocheter needs to determine which stitch works best to begin the next row.

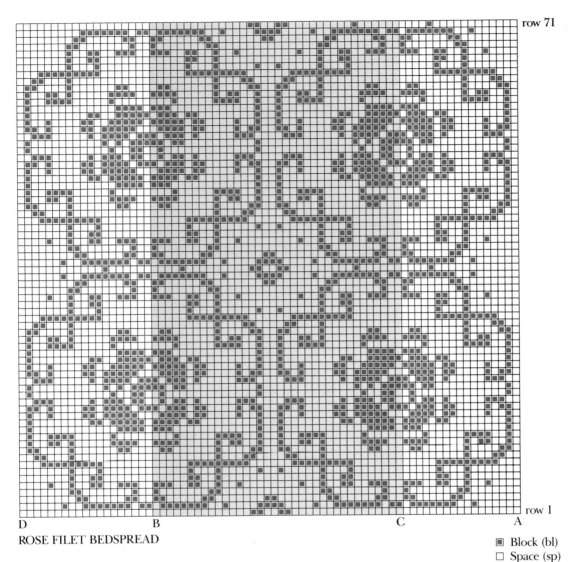

row 71

row 1

D   B   C   A

ROSE FILET BEDSPREAD

▣ Block (bl)
☐ Space (sp)

ROSE FILET BEDSPREAD

Shown on pages 80 and 81.

Bedspread measures approximately 88x92¼ inches.

MATERIALS
DMC Cordonnet Special crochet cotton, Size 10 (124-yard ball): 157 balls of off-white
Size 10 steel crochet hook

Abbreviations: See page 186.
Gauge: 6 spaces = 1 inch; 6 rows = 1 inch.

INSTRUCTIONS
For additional information for working filet crochet patterns, refer to the tip box, *opposite.*

Note: The scalloped edging is worked separately and hand-sewn to the center of the spread after all the crocheting is completed.

Beginning along the narrow edge of the spread, ch 1,301.

Row 1: Dc in eighth ch from hook; (ch 2, sk 2 ch, dc in next ch) 32 times; dc in next 6 ch; (ch 2, sk 2 ch, dc in next ch) twice; dc in next 6 ch; (ch 2, sk 2 ch, dc in next ch) 14 times—point B on chart, *above;* begin to work the pat rep
continued

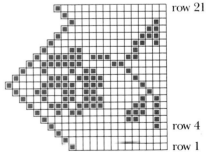

row 21

row 4

row 1

ROSE MOTIF BEDSPREAD EDGING
▣ Block (bl)
☐ Space (sp)

bet C and B as follows: * (ch 2, sk 2 ch, dc in next ch) 16 times; dc in next 6 ch; (ch 2, sk 2 ch, dc in next ch) twice; dc in next 6 ch; (ch 2, sk 2 ch, dc in next ch) 14 times; rep from * across row 9 times more; (ch 2, sk 2 ch, dc in next ch) 19 times; ch 5, turn.

Rows 2–71: Keeping to pat as established on chart, work all even-numbered rows from left to right and all odd-numbered rows from right to left.

When working even-numbered rows, work across chart from D to C; rep from B to C 11 times; work from C to A once. When working odd-numbered rows, work across chart from A to B; rep from C to B 11 times; work from B to D once.

Always ch 5 at ends of rows to turn.

Rep rows 2–71 for desired length or until 15 motifs are completed; fasten off.

EDGING: Ch 47.

Row 1: Dc in eighth ch from hook; (ch 2, sk 2 ch, dc in next ch) 12 times; dc in last 3 ch; ch 5, turn.

Row 2: **Dc in fourth and fifth ch from hook, dc in next dc—bl inc made at beg of row;** ch 2, sk 2 dc, dc in next dc; (ch 2, dc in next ch) 12 times; ch 2, sk 2 dc, dc in next ch; ch 5, turn.

Row 3: Sk first dc, dc in next dc; (ch 2, dc in next dc) 13 times; ch 2, sk 2 dc, dc in next dc; **yo hook, draw up lp in base of last dc made, yo, draw through 1 lp on hook—base ch made for next dc; (yo, draw through 2 lps on hook) twice; * yo hook, draw up lp in base ch, yo, draw through 1 lp on hook—base ch for next dc; complete st as for dc; rep from * once more—bl inc made at end of row;** ch 5, turn.

Rows 4–21: Work from edging chart on page 89. When beginning rows 12, 14, 16, and 18, do

not ch 5 to turn at the end of the previous row. Instead, turn work and sl st across the 4 dc; ch 3, and beg to work the first bl of the row.

Rep rows 4–21 for required length. Work 4 strip edgings—two to fit along the length of the spread and two to fit across the width of the spread. Use crochet thread to whipstitch the edging strips to the spread.

ROSE DOILY PILLOW

Shown on page 81.

Doily measures 20x22 inches; pillow measures 28½x30½ inches, including ruffles and piping.

MATERIALS
DMC Cebelia crochet cotton, Size 20 (405-yard ball): 3 balls
Size 11 steel crochet hook
Two *each* 21x23-inch pieces of chintz fabric for pillow front and back
1x86-inch strip of chintz to cover cotton cording for piping
2½ yards of cotton cording for piping
1¼ yards of printed chintz for pillow ruffle
Polyester fiberfill

Abbreviations: See page 186.
Gauge: 5 spaces = 1 inch; 5 rows = 1 inch.

INSTRUCTIONS
For additional information for working filet crochet patterns, refer to the tip box on page 88.

Note: The seven rounds of the edging are worked after the center of the doily is made. The edging is shaded on the pattern, *opposite.* Do not work these rounds when you work the doily center.

Ch 297.

Row 1: Dc in fourth ch from hook and in each ch across—295 dc, counting turning ch as dc; ch 3, turn.

Row 2: Sk first dc, dc in next 3 dc; * ch 2, sk 2 dc, dc in next dc; rep from * across until 4 sts remain—96 sp across; dc in next 3 dc and in top of turning ch; ch 3, turn.

Row 3: Sk first dc, dc in next 3 dc; (ch 2, dc in next dc) twice—2 sp; 2 dc in next ch-2 sp, dc in next dc—bl made; make 31 sp; 1 bl, 26 sp; 1 bl, 31 sp; 1 bl; 2 sp, dc in next 2 dc and top of turning ch; ch 3, turn.

Row 4: Following chart, *opposite,* and reading from left to right, work row across.

Row 5: Sk first dc, dc in next 3 dc; work 2 sp; 2 bl, 2 sp; 1 bl, 6 sp; 1 bl, 2 sp, 1 bl, 13 sp; 3 bl, 1 sp; 2 bl, 2 sp; 3 bl, 6 sp; **ch 3, sc in next dc, ch 3, dc in next dc—lacet st made;** complete row following chart; ch 3, turn.

Row 6: Work across row, following chart to first lacet st; **ch 5, dc in next dc—ch-5 lp made;** follow chart to complete row.

Note: Hereafter, when working lacet st, work the sc in the center ch of the ch-5 lp of the previous row.

Rows 7–98: Work from chart—295 dc across at end of Row 98.
At end of Row 98, ch 5, turn.

EDGING: *Rnd 1:* Sk next 2 dc, dc in next dc; * ch 2, sk 2 dc, dc in next dc; rep from * across—98 sp; **ch 5, dc in same st as last dc—corner made;** ** ch 2, dc in st at top of next row; rep from ** across side—98 sp; work corner; rep bet * along next side; work corner; rep between ** on next side; ch 2, dc in third ch of beg ch-5; do not turn.

Rnd 2: Ch 5, dc in same ch as last dc; * ch 2, dc in next dc; rep

rnd 1
row 98

row 7
row 5

row 1

ROSE DOILY PILLOW

▣ Block (bl)   ⋈ Lacet Stitch
☐ Space (sp)   ⊓ Ch-5 Loop

from * across row to ch-5 corner lp; ch 2, dc in third ch of ch-5; ch 5, dc in same ch as last dc; work remaining two sides as established; end ch 2, dc in third ch of beg ch-5; do not turn.

Rnds 3–7: Work from chart, continuing to work corners as established. At end of Rnd 7, fasten off; block doily.

PILLOW ASSEMBLY: Cover cotton cording with piping fabric; trim seam to ¼ inch. Sew piping to pillow front with right sides facing. Cut ruffle fabric into four 8½-inch-wide strips; sew strips together to make one circle. Fold fabric in half to make ruffle piece 4¼ inches wide, with wrong sides

facing. Gather ruffle to fit pillow front; sew ruffle to pillow front atop piping seam, with right sides facing. Sew pillow front to pillow back, leaving an opening for turning and taking care not to enclose ruffle in seams. Clip seams and turn pillow to right side; stuff and sew opening closed. Use sewing thread to hand-sew doily to pillow top next to piping edge.

BUTTERFLY AND POPPY CLOTH EDGING

Shown on page 82.

This edging fits a hemmed cloth that measures approximately 44x46 inches and is 11 inches across the widest point of each scallop.

MATERIALS

DMC Cordonnet crochet cotton, Size 50 (286-yard ball): 21 balls (1 ball makes 9½ inches of lace)
Size 14 steel crochet hook
47x49-inch piece of linen or fabric of your choice for cloth

Abbreviations: See page 186.
Gauge: 7 spaces = 1 inch; 8 rows = 1 inch.

INSTRUCTIONS

For additional information for working filet crochet patterns, refer to tip box on page 88.

FIRST SIDE: Ch 228.
Row 1: Dc in fourth ch from hook and in next 2 ch; **(ch 3, sk 2 ch, sc in next ch, ch 3, sk 2 ch, dc in next ch—lacet st made)** 3 times; dc in next 6 ch; (ch 2, sk 2 ch, dc in next ch) twice; dc in next 3 ch; (ch 2, sk 2 ch, dc in next ch) 34 times; dc in next 3 ch, ch 2, sk 2 ch, dc in next 4 ch; (ch 2, sk 2 ch, dc in next ch) twice; dc in next 6 ch, ch 2, sk 2 ch, dc in next 13 ch; (ch 2, sk 2 ch, dc in next ch) 3 times; dc in next 6 ch, ch 5, sk 5 ch, dc in next 7 ch, ch 5, sk 5 ch, dc in next ch, ch 2, sk 2 ch, dc in next 13 ch, ch 2, sk 2 ch, dc in last ch; ch 5, turn.
Row 2: Sk first dc, dc in next 13 dc, ch 2, dc in next dc, ch 5, dc in next 4 dc, ch 2, sk 2 dc, dc in next dc, ch 5, dc in next 7 dc; (ch 2, dc in next dc) 3 times; ch 2, sk 2 dc, dc in next 7 dc, ch 2, sk 2 dc, dc in next dc, 2 dc in ch-2 lp, dc in next 7 dc, ch 2, dc in next dc, 2 dc in ch-2 lp, dc in next 4 dc, ch 2, dc in next dc, ch 2, sk 2 dc, dc in next dc, 2 dc in ch-2 lp, dc in next dc; (ch 2, dc in next dc) 33 times; ch 2, sk 2 dc, dc in next dc, ch 2, dc in next dc, ch 2, dc in next 7 dc; (ch 5, dc in next dc) 3 times; dc in next 2 dc and in top of turning ch; ch 3, turn.
Row 3: Sk first dc, dc in next 3 dc, work 3 lacet st, dc in 6 dc; (ch 2, dc in next dc) 35 times; 2 dc in ch-2 lp, dc in next 4 dc; (ch 2, dc in next dc) twice; dc in 6 dc, ch 2, dc in next dc, ch 2, sk 2 dc, dc in next 7 dc, 2 dc in ch-2 lp, dc in next dc; ch 2, sk 2 dc, dc in next 4 dc, 2 dc in ch-2 lp, dc in next dc, (ch 2, dc in next dc) 3 times; dc in next 6 dc, 3 dc in ch-5 lp, ch 5, sk dc, dc in next 4 dc, ch 5, dc in next dc, ch 5, sk 3 dc, dc in next 7 dc, ch 2, sk 2 dc, **holding back last lp of each dc, dc in next dc, sk 2 ch of turning ch, dc in next ch— half-bl dec at end of odd-numbered row made;** ch 5, turn.
Row 4: Sk first dc, dc in next dc; reading from left to right, work from chart, *opposite.*
Rows 5–281: Work from chart. Rows 134–267 are on page 94; rows 268–281 are on page 95.
To work half-block increase at beginning of row (see rows 22, 26, 36, and 42): Ch 5 to turn at end of previous row, dc in first dc.
To work block and half-block increases at beginning of row (see rows 30 and 96): Ch 8 to turn at end of previous row, dc in sixth ch from hook, ch 2, dc in next dc.
To work block increase at end of row (see Row 35): Ch 2, dtr (yo hook 3 times) in base of last dc made.

CORNER: Following chart on page 95, work rows 282–338. Do not work shaded areas at this time; fasten off at end of Row 338.

TURNING THE CORNER: Join thread and work shaded rows 339–429, working these stitches perpendicular to the existing work. Row 339 is worked into the sides of the stitches of Row 338 and so are all subsequent rows as they are joined to the existing work. The shaded area on the chart shows the placement for the stitches for the corner and the beginning of the next side. When joining work in progress to work that is already made with a space block, work across row to last dc (do not ch 2); work hdc in dc— last sp made; ch 3, work hdc in next dc—first sp of next row made; turn work and complete row following chart. At end of Row 429, fasten off.

SECOND SIDE OF EDGING: Join thread at inside edge of Row 429 and work Row 1 of chart; rep rows 2–429 to complete next side of cloth edging.

Work this side and the remaining two sides as established for the first side. At end of Row 429 of fourth side, fasten off.

Whipstitch beginning and ending edges together.

EDGING ALONG SCAL-LOPED EDGE: Join thread in any turning-ch space along scalloped edge; ch 3, work 3 dc in same sp; * ch 3, sk next row, sc in next turning-sp row; ch 3, sk next row; 4 dc in next turning-sp row; rep from * around; end ch 3, join to top of beg ch-3; fasten off. Wash and block edging.

FINISHING: Wash fabric; hem to fit edging. With sewing thread, hand-sew edging to hemmed cloth.

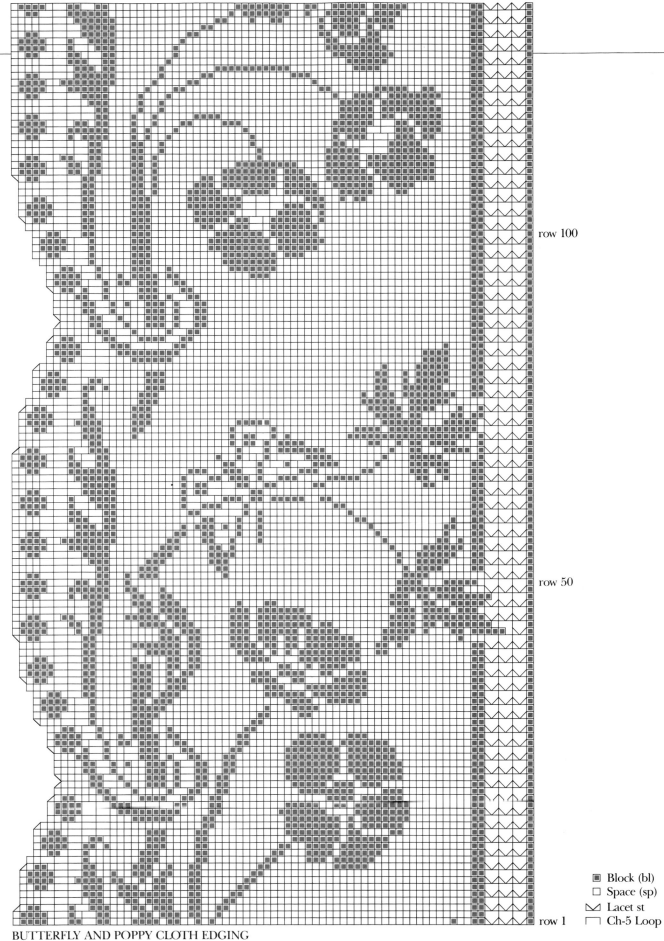

row 100

row 50

◨ Block (bl)
☐ Space (sp)
⋈ Lacet st
☐ Ch-5 Loop

row 1

BUTTERFLY AND POPPY CLOTH EDGING

93

row 250

row 200

row 150

Block (bl)
Space (sp)
Lacet st
Ch-5 Loop

BUTTERFLY AND POPPY CLOTH EDGING (continued)

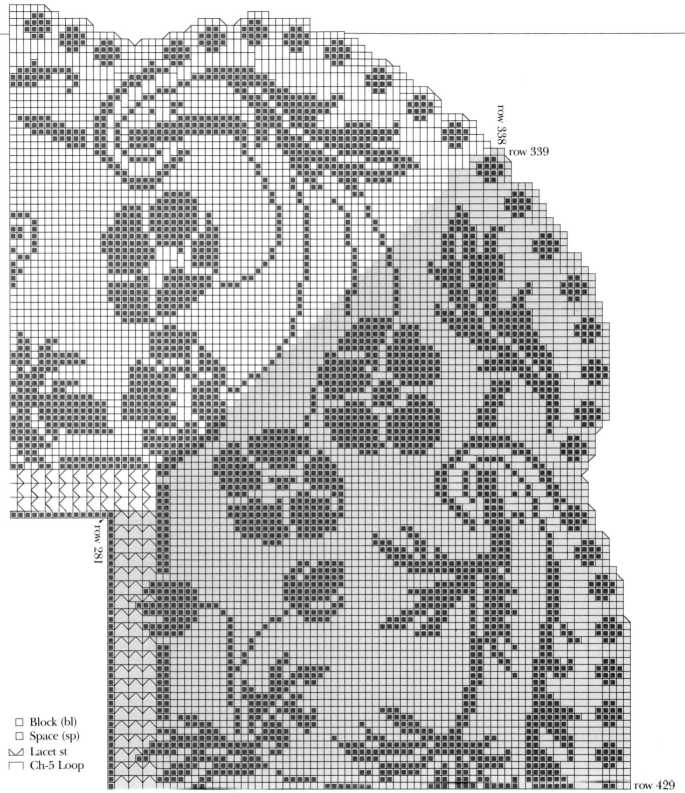

row 338

row 339

row 281

row 429

☐ Block (bl)
☐ Space (sp)
◁▷ Lacet st
☐ Ch-5 Loop

BUTTERFLY AND POPPY CLOTH EDGING (continued)

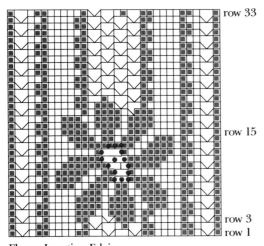

Flower Insertion Edging
FLOWER PILLOWCASE EDGINGS

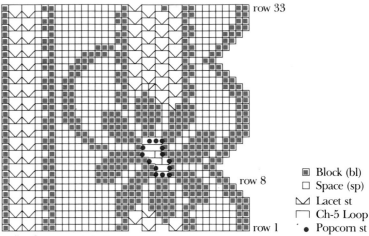

Flower Scalloped Edging

■ Block (bl)
□ Space (sp)
⋈ Lacet st
▭ Ch-5 Loop
● Popcorn st

FLOWER PILLOWCASE EDGING

Shown on page 83.

Insertion panel measures 5 inches across. Scalloped edging measures 5¾ inches across the widest points.

MATERIALS

DMC Cordonnet Special, Size 40 (249-yard ball): 1 ball makes 16 inches of lace
Size 14 steel crochet hook
Pair of pillowcases

Abbreviations: See page 186.
Gauge: 7 bls = 1 inch; 8 rows = 1 inch.

INSTRUCTIONS
For the insertion edging
Ch 99.

Row 1: Dc in fourth ch from hook and in next 3 ch; **ch 3, sk 2 ch, sc in next ch, ch 3, sk 2 ch, dc in next ch—lacet st made;** ch 2, sk 2 ch, dc in next 7 ch; (ch 2, sk 2 ch, dc in next ch) 4 times; dc in next 6 ch; (work lacet st, **ch 5, sk 5 ch, dc in next ch—ch-5 lp made)** 2 times; dc in next 6 ch; (ch 2, sk 2 ch, dc in next ch) 4 times; dc in next 6 ch, ch 2, sk 2 ch, dc in next ch, work lacet st, dc in last 3 ch; ch 3, turn.

Row 2: **Sk first dc, dc in next 3 dc—beg bl made; ch 5, dc in next dc—ch-5 lp over lacet st made;** ch 2, dc in next 7 dc; (ch 2, dc in next dc) 4 times, ch 2, sk 2 dc, dc in next 4 dc; **ch 3, sc in center ch of ch-5 lp, ch 3, dc in next dc—lacet st over ch-5 lp made;** ch 5, dc in next dc, ch 2, 3 dc over end of ch-5 lp, dc in next dc, ch 5, dc in next 7 dc; (ch 2, dc in next dc) 4 times; dc in next 6 dc, ch 2, dc in next dc, ch 5, dc in next 3 dc and top of turning ch-3; ch 3, turn.

Rows 3–8: Work from chart, *above left.*

Row 9: Work beg bl, 1 lacet st, 2 sp, 1 bl, 4 sp, 4 bl; (**work 5 dc in next dc, drop hook from work, insert hook in top of first dc of 5-dc grp, draw dropped lp through—popcorn [pc] made;** dc in next dc) 3 times; 2 dc in ch-2 sp; dc in next dc; complete row following chart; ch 3, turn.

Row 10: Work beg bl, ch-5 lp, ch 2, dc in next dc, 2 dc in ch-2 lp, dc in next 4 dc, 1 sp, 5 bl, 2 sp, dc in next 6 dc, pc over pc, ch 2, sk 2 st, dc in next dc, pc over pc, dc in next 4 dc, 7 sp; complete row following chart; ch 3, turn.

Row 11: Work beg bl, lacet st, ch 2, dc in 7 dc; 3 sp, 5 bl, pc over pc, ch 2, dc in ch-2 lp, ch 2, sk 2 st, pc in next dc, dc in next 5 dc; complete row following chart; ch 3, turn.

Row 12: Work beg bl, ch-5 lp, ch 2, dc in next dc, ch 2, sk 2 dc, dc in next 4 dc, 3 sp, dc in next 16 dc, pc in next dc, ch 3, pc in ch-2 lp, ch 3, pc in next ch-2 lp, dc in pc and in next 16 dc; complete row following chart; ch 3, turn.

Row 13: Work beg bl, lacet st, ch 2, dc in next dc, 2 dc in ch-2 lp, dc in next 4 dc, 1 sp, 5 bl, 2 sp, dc in next 2 st, pc in ch-3 sp, ch 5, dc in next pc, pc in next dc, dc in next 3 dc; complete row following chart; ch 3, turn.

Row 14: Work beg bl, ch-5 lp, ch 2, dc in 7 dc, 4 sp; (2 dc in ch-2 lp, dc in next dc) 3 times; dc in next 5 sts; in ch-5 lp work pc, 2 dc, pc, and 2 dc; pc in next pc, dc in next 3 dc; complete row following chart; ch 3, turn.

Rows 15–33: Work from chart.

Rep rows 3–33 for pat for desired length; fasten off.

For the scalloped edging
Ch 114.

Row 1: Dc in fourth ch from hook and in next 5 ch; (ch 2, sk 2 ch, dc in next ch) 6 times; dc in next 6 ch; **(ch 3, sk 2 ch, sc in next ch, ch 3, sk 2 ch, dc in next ch—lacet st made; ch 5, sk 5 ch, dc in next ch—ch-5 lp made)** 2 times; dc in next 6 ch; (ch 2, sk 2 ch, dc in next ch) 9 times, dc in 6 dc, ch 2, sk 2 ch, dc in next ch, work 2 lacet st, dc in last 3 ch; ch 3, turn.

Rows 2–33: Work from chart, *opposite, near left,* referring to instructions for Insertion Edging (rows 9–13) to work popcorn st in flower centers.

When decreasing bl at end of even-numbered rows, work across row leaving 3 sts unworked; turn.

When decreasing bl at beg of odd-numbered rows, sk first dc, sl st in each of next 3 dc, ch 3, and work from chart.

To increase bl at beg of odd-numbered rows, ch 5, turn at end of previous row; then dc in fourth and fifth ch from hook, dc in next dc.

Rep rows 3–33 for pat for desired length; fasten off.

Wash and block edgings. Baste, then sew insertion strips to pillowcases. Cut away fabric behind strips, leaving ½-inch seam allowances. Turn back ¼-inch seams twice; press and sew hems in place. Whipstitch the scalloped edgings to ends of cases.

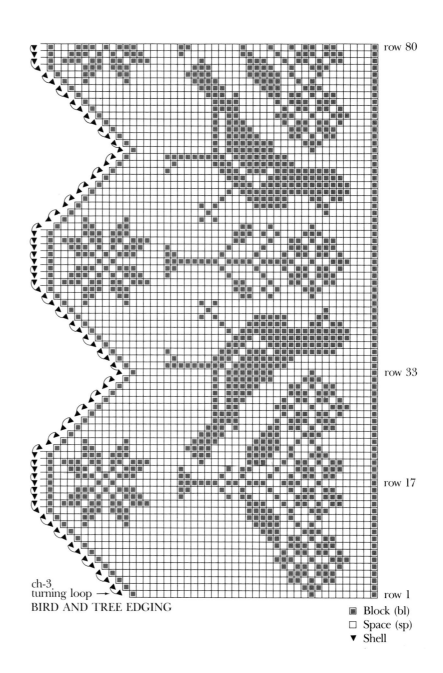

row 80

row 33

row 17

ch-3
turning loop →
BIRD AND TREE EDGING

row 1

■ Block (bl)
☐ Space (sp)
▼ Shell

BIRD AND TREE EDGING

Shown on pages 84 and 85.

Edging measures 8½ inches across the widest point of each scallop.

MATERIALS
DMC Cebelia crochet cotton, Size 30 (563-yard ball): 1 ball makes approximately 18 inches of edging
Size 12 steel crochet hook

Abbreviations: See page 186.
Gauge: 6 spaces = 1 inch; 6 rows = 1 inch.

continued

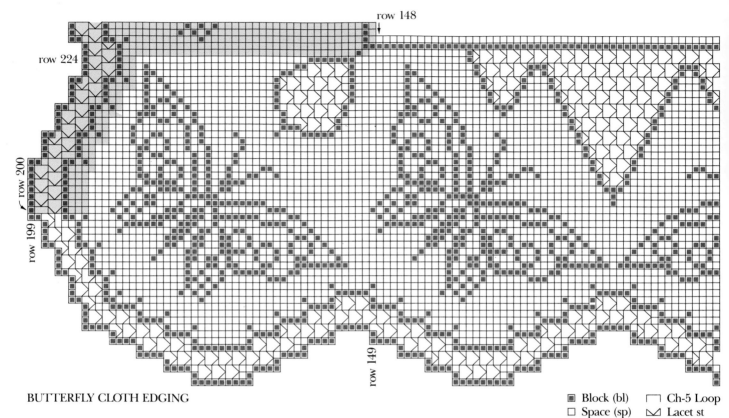

row 148

row 224

row 200

row 199

row 149

BUTTERFLY CLOTH EDGING

■ Block (bl)   ☐ Ch-5 Loop
☐ Space (sp)   ⋈ Lacet st

INSTRUCTIONS

Note: For additional information for working filet crochet patterns, refer to tip box on page 88.

Ch 114.

Row 1: Dc in fourth ch from hook and in next 2 ch; (ch 2, sk 2 ch, dc in next ch) 8 times; dc in next 3 ch; (ch 2, sk 2 ch, dc in next ch) 25 times; dc in next 3 ch, ch 2, in last ch work **3 dc, ch 2, and 3 dc—shell made;** ch 3, turn.

Row 2: Work shell in ch-2 sp of shell; ch 2, dc in last dc of shell, 2 dc in ch-2 sp, dc in next dc; ch 2, sk 2 dc, dc in next dc; (ch 2, dc in next dc) 24 times; 2 dc in next lp, dc in next 4 dc, 2 dc in next lp, dc in next dc; (ch 2, dc in next dc) 7 times; dc in next 2 dc and in top of turning ch; ch 3, turn.

Row 3: Work from chart on page 97; end with ch 2, shell in ch-2 sp of shell; ch 3, turn.

Row 4: Work shell in ch-2 sp of shell, ch 2, dc in last dc of shell, 2 dc in ch-2 lp, dc in next dc, ch 2, sk 2 dc, dc in next dc; continue to work across row following chart.

Rows 5–80: Work from chart.

Note: When working the rows along the edges that decrease along the scallops, do not work the ch-2 sp at the end of the odd-numbered rows before working the shells, and do not work the ch-2 sp after the shells on the even-numbered rows.

Rep rows 17–80 for desired length. If you want the end of your strip to match the beginning, finish the strip by working rows 17–33 *except* do not work the bird motif; complete the star and tree motifs and work open spaces for the blocks that fill the bird spaces.

Fasten off at end of strip; use sewing thread to whipstitch the edging to the desired item.

BUTTERFLY CLOTH EDGING

Shown on page 84.

Edging measures 7½ inches across the widest point of each scallop. The instructions are for edging that fits a hemmed cloth, approximately 32x33 inches.

MATERIALS

DMC Cordonnet Special crochet cotton, Size 30 (216-yard ball): 1 ball makes 10 inches of lace
Size 13 steel crochet hook
34x35-inch piece of linen or fabric of your choice for cloth

Abbreviations: See page 186.
Gauge: 6 spaces = 1 inch; 7 rows = 1 inch.

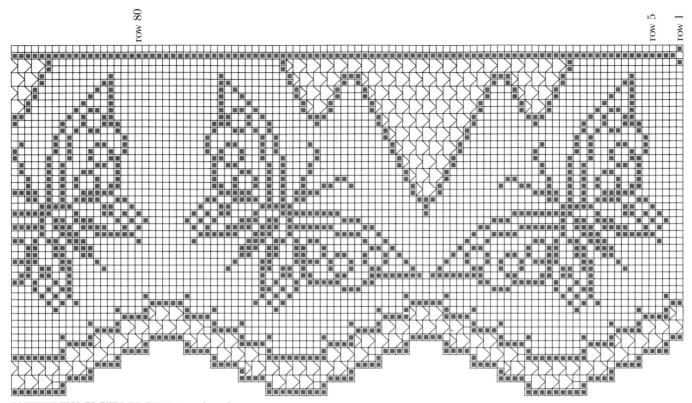

row 80

row 5

row 1

BUTTERFLY CLOTH EDGING (continued)

INSTRUCTIONS

FIRST SIDE OF EDGING: Ch 132.

Row 1: Dc in fourth ch from hook and in next 2 ch; ch 2, sk 2 ch, dc in next 4 ch; (ch 2, sk 2 ch, dc in next ch) 34 times; dc in next 3 ch; **ch 5, sk 5 ch, dc in next ch—ch-5 lp made; ch 3, sk 2 ch, sc in next ch, ch 3, sk 2 ch, dc in next ch—lacet st made;** dc in next 3 ch; ch 3, turn.

Row 2: Sk first dc, dc in next 3 dc, ch 5, dc in next dc, ch 3, sc in center ch of ch-5 lp, ch 3, dc in next 4 dc; (ch 2, dc in next dc) 34 times; ch 2, sk 2 dc, dc in next dc, 2 dc in ch-2 lp, dc in next dc, ch 2, sk 2 dc, dc in top of turning ch; ch 5, turn.

Rows 3–80: Work from chart, *above.*

To increase two blocks at ends of odd-numbered rows: * Yo hook, draw up lp in base of last dc made, yo, draw through 1 lp on hook—base ch for next dc; (yo, draw through 2 lps on hook) 2 times; working in base ch, rep from * 5 times more; ch 3, turn.

To decrease two blocks at beginning of even-numbered rows: Do not ch 3 to turn at end of previous row; turn and sl st across 7 dc, ch 3, and continue to work from chart.

Rep rows 5–80 once more.

Work rows 81–148 once following chart, *above and opposite.*

CORNER MOTIF: Following chart, work rows 149–199. Do not work shaded areas; fasten off at end of Row 199.

TO TURN THE CORNER: Join thread and work shaded rows 200–224, working these stitches perpendicular to the existing work. Row 200 is worked into the sides of the stitches of Row 199. Work across row to last dc (do not ch 2); work hdc in dc—last sp made; ch 3, work hdc in next dc—first sp of next row made; turn work and complete row following chart. When Row 224 is completed, fasten off.

SECOND SIDE OF EDGING: Join thread at inside corner of Row 150, and work rows 1–80 perpendicular to completed side. The shaded area on the chart shows the placement for the stitches for the next side. Work this side and the remaining two sides as established for the first side. At end of Row 224 of fourth corner, fasten off.

Whipstitch beginning and ending rows of crocheted edging together. Hem fabric to fit the edging. Hand-sew edging to hemmed cloth.

row 384
row 383
row 440
← row 346
← row 326
row 37
row 1

■ Block (bl)
□ Space (sp)
⋈ Lacet st
⬓ Ch-5 Loop

Thistle Border Edging
THISTLE CLOTH EDGINGS

Triangle Insertion
THISTLE CLOTH EDGINGS

THISTLE CLOTH
EDGINGS

Shown on page 87.

Border edging measures 7⅛ inches across. Insertion triangle measures 22 inches along the baseline (Row 1) of the triangle.

──────**MATERIALS**──────
DMC Cordonnet Special crochet cotton, Size 40 (249-yard ball): 22 balls (1 ball makes 13 inches of border lace)
Size 14 steel crochet hook
54-inch square of linen fabric for cloth

continued

■ Block (bl)
□ Space (sp)
⋈ Lacet st
⊓ Ch-5 Loop

row 132

row 5
row 3
row 1

Abbreviations: See page 186.
Gauge: 16 dc = 1 inch; 7 rows = 1 inch.

INSTRUCTIONS
Note: For additional information for working filet crochet patterns, see the tip box on page 88.

For the triangle insertion
Ch 401.

Row 1: Dc in eighth ch from hook; * ch 2, sk 2 ch, dc in next dc; rep from * across; ch 5, turn.

Row 2: Sk first dc, dc in next dc; * ch 2, dc in next dc; rep from * across; end ch 2, sk 2 ch of turning ch, dc in next ch; ch 5, turn.

Row 3: Sk first dc, dc in next dc; (ch 2, dc in next dc) 3 times; * **ch 3, sc in next dc, ch 3, dc in next dc—lacet st made**; (ch 2, dc in next ch) twice; rep from * across until 4 sp rem; (ch 2, dc in next dc) 2 times; ch 5, turn.

Row 4: Sk first dc, dc in next dc; (ch 2, dc in next dc) 3 times; * **ch 5; dc in next dc—ch-5 lp made**; work lacet st, working sc in next dc; rep from * across until 2 sp rem; ch 2, dc in next dc, ch 2, sk 2 ch of turning ch, dc in next ch; ch 5, turn.

Row 5: Sk first dc, dc in next dc, ch 2, dc in next dc; (ch 5, dc in next dc, work lacet st, working sc in center ch of ch-5 lp) 6 times; (work 3 dc in next ch-3 lp, work 2 dc in next ch-3 lp; dc in next dc, work 5 dc in next ch-5 lp) 18 times; work 3 dc in next ch-3 lp, work 2 dc in next ch-3 lp, dc in next dc; (work lacet st over ch-5 lp, work ch-5 lp over next lacet st) 6 times; ch 2, dc in center ch of ch-5 lp; (ch 2, dc in next dc) 3 times; ch 5, turn.

Rows 6–132: Work from Triangle Insertion chart on pages 100 and 101. Read all even-numbered rows from left to right and all odd-numbered rows from right to left. Follow chart across the page to complete each row; always ch 5 to turn. Fasten off at end of Row 132. In the same manner, make three more triangle insertions.

For the border edging
Ch 117.

Row 1: Dc in fourth ch from hook and in next 5 ch; **(ch 3, sk 2 ch, sc in next ch, ch 3, sk 2 ch, dc in next ch—lacet st made; ch 5, sk 5 ch, dc in next ch—ch-5 lp made)** 7 times; ch 2, sk 2 ch, dc in next 22 ch; ch 8, turn.

Row 2: **Dc in fourth ch from hook and in next 4 ch—2 bl inc at beg of even-numbered row;** dc in next 16 dc; ch 2, sk 2 dc, dc in next dc; (work ch–5 lp, work lacet st working sc in center ch of ch-5 lp) 7 times; ch 5, dc in next 6 dc and in top of turning ch-3; ch 3, turn.

Row 3: Work from Thistle Border Edging chart on page 100 as established, working alternating ch-5 lp and lacet st; end with 5 bl; ch 8, turn.

Row 4: Work 2 bl inc, dc in next 10 dc; ch 2, sk 2 dc, dc in next dc, ch 5, sk 3 dc, dc in next dc; (work lacet st, work ch-5 lp) 2 times; work lacet st, work 3 dc in next ch-3 lp, work 2 dc in next ch-3 lp, dc in next dc; work 3 dc in next ch-5 lp, ch 2, dc in next dc; (work ch-5 lp, work lacet st) 4 times; work ch-5 lp, dc in next 5 dc and in top of turning ch-3; ch 3, turn.

Rows 5–37: Work from chart.
Rep rows 2–37 eight times more—325 rows completed.

Rows 326–346: Work from chart to complete side and to establish pattern to begin corner.

Rows 347–383 (mitered corner): Continue to work from chart; do not work the shaded area. Work short rows to establish half of corner design; fasten off at end of Row 383.

Row 384: Join thread in top of ch-3 at beg of Row 383, ch 8, turn; work 2 bl inc at beg of row and complete row, working in sides of dc of Row 383 to complete 2 more bl.

Row 385: Sl st across side of next dc to set up bl for beg of row, ch 3, and complete bl and remaining st of row.

Rows 386–440: Continue to work from chart, joining ends of odd-numbered rows to existing corner sts.

Rep rows 2–440 to work next side and corner. Work as established to complete rem 2 sides; fasten off. Whipstitch beg and end rows together.

CLOTH ASSEMBLY: Wash and press fabric and edgings before assembly. Lay border edging atop cloth and baste in place, keeping edges of fabric straight and even on all sides; sew the border edging to the fabric. Trim fabric along edges, leaving ½ inch for hem. Turn under ¼ inch twice; press and hand-sew hem in place.

Place the triangle motifs evenly spaced on center portions of cloth so adjacent points of triangles meet (diagonal sides of triangles form the center square); baste, then sew in place. Cut fabric away from behind the triangle insertions, leaving ½ inch for hem. Turn under ¼ inch twice; press and hand-sew hems in place.

GRAPE INSERT EDGING

Shown on page 86.

Edging measures 4 inches across.

MATERIALS

DMC Cebelia crochet cotton,
  Size 20 (405-yard ball): 1 ball
  makes 30 inches of lace
Size 13 steel crochet hook
Pair of pillowcases

Abbreviations: See page 186.
Gauge: 6 bls = 1 inch; 7 rows =
1 inch.

INSTRUCTIONS

Note: For additional information
for working filet crochet patterns,
refer to tip box on page 88.
  Ch 80.
  Row 1: Dc in eighth ch from
hook; * ch 2, sk 2 ch, dc in next
ch; rep from * across; ch 5, turn.
  Row 2: Sk first dc, dc in next dc;
* ch 2, dc in next dc; rep from *
across; end sk 2 ch of turning ch,
dc in next ch; ch 5, turn.
  Row 3: Sk first dc, dc in next dc;
(ch 2, dc in next dc) 15 times; 2 dc
in ch-2 lp, dc in next dc; (ch 2, dc
in next dc) 2 times; (2 dc in ch-2
lp, dc in next dc) 4 times; ch 2, dc
in next dc, ch 2, sk 2 ch of turning
ch, dc in next ch; ch 5, turn.
  Row 4: Sk first dc, dc in next dc,
ch 2, dc in next dc, ch 2, sk 2 dc,
dc in next 10 dc, 2 dc in ch-2 lp,
dc in next dc; ch 2, dc in next 4 dc,
2 dc in ch-2 lp, dc in next dc; (ch
2, dc in next dc) 14 times; ch 2, sk
2 ch of turning ch, dc in next ch;
ch 5, turn.
  Row 5: Sk first dc, dc in next dc;
(ch 2, dc in next dc) 12 times; 2 dc
in ch-2 lp, dc in next dc, ch 2, dc in

next 7 dc, 2 dc in ch-2 lp, dc in
next 13 dc; (ch 2, dc in next dc) 2
times; ch 2, sk 2 ch of turning ch,
dc in next ch; ch 5, turn.
  Rows 6–38: Work from chart,
right.
  Rep rows 3–38 for pat until insertion strip measures the same as
the width across pillow slip plus
extra to allow for shrinkage.
  Wash and block strip.
  Baste, then sew to pillowcase.
Cut away fabric behind edging,
leaving ½-inch for hems. Turn
back ¼-inch seams twice; press
and sew hem in place.

CARING FOR HANDMADE LACE

To preserve the beauty of the
crocheted lace you've made,
treat it with the same tender
loving care that you would lavish on the heirloom laces in
your linen cupboard.
  Repair all damaged lace before washing it. If sewing is ad-
equate to repair the damage,
insert the needle *between*
threads rather than into them.
  Holes are best repaired by
darning. Use a thread close to
the color and weight of the
original, and weave the horizontal threads across the tear;
begin and end with three or
more meshes on each side of
the hole. Weave in and out of
these threads, duplicating the
original stitches as closely as
possible. Fasten threads to existing piece.

To remove stains, use a gen-
tle bleach, such as lemon juice
mixed with water. Or, use hy-
drogen peroxide, diluting it according to the manufacturer's
directions.
  You also can remove stains
using a weak solution of non-
chlorine household bleach. Begin with one teaspoon of
bleach per cup of water. Soak
the lace only long enough to
remove the stain.
  Store your handmade lace in
a cool, dry place. Lay small
pieces flat, without folding, between sheets of acid-free tissue
paper. Loosely roll larger
pieces around a cardboard cyl-
inder that has been wrapped
with tissue paper. Wrap another layer of tissue paper around
the outside of the lace.

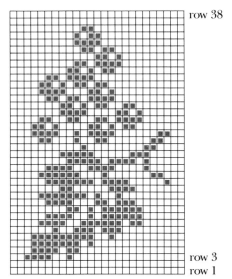

GRAPE INSERT EDGING
■ Block (bl)
□ Space (sp)

Just for Wee Folks

PRECIOUS DRESS-UPS, TOYS, AND BLANKETS

The celebrated delights of childhood, when, as Wordsworth exclaimed, "to be young was very heaven!" included dainty dresses lavished with lace, flower-strewn blankets, beribboned bonnets, handmade dolls, and cuddlesome animals. Here, and on the next six pages, are winsome gifts that evoke those halcyon days.

Pictured at *right* is a cozy crib-to-carriage set bursting with embroidered flowers. The blanket, cardigan, and prairie-style bonnet are embellished with simple cross-stitch motifs reminiscent of calico prints popular today and in great-grandmother's day. Instructions begin on page 112.

Modern-day parents and those of generations to come will delight in the fine handwork lavished on the heirloom christening set, *above.* The dainty gown, bonnet, and bib are fashioned of fine cotton batiste and trimmed with exquisite crocheted edgings, ribbon rosettes, rows and rows of tiny tucks, and lengths of double-faced satin ribbon. A pair of ribbon-tied bootees completes the baby's ceremonial attire.

If you don't have time to create the entire ensemble, consider making just the bonnet, bib, and bootees, or assign each piece of the outfit to a different stitcher and make the set as a friendship project for a baby shower. See page 114 to begin this project.

Named in honor of our 26th president, Theodore Roosevelt, the first "Teddy's Bear" was created in 1907 by a 32-year-old Russian immigrant, Morris Michtom, as a display piece for his Brooklyn toy store. Before the decade was out, the teddy bear had become the most popular toy in America, and bears were being manufactured in every size and shape imaginable by dozens of different companies all over the world.

The personable little teddy at the tea table, *above*, is crocheted using nubby tweed yarn and boasts classic black shoe-button eyes and a soft felt nose. Instructions for this teddy bear begin on page 117.

Manufactured toys had become widely available in America by the mid-1800s, and beautifully illustrated books were now a part of every well-stocked nursery. Many of these toys and books were imported from Europe, but a growing number were beginning to be produced right here at home.

Then as now, homemade toys fashioned with love, like the sweet little pair of dolls, *above*, were often a child's most treasured possessions. And despite the increasing availability of store-bought clothing for children, handmade outfits like the handsome sailor suit and hooded pullover, *opposite*, were still the order of the day.

See pages 117–121 for the instructions for these projects.

*n 1908, Francis
Thompson wrote about the English poet Percy Bysshe
Shelley: "Know you what it is to be a child?... It is to
be so little that the elves can reach to whisper in your ear;
it is to turn pumpkins into coaches, and mice into horses,
lowness into loftiness, and nothing into everything, for
each child has its fairy godmother in its soul."*

A familiar model for children's toys from the early 18th century on, rabbits began to proliferate in every nursery in the English-speaking world after publication of Beatrix Potter's delightful *Tale of Peter Rabbit* in 1902.

Our cuddly version of Miss Potter's infamous Peter, *opposite,* is a perfect complement to the springtime-fresh, heart-patterned ensemble over which he presides.

The bunny, as well as the blanket, bonnet, and sweater, is crocheted of washable yarns. The sweater is conveniently sized for babies from 3 to 24 months old. Take particular note of the sweet, heart-shaped back on the baby's bonnet. Even Miss Potter would have been charmed by such detail. See pages 121–123 for the rabbit and sweater, cap, and blanket set instructions.

SWEATER, CAP, AND BLANKET SET

Shown on pages 104 and 105.

Sweater and cap fit Size 3–6 months; changes for sizes 9–12 months and 18–24 months follow in parentheses.

MATERIALS

Coats & Clark Luster Sheen (1.75-ounce skein) in the following colors: 17 (18, 19) skeins vanilla (No. 7); 10 skeins aqua (No. 678); 2 skeins watermelon (No. 725); 1 skein yellow (No. 224)
Sizes D, F, and G crochet hooks or sizes to obtain gauge cited below
Five ½-inch-diameter buttons
1¾ yards of ¼-inch aqua satin ribbon

Abbreviations: See page 186.
Gauge: 16 sc = 3 inches with Size F hook.

INSTRUCTIONS

For the sweater
BACK: With Size F hook and vanilla, ch 55 (59, 65). Sc in second ch from hook and in each ch across—54 (58, 64) sc; ch 1, turn.
Cont working evenly in sc until back is 4½ (5, 5½) inches.
Next row (wrong side): Ch 3, turn, dc in *front* lps of each sc across. (This leaves the back lp to attach trim on right side of work.)
Cont working evenly in sc until back measures 4 (4½, 5) inches from bottom of dc row; fasten off.
Back ribbing: With Size D hook and vanilla, attach yarn along bottom edge, ch 3, dc in each st across—54 (58, 64) dc including beg ch-3; ch 2, turn.

Next row: In second dc, work dc around post *from the back;* * dc around post of next dc *from the front,* dc around post of next dc *from the back;* rep from * across; ch 2, turn. Cont in established post st ribbing until ribbing measures 1 inch; fasten off.

FRONT (make 2): With Size F hook and vanilla, ch 27 (29, 32).
Row 1: Sc in second ch from hook and in each ch across—26 (28, 31) sc; ch 1, turn.
Work as for Back until front is 2½ (3, 3½) inches from beg of dc row; end at armhole edge.
Neck shaping: Sc in each sc until 7 (7, 8) st rem; ch 1, turn.
Next row: Sc in each st across; ch 1, turn.
Next row: Sc across row working dec over last 2 sc; ch 1, turn.
Rep last 2 rows.
Work evenly on rem sts until front matches back; fasten off.
Work second front piece to match, reversing shaping.
Front ribbing: Work same as Back Ribbing, ending with dc around post of last dc from the front for largest size.

SLEEVES: With Size G hook and vanilla, ch 43 (49, 55).
Row 1: Sc in second ch from hook and in each ch across—42 (48, 54) sc; ch 1, turn.
Work evenly in sc until sleeve is 6 (7, 8) inches; fasten off.
Sleeve ribbing: With Size D hook, attach vanilla yarn at wrist edge; ch 3 (counts as first dc), dc in next 2 (0, 0) ch; *** keeping last lp on hook, work dc in each of next 2 ch, yo, draw through all lps on hook—dec made;** rep from * until last 3 (3, 1) dc; dc in last 3 (3, 1) dc—24 (26, 28) sts.
Work as for Back Ribbing; fasten off.

EMBROIDERY: Work cross-stitch and backstitch embroidery on yoke following Chart 1, *opposite, top.* Work cross-stitches over lower sweater pieces and sleeves following Chart 2, *opposite.*

YOKE EDGING: Beg at right side edge, with right side facing, and with top of sweater back closest to you, attach yarn and sc in first *front* lp of dc row; * sk next lp, ch 3, sc in next lp; rep from * across; ch 3, turn.
Next row: Sc in ch-3 lp; * ch 3, sc in next lp; rep from * across; join with sl st at edge of work.
Rep Yoke Edging on two fronts.

NECK EDGING: Sew shoulder seams. With Size D hook, join vanilla at right front neck with right side facing; ch 3, dc evenly spaced around neck edge, working even number of sts around; ch 2, turn.
Work in ribbing pat as established for 3 rows; fasten off.

BUTTON BAND (work on left front for girls and right front for boys): With Size D hook and vanilla, work 5 rows sc along appropriate front edge.
Buttonhole band (work on right front for girls, left front for boys): With Size D hook and vanilla, work 2 rows sc along appropriate front edge. Use pins to mark 5 buttonhole places evenly spaced. Make buttonholes as follows: Sc to marker; * ch 3, sk 2 sts at marker; sc to next marker; rep from * until all buttonholes are worked. Finish as for button band, working 2 sc in ch-2 lp on next row.

ASSEMBLY: Sew sleeves in at armholes between dc rows to form drop shoulders. Sew sleeve and body side seams. Thread ribbon through dc casing. Tack ends in place. Sew buttons in place.

For the cap

Beg at lower back with Size G hook and vanilla, ch 21 (24, 26).

Row 1: Sc in second ch from hook and in each ch across—20 (23, 25) sts; ch 1, turn.

Work evenly in sc until piece is 3½ (4, 4½) inches from beg.

Top shaping: Dec 1 st at both ends of every row until there are 10 (13, 15) sts rem; fasten off.

Cap sides: With Size G hook and vanilla, join yarn at right edge of back with right side facing; work 66 (74, 80) sc around side, top, and other side of back. (Do not work across bottom edge.)

Increase row: Sc in first st, work 2 sc in next st; * sc in next st, 2 sc in next st; rep from * across—99 (111, 120) sc.

Work even on these sts until 2 (2½, 3) inches from beg.

Decrease row: Sc in first st, dec over next 2 sts; * sc in next st, dec over next 2 sc; rep from * across—66 (74, 80) sts. Mark this row to beg the instructions for Finishing, *below.*

Work 13 rows even for brim.

Brim edging: With Size D hook, sc in first st; * sk sc, ch 3, sc in next sc; rep from * across; ch 3, turn.

Next row: * Sc in ch-3 sp, ch 3; rep from * across; join with sl st to edge of work; fasten off.

FINISHING: With Size D hook, join vanilla at right edge of marked row; draw up ch-lps to form a ch across entire width of brim; ch 1, turn.

Working in the chs, rep the Brim Edging, *above.*

Ribbon casing: With Size D hook, right side facing, join vanilla along bottom edge of bonnet; ch 3, work dc along bottom edge.

Rep Brim Edging in these sts.

EMBROIDERY: Work cross-stitch and backstitch embroidery along brim following Chart 1, *top right.* Cross-stitch 6 flowers evenly spaced on back of bonnet, using Chart 2 motif.

Thread ribbon through casing.

For the blanket

Make 40 squares with aqua; make 41 squares with vanilla.

With Size F hook, ch 25.

Row 1: Sc in second ch from hook and in each ch across—24 sc; ch 1, turn.

Work evenly in sc until there is a total of 27 rows; fasten off.

Join yarn at upper right-hand corner with Size D hook, work 3 sc in corner, sc across top of square, 3 sc in corner; cont to sc in every st or row around the square, working 3 sc in each corner st; join with sl st to first sc; fasten off.

EMBROIDERY: Work cross-stitch and backstitch embroidery on vanilla squares following Chart 3, *right.*

ASSEMBLY: Join squares, alternating colors, by sl st tog on *wrong side,* working through the *back* lps only. Assemble nine rows with nine squares in each row.

Edging (on vanilla squares in center of blanket): With Size D hook, attach vanilla in front lp of corner sc, sc in same lp; * ch 3, sk next st, sc in next front lp; rep from * around; do not join.

Next rnd: * Ch 3, sc in next ch-3 lp; rep from * around; join with sl st to beg ch-3 lp; fasten off.

Edging (on vanilla squares around edges of blanket): Join yarn at outside edge, sc in first top lp; * ch 3, sk next st, sc in next front lp; rep from * around 3 sides of square or 2 sides on corner squares; turn.

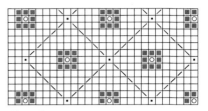

Chart 1
Sweater Yoke and Cap Brim

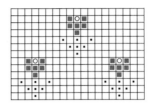

Chart 2
Sleeves and Lower
Part of Sweater

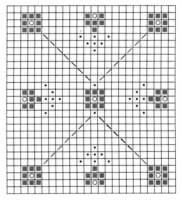

Chart 3
Blanket Squares

SWEATER CAP AND BLANKET SET
1 block = 1 single crochet and
1 cross-stitch

☑ Aqua Backstitches
⊡ Aqua
▣ Watermelon
◉ Yellow

Next row: * Ch 3, sc in ch-3 lp; rep from * across; fasten off.

BORDER: With Size D hook, join vanilla at any corner and work as for Edging on squares in center of blanket, working sc in *top* lps on first rnd of both colored squares.

CHRISTENING SET

Shown on page 106.

Instructions are for Size Newborn to 6 months.

MATERIALS

DMC Cebelia crochet cotton, Size 30 (563-yard ball): 3 balls of white
Sizes 5, 9, 10, and 12 steel crochet hooks
2¾ yards of cotton batiste fabric
Six ¼-inch-diameter pearl shank buttons
½ yard of narrow elastic
Double-faced white satin ribbon in following amounts: 1 yard of ⅛-inch-wide; 6 yards of ½-inch-wide; 1½ yards of 1-inch-wide; and 6½ yards of 1½-inch-wide
Satin ribbon roses as desired
Water-erasable marking pen
White thread and hand-sewing supplies

Abbreviations: See page 186.
Gauge: With 1 strand of thread and Size 9 hook, 13 dc = 1 inch; 5½ rows = 1 inch.

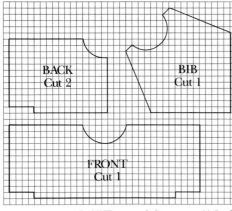

CHRISTENING SET   1 Square = ½ Inch

INSTRUCTIONS

For the bootees

SOLE (make 2): Beg at toe with doubled thread and Size 5 hook, ch 10.

Row 1: Sc in second ch from hook and in each ch across—9 sc; ch 1, turn.

Note: Unless otherwise stated, all sc rows end with ch 1 to turn.

Row 2: Sc in first sc, 2 sc in next sc, sc in next 5 sc, 2 sc in next sc, sc in last sc—11 sc.

Rows 3 and 4: Sc in each sc.

Row 5: Sc in first sc, 2 sc in next sc, sc in next 7 sc, 2 sc in next sc, sc in last sc—13 sc.

Rows 6 and 7: Sc in each sc.

Row 8: Sc in first sc, 2 sc in next sc, sc in next 9 sc, 2 sc in next sc, sc in last sc—15 sc.

Rows 9–13: Sc in each sc.

Row 14: Sc in first sc; **draw up lp in each of next 2 sc, yo, draw through all lps on hook—dec made;** sc in each sc until 3 sc rem; work dec, sc in last sc—13 sc.

Rows 15 and 16: Sc in each sc.
Row 17: Rep Row 14—11 sc.
Rows 18–21: Sc in each sc.
Row 22: Rep Row 5—13 sc.
Rows 23–29: Sc in each sc.
Rows 30, 32, 34: Rep Row 14.
Rows 31, 33, 35: Sc in each sc.

Do not turn work at end of Row 35. Instead, cont down side and work 2 rows of sc around entire sole; join with sl st; fasten off.

Top of sole: Ch 2.

Row 1: Make 4 sc in second ch from hook; ch 1, turn. (All rows end with ch 1 to turn.)

Row 2: Working in *back* lp only until indicated otherwise, work 2 sc in each sc—8 sc.

Row 3: Sc in first sc; * 2 sc in next sc, sc in next sc; rep from * across; 2 sc in last sc—12 sc.

Row 4: Rep Row 3—18 sc.
Row 5: Rep Row 3—27 sc.
Rows 6–22: Sc in each sc.

Bootee sides: Work back and forth on first 13 sc for 21 more rows; fasten off.

Sk center sc of Row 22. Attach thread with sc in next st and work back and forth on 13 sc for 21 rows. Sl st ends of side pieces tog to form back seam; fasten off.

With right side facing, join thread at bottom of center back seam. Loosely work a row of sl st around lower edge of foot section, working 1 sl st for every other row of sc; fasten off.

With wrong sides together, pin sole to sides, lining up center front and center back. Beg at center back, sc the 2 pieces tog, working in *both* lps of sides and *back* lps on sole; sl st to join; fasten off.

Cuff: Join thread at center back, ch 5.

Rnd 1 (beading rnd): * Dc in ridge formed by sc rows, ch 2; rep from * around bootee top, join with sl st in third ch of beg ch-5.

Rnd 2: Ch 1, sc in same place as join; * 2 sc in ch-2 sp, sc in next dc; rep from * around, join to first sc.

Rnd 3: Ch 3, dc in joining sc and in each sc around; join to top of beg ch-3.

Rnd 4: Ch 1, sk first dc, * dc around post of next dc; cross over in front of post st just made and dc around post of skipped dc, sk next unworked dc; rep from * around; join to first dc.

Rnd 5: Ch 3; work dc around each post of each dc around; join to top of beg ch-3.

Top edge: Drop 1 strand of thread and change to Size 10 hook, work as follows:

Rnd 6: Ch 1, sc in first dc; * ch 5, sc in same dc as last sc; sc in next 2 dc; rep from * around; join with sl st in first sc; fasten off.

Fold ½ yard of 1½-inch-wide ribbon in half lengthwise and weave through beading row. Tie bow; trim ends.

For the gown and bonnet

CUTTING: On cotton batiste, draw one 18x14-inch piece (for bonnet) and two 45x26-inch pieces (for skirt) using the water-erasable pen.

Enlarge bodice front and back patterns, *opposite, bottom left,* onto graph paper. Do not add seam allowances. Trace patterns onto fabric using same pen.

Cut out all pattern pieces.

Note: Sew pattern pieces together with right sides facing, and use ¼-inch seams unless otherwise indicated.

GOWN: *Skirt:* Join side seams (short sides) of skirt pieces with narrow French seams.

For horizontal tucks, with wrong sides together, fold up 9½ inches along lower edge of skirt, stitch ½ inch from fold. * Fold fabric again 1½ inches from last fold line; stitch ½ inch from new fold. Rep from * twice to make four tucks.

Run two gathering threads along top edge of skirt. Pull threads until skirt measures 21 inches across; distribute gathers evenly; stay-stitch in place.

Bodice (make 2; 1 is for the lining): Join front and back pieces at shoulder and underarm seams; repeat for lining. Place bodice and lining together. Sew together, starting 1 inch from bottom edge of center back. Stitch up back to neck corner, around neck, and down other side of center back, ending 1 inch from bottom. Clip corners and neckline curve. Turn right side out and press.

Pin, then sew bodice to skirt, leaving lower edge of lining loose. Turn gown to wrong side. Turn under ¼ inch on lining; tack along waist seam. Hand-stitch the 1-inch opening of the lining along the center back seams in place.

Roll a fine hem on sleeve edge and stitch by hand. (Leave sleeve edge of lining unfinished at this time.) Measure baby's upper arm for correct size, and cut a piece of elastic to form ring.

Rnd 1: Hold sleeve with right side facing and elastic along edge underneath. With Size 12 hook and 1 strand of thread, start at underarm and work sc directly into sleeve fabric and over elastic.

Sleeve trim: Make 96 sc around edge; join.

Rnd 2 (beading rnd): With Size 9 hook, ch 7, sk 2 sc; * dtr (yo hook 3 times) in next sc, ch 2, sk 2 sc; rep from * around; join to fifth ch of beg ch-7—32 sps.

Rnd 3: Ch 1, sc in same st as join; sc in first sp, sc in dtr; * 2 sc in next sp, sc in next dtr; rep from * around; end with 1 sc in last sp; join to first sc—94 sc.

Rnd 4: Ch 3, sk 3 sc; (in next sc make **dc, ch 1, and dc—V-st made;** sk 2 sc) 30 times; dc in last sc; ch 5, turn—30 V-st.

Begin to work edging in rows.

Row 5: Sc in first ch-1 sp; * ch 5, sc in next ch-1 sp; rep from *; end ch 5, sc in top of ch-3; ch 3, turn.

Row 6: Work 3 dc in first ch-5 lp, sc in next lp; * (ch 5, sc in next lp) 3 times, 7 dc in next sp, sc in next sp; rep from *; end 4 dc in beg ch-5 lp; ch 4, turn.

Row 7: Dc in second dc; (ch 1, dc in next dc) twice; * ch 1, sc in ch-5 sp; (ch 5, sc in next ch-5 sp) twice; (ch 1, dc in next dc) 7 times; rep from *; end with (ch 1, dc in next dc) 3 times, ch 1, dc in top of turning ch; ch 5, turn.

Row 8: Dc in second dc, (ch 2, dc in next dc) twice; * ch 2, sc in ch-5 sp, ch 5, sc in next ch-5 sp; (ch 2, dc in next dc) 7 times; rep from *; end with (ch 2, dc in next dc) 3 times, ch 2, dc in turning ch; ch 5, turn.

Row 9: Dc in sp; * ch 2, dc in next sp; rep from *; ch 5, turn.

Row 10: * Dc in next sp, **ch 5, sc in top of dc just made—picot**

made; rep from * to end of row, dc in last sp; fasten off; sew ends of edging tog.

Finishing sleeve: Turn dress inside out. Turn under ½ inch on lower edge of sleeve lining and tack down carefully to first row of sc. Weave 18-inch length of ½-inch-wide ribbon through beading row and tie into bow.

Neck and placket edging: Row 1: With Size 12 hook and right side facing, use one strand of thread to work sc into fabric close to edge at bottom left side of center back.

Work sc evenly spaced up center back edge, 2 sc at corner, and sc around neck to opposite center back corner; ch 1, turn. (Do not work sc down right back edge.)

Row 2: Work sc, ch 5, and sc in first sc; * sk sc, 2 sc in next sc, sk sc; work sc, ch 5, and sc in next sc; rep from * around neck to other corner; work sc in each sc down center back; ch 1, turn.

Row 3: Sc in first 2 sc, ch 8, sc in next sc (button lp made). Use pins to mark placement for rem button lps—1 at top corner and 4 more evenly spaced along back edge. Sc to corner, making button lps as marked; then work 6 sc in each ch-5 sp along neck; fasten off. Sew 6 pearl buttons on right edge opposite button lps.

Hem edging: With Size 10 hook and single strand of thread, loosely ch 23.

Row 1 (heading): Dc in fourth ch from hook, ch 5, sk 5 ch; make dc, ch 3, and dc in next ch; ch 5, sk 5 ch, sc in next ch; **(ch 5, sc in same ch as last sc) 3 times—3 scallop lps made;** ch 5, sk 5 ch, dc in last 2 ch; ch 4, turn.

Row 2: Dc in next dc, ch 5; make dc, ch 3, and dc in center scallop lp; ch 5, sc in ch-3 lp; **(ch 5, sc in same lp) 3 times—3 scallops made;** ch 5, dc in last dc and in top of turning ch; ch 4, turn.

continued

115

Rep Row 2 until edging fits hem. Ch 1 at end of last row and work in sp along side as follows for beading.

Row 1: Sc in corner of heading; * 2 sc in next sp, 3 sc in next sp; rep from * across; ch 7, turn.

Row 2 (beading row): Sk first 3 sc, dtr in next sc; * ch 2, sk 2 sc, dtr in next sc; rep from * across; fasten off.

Row 1 (edging trim): Sc in corner at opposite end of heading; * 2 sc in next sp, 3 sc in next sp; rep from * across; ch 3, turn.

Row 2: Sk first 2 sc of row; * in next sc make V-st, sk 2 sc; rep from * across; end V-st in second sc from end, dc in last dc; ch 5, turn—5 V-st.

Rows 3–8: Same as rows 5–10 of Sleeve Trim under Gown instructions on page 115; fasten off at end of last row.

FINISHING: Press completed lace; join ends. Sew lace to skirt just under bottom tuck, with beading row below hem. Press under ¼ inch on lower raw edge. Turn up hem on skirt so that fold of fabric is at bottom of lace. Hand-sew hem. *Note:* Hem will be about 4 inches deep.

Make belt carriers for each side seam and center back by crocheting a ch about 2 inches long. Pull thread ends through fabric at waistline and tie off on wrong side. Using 1½-inch-wide ribbon for sash, pull ribbon through carriers and tie in bow at back. Sew 1-inch-wide ribbon to skirt just above top tuck. Use ½-inch-wide ribbon to run through beading on hem lace; tie bow in front. Tack on ribbon roses and additional bows as desired for decoration.

BONNET: With right sides together, fold fabric in half lengthwise and stitch around the three open sides, leaving a small opening for turning. Turn right side out, slip-stitch opening closed, and press.

Locate the center of a 1-yard length of ⅛-inch-wide ribbon and the center on the long side of the bonnet. Matching centers, place ribbon along edge of long, stitched side; turn ribbon around corners, keeping ribbon along edge on both short sides of bonnet. Starting at *center point* on short side, use machine zigzag and work toward corner, across long edge, and *halfway* down other short side. When stitching, be careful to go through fabric with both sides of zigzag so that ribbon is enclosed, but take care not to stitch through the ribbon. Be sure first and last sts are firmly anchored. When finished, pull ribbon up to gather and tie in a bow.

Bonnet edging: Row 1: With Size 12 hook and 1 strand of thread, start at corner and work 152 sc directly into fabric along folded edge; ch 3, turn.

Row 2: Change to Size 9 hook, sk first 2 sc on row; * work V-st in next sc, sk 2 sc; rep from * across; end with V-st in third st from end, dc in last sc; ch 5, turn.

Rows 3–8: Same as rows 5–10 of Sleeve Trim under Gown instructions on page 115; fasten off at end of last row.

Use 19-inch lengths of 1½-inch-wide ribbon for ties.

Turn under 1½ inches of ribbon on one end; gather (through both layers of ribbon) across raw edge and secure. Tack ribbon to corners of bonnet and trim with ribbon roses atop gathers.

For the bib
Enlarge bib pattern on page 114 onto graph paper. Do not add seam allowances. Trace pattern onto fabric using marking pen.

Turn under and baste ¹⁄₁₆-inch hem all around bib. Turn under another ¹⁄₁₆ inch and press.

BIB EDGING: *Rnd 1:* With Size 12 hook and right side facing, use 1 strand of thread to work sc directly into fabric at left neck corner. Work sc evenly spaced across neckline curve and around outer edge of bib; join to beg sc.

Rnd 2: Change to Size 9 hook. Ch 1, sc in first sc, ch 5, sc in same st; * sk 2 sc, 2 sc in next sc, sk 2 sc; sc, ch 5, and sc in next sc; rep from * across neck edge only, adjusting spacing to end with sc, ch 5, and sc in opposite neck corner; ch 3 and continue around outside edge as follows.

First side: * Sk 2 sc, work V-st in next dc; rep from * across first side until there are 20 V-sts, adjusting spacing so the last V-st is at next corner.

Second side: Make another V-st at corner in next sc after last V-st of first side; rep from * of First Side until there are 25 V-sts on second side, with last V at next corner.

Third side: Make 25 V-sts as for the second side.

Fourth side: Make 20 V-sts, with last V-st in second sc from corner; ch 3, sl st in first sc on row.

Rnd 3: Work 6 sc in each ch-5 lp across neck edge, sl st to top of ch-3 on previous row; ch 5, sc in ch-1 sp of first V-st; * ch 5, sc in next ch-1 sp; rep from * around; end with ch 5, sc in top of ch-3 at end of fourth side; ch 3, turn. Edging now works back and forth in rows.

Rows 4–8: Work same as rows 6–10 of Sleeve Trim under Gown instructions on page 115; fasten off at end of last row. Tack a 32-inch length of 1-inch-wide ribbon to each neck corner for ties; trim with ribbon roses.

TEDDY BEAR

Shown on page 107.

Bear stands 14 inches tall.

MATERIALS
Reynolds Tipperary Tweed worsted-weight yarn (3½-ounce): 1 skein brown
Size G crochet hook
Polyester stuffing
Two ⅜-inch-diameter black shank buttons or black felt circles
Scrap of black felt
Black sewing thread
½ yard of ⅞-inch-wide blue satin ribbon

Abbreviations: See page 186.
Gauge: 3 sc = 1 inch.

INSTRUCTIONS
HEAD: Begin at back of head, ch 4; join with sl st to form ring.

Rnd 1: Ch 1, work 8 sc in ring; join to first sc.

Rnd 2: Ch 1, work 2 sc in each sc; join to first sc.

Rnd 3: Ch 1, * sc in first sc, 2 sc in next sc; rep from * around; join to first sc—24 sc around.

Rnds 4–11: Ch 1, sc in each sc around; join to first sc.

Rnd 12 (nose): Ch 1, * **draw up lp in each of next 2 sc, yo, draw through all lps on hook—dec made;** rep from * around; join to first dec—12 sc around.

Rnds 13–17: Ch 1, sc in each sc around; join to first sc.

Rnd 18: Rep Rnd 12; join to first sc; fasten off—6 sts around.

Stuff head and nose. Use yarn to darn nose and back of head closed if there is a gap.

Ears: Using photo on page 107 as guide, work 8 sc in a curve across top of one side of head.

Working in rows, dec 1 sc at end of each row until 6 sts rem; fasten off. Weave in yarn end and push end inside head. Rep second ear along opposite side of head.

Eyes and nose: Sew buttons along edge of nose, about 1 inch apart. If this bear is for a child younger than 3, use hand-cut rounds of black felt; sew to head with black sewing thread. Cut a ¾-inch-diameter circle of black felt and sew to end of nose. Set head aside.

BODY: Ch 10, join with sl st to form ring.

Rnd 1: Ch 1, work 15 sc in ring; join to first sc.

Rnd 2: Ch 1, work 2 sc in each sc around; join—30 sc.

Rnds 3–17: Ch 1, sc in each sc around; join; do not fasten off. Stuff body.

Legs—Rnd 1: Working on half the body sts for one leg, ch 1, sc in next 15 sc; join to first sc.

Rnds 2–8: Ch 1, sc in each st around; join.

Rnd 9: Ch 1, sc in first sc; (dec over next 2 sc, sc in next 2 sc) 3 times; dec in last 2 sc; join.

Rnds 10–16: Ch 1, sc in each sc around; join; fasten off.

Rep leg on opposite side of body on rem 15 sts.

Stuff legs; darn shut. Backstitch across top of legs.

Arms: Ch 15, join.

Rnd 1: Ch 1, sc in each ch around; join to first sc—15 sc.

Rnds 2–13: Ch 1, sc in each sc around; join.

Rnds 14–21: Rep rnds 9–16 of Legs instructions, *above;* fasten off.

Stuff arms and darn shut. Sew arms to body at an angle, using photo as a guide.

FINISHING: Sew head to body. Tie ribbon around neck.

CROCHETED DOLLS

Shown on page 108.

Dolls stand 6¾ inches tall.

MATERIALS
Plymouth's Sun Day cotton acrylic yarns (3.5-ounce skein): 1 skein *each* of flesh, black, white, red, and blue
Scraps of yellow, acrylic, brushed yarn for hair
Size F crochet hook
Polyester stuffing

Abbreviations: See page 186.
Gauge: 5 sc = 1 inch.

INSTRUCTIONS
HEAD (for both dolls): Beg at top of head with flesh, ch 4; join with sl st to form ring.

Rnd 1: Ch 1, work 8 sc in ring; join to first sc.

Rnd 2: Ch 1; work 2 sc each sc around; join to first sc—16 sc.

Rnd 3: Ch 1; * sc in 3 sc, 2 sc in next sc; rep from * around; join to first sc—20 sc around.

Rnds 4–8: Ch 1, sc in each sc around; join to first sc.

Rnd 9: Ch 1; * sc in 2 sc, **draw up lp in each of next 2 sc, yo, draw through all lps on hook— dec made;** rep from * around; join to first sc—15 sc.

Rnd 10: Ch 1; (sc in 3 sc, dec over next 2 sc) 3 times; join to first sc; fasten off—12 sc around.

For the girl doll
DRESS BODICE: *Rnd 1:* Join red, ch 1, sc in 12 sc around; join.

Rnd 2: Ch 1, work 2 sc in each sc around; join—24 sc.

Rnds 3–12: Ch 1, sc in each sc around; fasten off.

continued

LEGS: *Rnd 1:* Join white, ch 1; working in back lps only, sc in each sc around; join.

Rnd 2: Ch 1; sc in each sc; join.

Rnd 3: Ch 1; * sc in next 2 sc, dec over next 2 sc; rep from * around; join—18 sc.

Rnds 4–9: Ch 1, sc in each sc around; join; fasten off.

Shoes: Rnd 10: Join black, ch 1; sc in each sc around; join—18 sc.

Rnd 11: Ch 1; (2 sc in next sc, sc in next 8 sc) twice; join—20 sc.

Rnds 12 and 13: Ch 1, sc in each sc around; join; fasten off.

Stuff head and body. With white yarn, sew down center of legs; with black, sew down center of shoes. Stuff each leg; sew legs closed.

DRESS RUFFLE: *Rnd 1:* Join red yarn at center back of doll in *front* lp of Rnd 1 of legs; ch 3, work 2 dc in same st as join; work 3 dc in each lp around; join to top of beg ch-3; fasten off.

Sash: Join white at center front above dress ruffle, leaving a 6-inch tail; sl st around dress; fasten off leaving a 6-inch tail; tie ends into bow; trim ends even.

DRESS SLEEVES (arms): With red, ch 8; join to form ring.

Rnd 1: Ch 1, work 10 sc in ring; join to first sc.

Rnd 2: Ch 1, work 2 sc in each sc around; join—20 sc.

Rnds 3–5: Ch 1, sc in each sc around; join.

Rnd 6: Ch 1; * dec in next 2 sc; rep from * around; join—10 sc.

Rnds 7–10: Ch 1, sc in each sc around; join; fasten off.

Hands: Rnd 11: Join flesh, ch 1; sc in each sc; join.

Rnd 12: Ch 1, sc in each sc around; join.

Rnd 13: Ch 1; (dec over next 2 sc) around; join; fasten off.

Lightly stuff upper sleeve; firmly stuff lower sleeve. Sew sleeve to body at shoulder. Make another sleeve in same manner.

HAIRDO: Cut one hundred 10-inch lengths of brushed yellow yarn. Arrange in bundle to fit down center of back of head; backstitch hair in place. Braid each side and tie ends with red yarn bows. Make small loops for bangs and tack in place.

For the boy doll

SUIT: *Rnd 1:* Join blue, ch 1, sc in 12 sc around; join.

Rnd 2: Ch 1, work 2 sc in each sc around; join—24 sc.

Rnds 3–10: Ch 1, sc in each sc around; join; fasten off blue.

Belt: Rnds 11 and 12: Join black, sc in each sc around; join; fasten off at end of Rnd 12.

Rnds 13 and 14: Join blue, ch 1; sc in each sc around; join.

Rnd 15: Ch 1; * sc in next 2 sc, dec over next 2 sc; rep from * around; join—18 sc.

Rnds 16 and 17: Ch 1, sc in each sc around; join.

Rnd 18: Ch 1; * sc in next 2 sc, dec over next 2 sc; rep from * around; join—14 sc.

Rnd 19: Ch 1, dec over next 2 sc, sc in next 8 sc; dec over next 2 sc, sc in last sc; join; fasten off.

SHOES: *Rnd 1:* Join black; ch 1, sc in each sc around; join.

Rnd 2: Ch 1, 2 sc in first sc; * sc in next sc, 2 sc in next sc; rep from * around; join—18 sc around.

Rnd 3: Ch 1, sc in first sc, 2 sc in next sc; sc in next 14 sc; 2 sc in next sc, sc in next sc; join—20 sc.

Rnd 4: Ch 1, sc in each sc around; join; fasten off.

Stuff body. With blue yarn, sew down center of legs; with black, sew down center of shoes. Stuff each leg; sew legs closed.

SLEEVES (arms): With blue, ch 8; join to form ring.

Rnd 1: Ch 1, work 10 sc in ring; join with sl st to first sc.

Rnds 2–8: Ch 1, sc in each sc around; join; fasten off.

Hands: Rnd 9: Join flesh, ch 1; sc in each sc around; join.

Rnd 10: Ch 1, sc in each sc around; join.

Rnd 11: Ch 1; * dec over next 2 sc; rep from * around; join; fasten off. Stuff and sew closed. Sew sleeve to body at shoulder. Make another sleeve in same manner.

SAILOR COLLAR: With white, ch 11. *Row 1:* Sc in second ch from hook and in each ch across; ch 1, turn.

Rows 2–4: Sc in each sc across; ch 1, turn.

Row 5: Sc in 4 sc; ch 1, turn.

Rows 6–12: Sc in 4 sc across; fasten off.

Sk next 2 sc of Row 4 and rep rows 5–12 on opposite side of collar; fasten off. Sew collar around neck of doll, matching corners at front. With red, backstitch around collar edges for stripe. Tie red yarn bow and tack to center front.

HAIRDO: With brushed yellow yarn, make short loops all over head; tack each loop in place.

HOODED SWEATER

Shown on page 109.

Directions are for Size 6 months. Changes for sizes 12 and 18 months are in parentheses. For body chest measurement of 19 (20, 21) inches, the stitched measurement is 21½ (23, 24) inches.

MATERIALS
Coats & Clark Softspun Baby yarn (3-ounce skein): 5 (6, 7)

ounces of red (No. 905); 1 ounce of white (No. 1)
Size E crochet hook or size to obtain gauge cited below
18-inch-long red zipper
Red sewing thread
Tapestry needle for embroidery

Abbreviations: See page 186.
Gauge: 5 sts = 1 inch; 4 rows = 1 inch.

──────**INSTRUCTIONS**──────
Note: Back is two pieces with a zipper at center back that extends about halfway up the center back of the hood.

LEFT BACK: Beg at bottom edge with red, ch 26 (28, 30).
Row 1: Sc in second ch from hook; * dc in next ch, sc in next ch; rep from * across; turn.
Row 2: Sl st in first sc, ch 3 for first dc; * sc in next dc, dc in next sc; rep from * across; ch 1, turn.
Row 3: Sc in first dc; * dc in next sc, sc in next dc; rep from * across.
Rep rows 2 and 3 for pat until 5⅜ (6¼, 7) inches from beg; end at arm edge; fasten off.
Sleeve: Ch 29 (33, 35). Work in Left Back pat as established across ch; then across back—53 (59, 63) st across. Cont in pat across all sts until 10 (10¾, 11½) inches from beg; fasten off.

RIGHT BACK: Make same as Left Back and Sleeve, reversing shaping.

FRONT: Beg at bottom edge, ch 54 (58, 60). Work in pat same as Left Back until same length as from back to sleeve; fasten off.
Sleeves: Ch 29 (33, 35); work across ch in pat, then across front. With separate strand of yarn, ch 28 (32, 35) and join to opposite side for second sleeve; rejoin yarn at beg of ch and cont in pat across

front and opposite sleeve—109 (121, 128) sts. Keeping to pat, work until 1½ inches less than back to shoulder.
Shape neck: Mark center 29 (29, 31) sts for front neck. Work in pat to first marker; leave remainder of row unworked; turn.
Next row: **Draw up lp in each of first 2 sts, yo, draw through 3 lps on hook—dec at neck edge;** work in pat across; turn.
Following row: Work in pat to last 2 sts, work dec. Cont in pat until same length as back; fasten off.
Return to last long row worked; join yarn at second marker; work as first side, reversing shaping.

HOOD: Beg at front edge, ch 90 (94, 98). Work in same pat as Left Back until 7 (7½, 8) inches from beg; fasten off.

ASSEMBLY: Sew shoulder and top of sleeve seams; sew underarm and side seams. Fold hood in half lengthwise, then sew a 2-inch-long seam at top of center back; cut yarn, leaving an 8-inch end to sew remainder of back seam later. Matching back of hood to back opening and front of hood to center front of neck, sew hood in place around neck, easing as necessary to fit.

BOTTOM RIBBING: Ch 12.
Row 1: Sc in second ch from hook and in each ch across—11 sc; ch 1, turn.
Row 2: Sc in *back* lps of each sc across; ch 1, turn.
Rep Row 2 until the piece, when slightly stretched, fits around bottom edge; fasten off.
Sew ribbing to bottom of sweater. Place zipper at back opening; mark where zipper ends on hood. With 8-inch end of yarn, sew remainder of back hood closed to zipper marker.

With red, sc evenly around back opening. With opening at bottom of sweater, sew zipper in place.

SLEEVE RIBBING (make 2): Ch 11. Working on 10 sc, make same as Bottom Ribbing until the piece, slightly stretched, fits around wrist; fasten off. Sew short edges of ribbing tog; sew ribbing to end of sleeve.

FRONT POCKET: Beg at side edge, ch 12.
Row 1: Work in pat same as Left Back on 11 sts. Mark this edge for inc edge (opposite edge will remain straight); turn.
Row 2: **Sc and dc in first st— inc made;** work in pat across—12 sts; turn.
Row 3: Work in pat across, work inc in last st—13 sts.
Rep rows 2 and 3 until 19 (20, 21) sts are across row.
Work even in pat until 6 (6½, 7) inches from beg. Working at inc edge only, dec 1 st on same edge every row until 11 sts rem; fasten off.
Pocket border: With red, sc evenly spaced around pocket, working 3 sc at each corner; join with sl st to first sc; fasten off.
With white yarn and tapestry needle, working about ¼ inch from edge, embroider a chain stitch around edge of pocket.
Center bottom edge of pocket at top of ribbing; sew in place; sew short side edges and center top edge (leaving the inc/dec edges open for hands).

FINISHING: Make a red ch about 35 inches long for the tie. Beg at center front, weave ch around front of hood (excess at ends is for tying).
For tassels, wrap white yarn around a 2-inch strip of card-
continued

119

board 20 times. Tie one end; cut opposite end. Wrap another strand of yarn around tassel ½ inch below the first tie. Secure yarn ends. Sew a tassel to each tie.

SAILOR SUIT

Shown on page 109.

Directions are for Size 6 months. Changes for sizes 12 and 18 months are in parentheses.

MATERIALS
Patons Astra (50-gram or 182-yard skein): 2 (3, 3) skeins *each* of white (No. 2751) and blue (No. 2733); 1 skein of red (No. 2756)
Sizes F and G crochet hooks or sizes to obtain gauge below
Five ⅜-inch-diameter snaps
¾ yard of ⅜-inch-diameter elastic
Sewing needle and thread
Yarn needle

Abbreviations: See page 186.
Gauge: With Size G hook, 4 sc = 1 inch.

INSTRUCTIONS
For the pullover
BACK: With Size G hook and blue, ch 41 (45, 49).
Row 1: Sc in second ch from hook and in each ch; ch 1, turn.
Row 2: Sc in each sc; fasten off.
Join white and cont in sc until back measures 8½ (9½, 10½) inches; fasten off.

FRONT: Work same as Back to 4½ (5, 5½) inches from beg.
Neck shaping: Work across first 20 (22, 24) sts; ch 1, turn.
Dec 1 st at neck edge every other row until 12 (13, 14) shoulder sts rem. Work even until front

measures 4 (4½, 5) inches from beg of neck shaping; fasten off.
Join yarn and complete opposite neck and shoulder to match over rem 20 (22, 24) sts.

BACK AND FRONT RIBBING: *Row 1* (right side): With Size G hook, join white at bottom edge; ch 3; dc in each ch across; ch 2, turn.
Row 2: Dc *from the back* around post of second dc; * dc *from the front* around post of next dc, dc *from the back* around post of next dc; rep from * across; fasten off.

SLEEVE (make 2): With Size G hook and blue, ch 21 (25, 25).
Row 1: Sc in second ch from hook and in each ch; ch 1, turn.
Row 2: Sc in first sc; * 2 sc in next sc, sc in next sc; rep from * across—30 (36, 36) sts; fasten off.
Join white, cont in sc and, at the same time, inc 1 st at each end of every fourth row 1 (0, 2) time.
Work even on 32 (36, 40) sts until sleeve measures 6 (7, 8) inches from beginning; fasten off.

SLEEVE RIBBING: With right side facing, Size G hook, and white, attach yarn at bottom of wrist edge, ch 3, work across edge with dc—20 (24, 24) dc, including beg ch-3; ch 2, turn. Finish as for Back Ribbing.
Join shoulders; sew in sleeves, placing center at shoulder. Sew underarm and body side seams.

COLLAR (left side): With Size G hook and blue, ch 3.
Row 1: Sc in second and third ch from hook; ch 1, turn.
Row 2: Sc in each sc; ch 1, turn.
Row 3: 2 sc in first sc, sc in each st across; ch 1, turn.
Row 4: Sc in each sc; ch 1, turn.
Rep rows 3 and 4 until 12 (13, 14) sc across row. Work even until straight edge (side without in-

creases) is the same as the left front neckline; set aside.
Collar (right side): Rep rows 1 and 2 of left side.
Row 3: Sc in each sc, working 2 sc in last st; ch 1, turn.
Row 4: Sc in each sc; ch 1, turn.
Rep rows 3 and 4 until right side corresponds with left side.
Sew straight edge of left side to left front neck edge. Sew straight edge of right side to right front neck edge.
Beg at outside edge of left collar, sc in 12 (13, 14) sc, sc in back neck sts, sc in 12 (13, 14) sc of right side collar. Cont working in sc on all sts until collar measures 4½ (5, 5½) inches from beg of back neck; fasten off.
With Size F hook, beg at front of left side collar, sc around collar, working 3 sc in corner; join with sl st to first sc; fasten off.

INSERT: Rep rows 1 and 2 of left side of Collar; fasten off. Change to white.
Row 3: 2 sc in first sc, sc in each sc across, working 2 sc in last sc; ch 1, turn.
Row 4: Sc in each sc across; ch 1, turn. Rep rows 3 and 4, alternating white and blue every rep, until there is a total of 14 sc across row; fasten off.
With smaller hook and white, work 1 row sc around insert, working 2 sc in corners; join with sl st to first sc; ch 1, turn. Work sc around; sl st to join; fasten off.
Sew 1 snap at bottom of triangle, and 2 snaps along each edge. Sew matching snaps on inside front neck to correspond.

TIE: Rep rows 1–4 of left side of Collar. Rep rows 3 and 4 of Collar until 6 sts across row. Rep Row 4 twice.
Next row: Work 2 sc tog, sc in each st across; ch 1, turn.
Following row: Sc in each st

across; ch 1, turn.

Rep last two rows until 2 sts rem. Sc in 2 sc; fasten off.

With F hook, work sc around tie; join to beg sc; fasten off.

For tie knot: With Size G hook and red, ch 3.

Sc in second ch from hook and in each ch across; ch 1, turn.

Cont to work evenly in sc until piece measures 1¼ inches. Change to smaller hook; sc around piece; join with sl st to first sc; fasten off. Gather tie at middle with tie knot; sew ends of knot tog. Tack tie at front neck.

SHORTS (make 2): With Size G hook and blue, ch 41 (45, 49).

Row 1: Sc in second ch from hook and in each ch across; ch 1, turn.

Inc 1 st at each edge of every row 3 times—46 (50, 54) sts.

Sl st in next 2 sts, ch 1, sc in each sc until 2 sc rem (mark this row for crotch); ch 1, turn.

Work even on 42 (46, 50) sts until piece measures 7½ (8½, 9½) inches from crotch; fasten off. Make another piece.

Join yarn and attach ribbing following instructions for Back and Front Ribbing, *opposite.*

Sew front, back, and leg seams. Turn top edge under ½ inch to form casing. Sew, leaving an opening for elastic. Thread elastic through casing; adjust to fit. Secure elastic; sew opening closed.

CROCHETED BUNNY

Shown on page 110.

Bunny is 25 inches tall.

MATERIALS
Reynolds Kitten worsted-weight yarn (160-yard skein): 4 skeins of yellow (No. 39)
Size G crochet hook
Black and white sewing thread
Tapestry and sewing needles
Scraps of black felt
Polyester fiberfill
1 yard of 1½-inch-wide pink satin ribbon

Abbreviations: See page 186.
Gauge: With 2 strands of yarn held tog, 3 sc = 1 inch.

INSTRUCTIONS
Note: Bunny is worked using 2 strands of yarn held tog. All rnds begin with ch 1 before first sc.

HEAD: Beg at nose, ch 4, join with a sl st to form ring.

Rnd 1: Work 6 sc into ring; join.

Rnd 2: Work 2 sc in each sc; join—12 sc.

Rnds 3 and 4: Sc in each sc; join.

Rnd 5: * 2 sc in next st, sc in next st; rep from *; join—18 sc.

Rnds 6 and 7: Sc in each sc; join.

Rnd 8: 2 sc in each st—36 sts.

Rnds 9 and 10: Sc in each sc; join.

Rnd 11: * Sc in next 6 sc, **draw up lp in each of next 2 sc, yo, draw through all lps on hook— dec made;** rep from * across; sc in last sc; join—32 sc.

Rnds 12 and 13: Sc in each sc; join.

Rnd 14: Dec 6 sts evenly spaced; join—26 sc.

Rnd 15: Sc in each sc; join.

Rnd 16: Dec 6 sts evenly spaced; join—20 sc.

Rnd 17: Rep Rnd 15.

Rnd 18: Dec 4 sts evenly spaced; join; fasten off—16 sc.

Stuff head and nose firmly. Darn back of head closed.

BODY: *Rnd 1:* On bottom edge of head work a circle of 22 sc, beg at center back of head; join.

Rnd 2: 2 sc in each sc—44 sc.

Work even for 20 rnds. Fasten off. Stuff body. Do not close.

Leg: Working from center back to center front, attach yarn and work 22 sc; join.

Work 15 rnds even.

Next 2 rnds: Dec 11 sts evenly spaced. Work 1 rnd on the 11 sts.

Work in rnds, working * sc in next sc, 2 sc in next sc; rep from * until 18 sc. Work 1 rnd even.

Heel: Work 6 sc across 6 center back leg sts; turn, ch 1, * sc in next st, dec over next 2 sc; rep from * until 2 sc rem, ending on right side of work.

Foot: Beg at shaped edge of left heel, work 3 sc along edge, 12 sc to right heel edge, 3 sc along edge, 2 sc at top of heel—20 sc.

Work 3 rnds even.

* Sc in next sc, dec over next 2 sc; rep from * until 9 sc rem; fasten off. Make a second leg on rem 22 sc of body. Stuff legs and feet, sew openings closed.

Arm: Work 20 sc around surface stitches of bunny's body below neck (see photo on page 110).

Work even for 18 rnds.

Next rnd: Dec 10 sts evenly spaced. Work 1 rnd even.

Next rnd: Inc to 20 sts. Work 1 rnd even.

Next rnd: * Sc in next sc, work dec over next 2 sc.

Rep from * until 9 sc rem.

Make second arm on other side of body; sew openings closed.

FINISHING: *Ears* (make 2): In an inverted V shape on top of head, work 7 sc onto surface. Work 5 rows of sc.

Dec row: * Sc to center st, work dec, sc to end of row. Rep from * until 1 sc rem; fasten off. Work reverse sc around each ear.

Eyes and nose: Using photo on page 110 as a guide, cut and sew in place three ½-inch-diameter felt circles for eyes and nose. Highlight eyes with a ¼-inch straight stitch of white thread.

continued

Tail: For a yarn tassel, wrap yarn around a 2½-inch strip of cardboard about 75 times. Tie a strand of yarn around bundle. Slip bundle from cardboard and cut the ends. Shape and sew tail to back of bunny.

Tie bow around bunny's neck.

BABY SET

Shown on pages 110 and 111.

Sweater and cap fit Size 3–6 months; changes for sizes 9–12 months and 18–24 months follow in parentheses. Blanket measures approximately 33x38 inches.

MATERIALS
Coats & Clark Luster Sheen (1.75-ounce skein) in the following amounts and colors: 20 (21, 22) skeins of vanilla (No. 7); 2 skeins of yellow (No. 232); 1 skein *each* of jade (No. 650) and pink (No. 206)
Sizes D, F, and G crochet hooks
Six ⅜-inch-diameter heart buttons
½ yard of ¼-inch-wide pink satin ribbon
Tapestry needle

Abbreviations: See page 186.
Gauge: With Size G hook, 5 sc = 1 inch; 6 rows = 1 inch.

INSTRUCTIONS
For the sweater
BACK: With Size G hook and vanilla, ch 53 (57, 63).

Row 1: Sc in second ch from hook and in each ch across—52 (56, 62) sc; ch 1, turn.

Cont to work evenly in sc until there is a total of 7 sc rows; ch 3, turn at end of last row.

Next row: Dc in second sc and in each sc across; ch 1, turn.

Following row: Sc in each dc across; ch 3, turn.

Rep these last 2 rows for pat until 4½ (5, 5½) inches from beg, ending with a sc row.

Armhole shaping: Sl st into next 5 sts, ch 3; keeping to pat as established, work across row until within last 4 sts; turn.

Dec 1 st at both ends of next row.

Work even in sc for 13 rows. Cont in dc/sc row pat until back measures 4 (4, 5) inches from beg of armhole shaping; fasten off.

Back ribbing: Row 1: With Size F hook, join vanilla at bottom edge; ch 3, dc in each ch across—52 (56, 62) dc including beg ch-3; ch 2, turn.

Row 2: Work dc around post *from the back* of second dc; * dc around post of next dc *from the front* of next dc; dc around post of next dc *from the back;* rep from * across; ch 2, turn.

Rep Row 2 until ribbing measures 1 inch; fasten off.

FRONT (make 2): With Size G hook and vanilla, ch 26 (28, 32).

Row 1: Sc in second ch from hook and in each ch across—25 (27, 31) sc; ch 1, turn.

Cont working as for back, working armhole shaping with sl sts and working to within last 5 sts on opposite fronts. Work even until 3 (3½, 4) inches from beg of armhole shaping.

Neck shaping: Sk 8 sts at neck edge, either with sl sts or by only working up to last 8 sts.

Dec 1 st at neck edge on next 2 rows.

Work even until fronts correspond to back; fasten off.

Front ribbing: With Size F hook, join vanilla at bottom edge; ch 3, dc in every ch across—25 (27, 31) dc; ch 2, turn. Rep Row 2 of Back Ribbing, ending with front post dc around last st; ch 2, turn.

Cont in ribbing pat until ribbing measures 1 inch; fasten off.

SLEEVES: With Size G hook and vanilla, ch 41 (43, 49).

Row 1: Sc in second ch from hook and in each ch across—40 (42, 48) sc; ch 1, turn.

Cont in sc until there is a total of 7 sc rows.

Work in alternating dc/sc row pat as for back, *and at same time* inc 1 st at both ends of every other row 0 (2, 2) times.

Work even in pat until sleeve measures 5 (6, 7) inches, ending with a sc row.

Armhole shaping: Sl st in first 5 sts, ch 3, dc across row until 4 sts rem; turn.

Dec 1 st at both ends of next row.

Cont in established dc/sc row pat until sleeve is 2¼ (2½, 2¾) inches, ending with a sc row.

Dec row: Ch 3, * **keeping last lp on hook, dc in each of next 2 dc, yo, draw through all lps on hook—dec made;** rep from * across; dc in last st; ch 1, turn.

Sc in each st across; fasten off.

Sleeve ribbing: With Size F hook, join vanilla at wrist edge; ch 3, dc in next ch for sizes 3–6 months and 9–12 months only; for all sizes: * Dec over next 2 ch, dc in next ch; rep from * across, ending with dc in last 2 ch for size 9–12 months—27 (29, 32) dc counting beg ch-3 as dc; ch 2, turn.

Cont in established ribbing pat until ribbing is 1 inch; fasten off.

EMBROIDERY: Work cross-stitches over all pieces following charts 1–3, *opposite.*

Sew shoulder seams.

NECK EDGING: With Size F hook, join yarn at right front neck; ch 3, dc in each st around neck; ch 2, turn. Work 2 rows of ribbing; fasten off.

BUTTON BAND: With Size D hook and vanilla, work 5 rows of sc along left front edge.

Buttonhole band: Work same as for Button Band along right front edge for 2 rows. Use pins to mark 6 buttonhole places evenly spaced along band. Make buttonholes as follows: * Sc in each sc to marker, ch 1, sk st, sc to next marker; rep from * until 6 holes are worked.

Next row: Sc in each sc and ch-1 sp; ch 1, turn. Work even for a total of 5 rows; fasten off. Sew buttons on band.

Sew sleeves along armhole openings. Sew sleeve and body side seams.

For the cap
With Size G hook and pink, ch 3. *Row 1:* Sc in second ch from hook and next ch; ch 1, turn.

Row 2: Sc in 2 sc; ch 1, turn.

First inc row: Work 2 sc in each of next 2 sc; ch 1, turn.

Second inc row: Work 2 sc in first sc, work across in sc until last st, work 2 sc into last st; ch 1, turn.

Rep Second Inc Row until there are 22 (24, 26) sts across row. Work 5 rows sc.

Divide for top of heart: * Dec over first 2 sc, sc across 7 (8, 9) sts *, dec over next 2 sts; attach another ball of yarn; rep bet * to work second side of heart.

Working both tops simultaneously, cont to dec on both sides of each top of every row until 3 (2, 3) sts rem; fasten off.

Beg at bottom point, join pink, sc around heart, working 2 sc in corner st; join with sl st to beg sc; fasten off.

Brim: Join vanilla at side of heart bottom (tip); ch 3, work 64 (70, 76) dc around outside edge of heart; ch 1, turn.

Work even in sc/dc row pat until 2 (2½, 3) inches from beg, ending with a dc row; ch 1, turn.

Work 9 rows of sc. Turn work so bottom edge faces you; ch 3, dc along bottom edge of cap to form ribbon casing, turn.

Edging (wrong side): Change to Size D hook; * **ch 2, sl st into second ch from hook—picot made;** sk st, sl st into next st; rep from * across; cont in picot pat across front of brim.

Work cross-stitch embroidery on sc panel of brim following Chart 4, *right.*

Thread ribbon through dc casing on cap bottom.

For the blanket
With Size G hook and vanilla, ch 198. *Row 1:* Sc in second ch from hook and in each ch across—198 sc; ch 1, turn.

Work evenly in sc until there is a total of 22 rows.

Divide for borders and center: Work across first 23 sts in sc—side panel; attach another ball of yarn, dc over center 151 sts—center panel; attach another ball of yarn and sc across rem 23 sts—side panel.

Work even in sc on side border panels until there is a total of 175 rows; fasten off. Work even in alternating sc/dc row pat on center panel sts until center measures the same length of the outside panels; fasten off.

Sew borders to center panel; join vanilla and sc across all 197 sts. Work even in sc for top border until there are 22 rows; turn to work on right side.

Edging: Change to Size D hook; * **ch 2, sl st in second ch from hook—picot made;** sk st (or row), sl st into next st (or row); rep from * around outside edge of blanket; join with sl st to beg sc.

Work cross-stitches on borders following Chart 5, *above right,* and on center panel following Chart 6, *above.*

Border inside edging: With Size D hook, draw up vanilla lp from

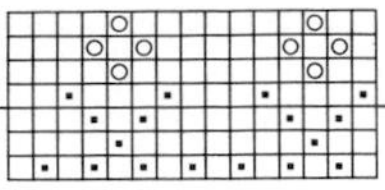

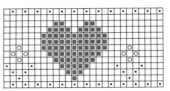

Cuff and
Sweater Trim
Chart 1

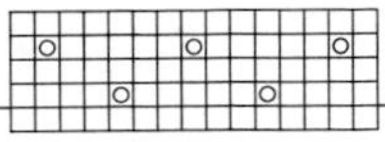

Cap, Sweater,
and Sleeve
DC/SC Pat
Chart 2

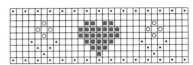

Sweater Yoke
Chart 3

Cap Brim
Chart 4

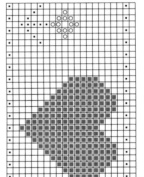

Blanket
Center Panel
DC/SC Pat
Chart 6

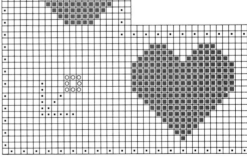

Blanket Border
Chart 5

BABY SET   1 block = 1 single crochet and 1 cross-stitch
⊡ Jade
■ Pink
⊙ Yellow

wrong side of blanket at inside corner of sc border; cont to draw up lps every row (or st) along inside edge of border to form a surface ch; fasten off.

Join yarn in any corner ch; * work picot, sk ch, sl st into next ch; rep from * around inside edge so that points of picots point inward; fasten off.

Nostalgic Charm

FANCYWORK
TREASURES

❖

Lacy curtains fluttering at the window on a hot summer day, freshly laundered place mats, a show of pretty doilies in the parlor, and the "company best" bedspread on display in the guest room—these were the cozy touches that confirmed even the humblest house as home at the turn of the century.

The sprightly stepping-stone pattern used for the curtains, *right,* is a charming repeat design that can be adapted to create any size panel you wish. The lacy windowpane pattern on the picot-edged place mat, *near right,* is equally versatile.

The Victorian "cottage look"—popular across America at the turn of the century (and again today)—mandated a smattering of crocheted doilies and antimacassars as part of the parlor decor. Smoothed like drifts of new-fallen snow across the backs and armrests of every sofa and soft easy chair in sight, these airy fancies were designed to protect fine old furnishings.

The pineapple motif (the traditional symbol of hospitality) is fashioned into a sumptuous antimacassar set, *above*. Sets like this one are one way to add a touch of old-fashioned charm to even the most contemporary sofa or chair.

Doily rounds, *above,* stretched over store-bought pillow forms make inviting accent pillows to plump down on a straight-back settee in an entryway or cozy nook. Be sure to cover the pillow forms with a contrasting fabric to showcase the patterns to their best advantage.

The pineapple antimacassar instructions begin on page 134; the pillow instructions begin on pages 137 and 139.

*M*iss Addie Heron said in *her popular 1905 pattern book,* Fancy Work for Pleasure and Profit, *". . . We have tried to give instructions in all things pertaining to the home beautiful so clear and simple that no household, however humble, need be without the refining influences of dainty environments."*

Crystal flacons of fragrant perfume and other boudoir treasures are elegantly displayed atop a fancy crocheted dresser set in the familiar pineapple pattern, *above.* The three-part set includes a graceful diamond-shaped center doily and a pair of companion coaster-size rounds worked in pale blue cotton thread. (Crochet worked in colored threads was especially popular in the 1920s, '30s, and '40s, and hundreds of patterns for multicolored designs were published in needlework magazines of that period.)

The delicate filigree doily, *opposite,* also is worked in blue and is perfect as the centerpiece for a tea or luncheon table setting when layered over a crisp white lace cloth. Instructions for these patterns begin on pages 141 and 142.

Nostalgic Charm

"A room where one sleeps and dreams and grieves and rejoices becomes inseparably connected with those processes and acquires a personality of its own," wrote L. M. Montgomery, author of **Anne of Green Gables.** *"This room . . . has always been a retreat for me, the one spot . . . where I might be alone and possess my soul in quietness."*

Just such a retreat is the bedroom pictured at *left,* where plain and fancy pieces and patterns mix companionably to create a cozy sanctuary. It is the sort of room that invites one to withdraw for a time from the cares of the world and indulge in private reveries.

The bed is dressed in medallion circlets trimmed with pink satin cording and all tied up in bows—a crocheted fantasy guaranteed to make one dream of summer meadows and spills of Queen Anne's lace.

Tossed across the foot of the bed is a snuggly throw of handsome but humbler design, just right to wrap up in against the unexpected chill of an autumn evening or the bone-numbing cold of a long winter's night.

Instructions for these two projects begin on pages 144 and 145.

BREAKFAST PLACE MATS

Shown on pages 124 and 125.

Place mats measure 14x18 inches.

MATERIALS

Clark's Big Ball 3-cord crochet cotton, Size 20 (400-yard ball): 1 ball makes 1 mat
Size 11 steel crochet hook

Abbreviations: See page 186.
Gauge: 10 dc = ⅞ inch; 4 rows = ¾ inch.

INSTRUCTIONS

Beg along bottom edge, ch 192.

Row 1: Dc in fourth ch from hook and in next 8 ch; * ch 10, sk 8 ch, dc in next 10 ch; rep from * across; ch 3, turn.

Row 2: Sk first dc, dc in next 3 dc; * ch 2, sk 2 dc, dc in next 4 dc; ch 10, dc in next 4 dc; rep from * across; end ch 2, sk 2 dc, dc in last 3 dc and in top of turning ch; ch 3, turn.

Row 3: Sk first dc, dc in next dc, * ch 2, 2 dc in ch-2 sp, ch 2, sk 2 dc, dc in next 2 dc; ch 10, dc in next 2 dc; rep from * across; end ch 2, 2 dc in ch-2 sp, ch 2, sk 2 dc, dc in next dc and in top of turning ch; ch 3, turn.

Row 4: Sk first dc, dc in next dc; * 2 dc in ch-2 sp, ch 2, 2 dc in next ch-2 sp; dc in next 2 dc; ch 5, sc around 3 ch-10 lps below; ch 5, dc in next 2 dc; rep from * across; end 2 dc in ch-2 sp, ch 2, 2 dc in next ch-2 sp; dc in next dc and in top of turning ch; ch 3, turn.

Row 5: Sk first dc, dc in next 3 dc; * 2 dc in ch-2 lp, dc in next 4 dc; ch 8, dc in next 4 dc; rep from * across; end 2 dc in ch-2 lp, dc in

next 3 dc and in top of turning ch; ch 13, turn.

Row 6: * Dc in 10th dc of 10-dc grp, 8 dc in next ch-8 lp, dc in next dc, ch 10; rep from * across; end dc in top of turning ch; ch 13, turn.

Row 7: Dc in first dc of 10-dc grp; dc in next 3 dc; * ch 2, sk 2 dc, dc in next 4 dc; ch 10, dc in next 4 dc; rep from * across; end ch 2, sk 2 dc, dc in next 4 dc; ch 10, sk 10 ch; dc in next ch; ch 13, turn.

Row 8: Sk first dc, * dc in first 2 dc of 4-dc grp; ch 2, 2 dc in ch-2 sp, ch 2, sk 2 dc, dc in next 2 dc, ch 10; rep from * across; end ch 10, sk 10 ch; dc in next ch; ch 8, turn.

Row 9: Sc around 3 ch-10 lps below, ch 5; * dc in next 2 dc, 2 dc in ch-2 sp, ch 2, sk 2 dc, 2 dc in ch-2 sp, dc in next 2 dc, ch 5, sc around 3 ch-10 lps below, ch 5, rep from * across; end dc in top of third ch of turning ch; ch 11, turn.

Row 10: Sk first dc, * dc in first 4 dc of 4-dc grp; 2 dc in ch-2 lp, dc in next 4 dc, ch 8; rep from * across; end dc in top of third ch of turning ch; ch 3, turn.

Row 11: * 8 dc in ch-8 lp, dc in next dc; ch 10, sk 8 dc, dc in next dc; rep from * across; end 8 dc in turning-ch lp, dc in top of third ch of turning ch; ch 3, turn.

Rep rows 2–11 seven times more; end last rep with Row 10; ch 4, turn.

EDGING: *Rnd 1:* Sc in ch-8 lp, * ch 4, sc in next dc, ch 4, sc between fifth and sixth dc; ch 4, sc in last dc of grp, ch 4, sc in next lp; rep from * across row; ch 4, sc in same ch-8 lp—2 ch-4 lps in corner, ** ch 4, sc around turning ch between the 4 ch-10 lps; ch 4, sk next turning lp, sc in next lp, ch 4, sk next 2 rows, sc around turning

ch of next row; ch 4, sk 2 rows, sc around turning ch of next row; rep from ** to complete this side, ending with sc in base ch of first row of mat. Continue to work as established around remaining two sides; join with sl st to first ch of beg ch-4.

Rnd 2: In *each* ch-4 lp around, work 2 sc, ch 3, and 3 sc; join to beg sc; fasten off.

LACY CURTAINS

Shown on page 125.

Curtains measure 34½ inches long and 36 inches wide. But this pattern can be crocheted in any length and width needed for a curtain panel of any size.

MATERIALS

Coats & Clark South Maid crochet cotton, Size 10 (350-yard ball): 1 ball makes approximately one 16-inch square
Size 7 steel crochet hook or size to reach gauge below
Packaged bias hem facing for rod pocket that matches color of crochet thread

Abbreviations: See page 186.
Gauge: 10 dc = 1 inch; 5 rows = 1 inch.

INSTRUCTIONS

Pattern is repeat of 41 sts. Curtain width can be in increments of 3½ inches by adding 41 chains to the beginning chain length. To make the curtain width of our curtain panel, ch 415.

Row 1: Dc in fourth ch from hook, * ch 5, sk 5 ch, dc in next 3 ch, ch 5, sk 5 ch, dc in next 14 ch;

ch 5, sk 5 ch, dc in next 3 ch, ch 5, sk 5 ch, dc in next ch; rep from * across; end ch 5, dc in last 2 ch; ch 3, turn.

Row 2: Dc in next dc, 2 dc in first ch-5 lp; * ch 5, 2 dc in next ch-5 lp, ch 5, sk 2 dc, dc in next 10 dc; ch 5, 2 dc at end of next ch-5 lp, ch 5, 3 dc in next ch-5 lp; ch 1, 3 dc in next ch-5 lp; rep from * across; end with dc in last grp of 10 dc, then work (ch 5, 2 dc in next ch-5 lp) 2 times; dc in next dc and in top of turning ch-3; ch 8, turn.

Row 3: * (Work 2 dc in next ch-5 lp, ch 5) 2 times; sk 2 dc, dc in next 3 dc, ch 1, sk next dc, dc in next 3 dc; (ch 5, 2 dc in next ch-5 lp) 2 times; ch 5, dc in ch-1 sp, ch 5; rep from * across; end with ch 5 and dc in top of turning ch-3; ch 3, turn.

Row 4: Work 2 dc in first ch-5 lp; * (ch 5, 2 dc in next ch-5 lp) 2 times; ch 5, dc in ch-1 sp; (ch 5, 2 dc in next ch-5 lp) 2 times; ch 5; (3 dc in next ch-5 lp) 2 times; rep from * across; end ch 5, 2 dc in last lp, dc in third ch of turning ch-8; ch 3, turn.

Row 5: Sk first dc, dc in next 2 dc; * (work 2 dc in next ch-5 lp, ch 5) 2 times; 3 dc in next ch-5 lp, ch 1, 3 dc in next ch-5 lp; (ch 5, 2 dc in next lp) twice, dc in next 6 dc; rep from * across; end ch 5, dc in last 2 dc and in top of ch-3; ch 3, turn.

Row 6: Sk first dc, dc in next 4 dc; * work 2 dc in next ch-5 lp, ch 5, 3 dc in next lp, ch 5, dc in ch-1 sp, ch 5, 3 dc in next lp; ch 5, 2 dc in next lp, dc in 10 dc; rep from * across; end dc in last 4 dc and in top of ch-3; ch 3, turn.

Row 7: Sk first dc, dc in next 6 dc; * ch 5, dc in 3 dc, ch 5, dc in next dc; ch 5, dc in 3 dc, ch 5, dc in 14 dc; rep from * across; end dc in last 6 dc and in top of ch-3; ch 3, turn.

Row 8: Sk first dc, dc in next 4 dc; * ch 5, 2 dc in next lp, ch 5, 3 dc in next lp, ch 1, 3 dc in next lp; ch 5, 2 dc in next lp, ch 5, sk 2 dc, dc in next 10 dc; rep from * across; end sk 2 dc, dc in last 4 dc and in top of ch-3; ch 3, turn.

Row 9: Sk first dc, dc in next 2 dc; * (ch 5, 2 dc in next lp) 2 times; ch 5, dc in ch-1 sp; (ch 5, 2 dc in next lp) 2 times; ch 5, sk 2 dc, dc in next 3 dc, ch 1, sk dc, dc in next 3 dc; rep from * across; end ch 5, sk 2 dc, dc in last 2 dc and in top of ch-3; ch 8, turn.

Row 10: * (Work 2 dc in next lp, ch 5) 2 times; (3 dc in next lp) 2 times; (ch 5, 2 dc in next lp) 2 times, ch 5, dc in ch-1 sp, ch 5; rep from * across; end ch 5, sk 2 dc, dc in top of ch-3; ch 3, turn.

Row 11: Work 2 dc in first ch-5 lp; * (ch 5, 2 dc in next lp) 2 times, dc in next 6 dc; (2 dc in next lp, ch 5) 2 times; 3 dc in next lp, ch 1, 3 dc in next lp; rep from * across; end 2 dc in last lp, dc in third ch of turning ch-8; ch 8, turn.

Row 12: * Work 3 dc in next lp, ch 5, 2 dc in next lp, dc in next 10 dc, 2 dc in next lp; ch 5, 3 dc in next lp, ch 5, dc in ch-1 sp, ch 5; rep from * across; end ch 5, 3 dc in last lp, ch 5, dc in top of ch-3; ch 8, turn.

Row 13: Dc in next 3 dc, * ch 5, dc in 14 dc; ch 5, dc in next 3 dc, ch 5, dc in next dc, ch 5, dc in next 3 dc; rep from * across; end ch 5, dc in third ch of turning ch-8; ch 3, turn.

Row 14: Work 2 dc in first lp; * ch 5, 2 dc in next lp, ch 5, sk 2 dc, dc in next 10 dc; ch 5, 2 dc in next lp, ch 5, 3 dc in next lp; ch 1, 3 dc in next lp; rep from * across; end ch 5, 2 dc in last lp, dc in third ch of turning ch-8; ch 8, turn.

Row 15: * (Work 2 dc in next ch-5 lp, ch 5) 2 times; sk 2 dc, dc in next 3 dc, ch 1, sk dc, dc in next 3 dc; (ch 5, 2 dc in next ch-5 lp) 2 times; ch 5, dc in ch-1 sp, ch 5; rep from * across; end ch 5, sk 2 dc, dc in top of turning ch-3; ch 3, turn.

Rep rows 4–15 for desired length, ending with Row 12. Do not fasten off.

BORDER: Border is worked around sides and bottom edges only.

Row 1: At end of last repeat of Row 12, ch 5, turn; dc on side of top corner of previous row; * ch 2, dc in top corner of next row; rep from * along the side of curtain; work (dc, ch 5, dc) in bottom corner. There should be a multiple of 12 spaces along the side before the corner space. Continue with spaces across lower edge, making 12 ch-2 spaces over each pat rep and working dc, ch 5, and dc in next corner. Work up third side as for first, having a multiple of 12 spaces; ch 3, turn.

Row 2: (Work 2 dc in sp, dc in next dc) 2 times; * ch 5, sk dc, dc in next dc; (2 dc in next sp, dc in next dc) 4 times; rep from * along the side to within next 4 sp before corner; ch 5, sk dc, dc in next dc; (2 dc in next sp, dc in next dc) 2 times; (ch 1, dc) 3 times in corner lp; ch 1, dc in next dc; (2 dc in next sp, dc in next dc) 2 times. Rep from first * to work rem sides and corner in same manner; end last rep with 2 dc in sp, dc in next dc, 2 dc in last sp, dc in third ch of ch-5; ch 5, turn.

Row 3: Sk first 3 dc; * dc in rem 4 dc, 3 dc over ch-5 lp; ch 5, sk 3 dc, dc in next 7 dc; ch 5, 3 dc in next ch-5 lp, dc in first 4 dc, ch 2, sk 2 dc, dc in next dc; ** ch 2, sk 2 dc; rep from * across side; end

continued

last rep at **; beg corner as follows: (ch 1, dc in next dc, ch 1, dc in next sp) 2 times; (ch 1, dc in next dc) 2 times; ch 2, sk 2 dc; rep from first * and work rem 2 sides and corner as established; end ch 2, sk 2 dc, dc in top of ch-3; ch 5, turn.

Row 4: Sk first dc, dc in next dc; ch 2, sk 2 dc, * dc in next 4 dc, 3 dc over ch-5 lp, ch 5, sk 3 dc, dc in center dc, ch 5, sk 3 dc, 3 dc over ch-5 lp, dc in first 4 dc; ** ch 3, sk 3 dc, dc in center dc; (ch 1, dc in same center dc) 4 times; ch 3, sk 3 dc; rep from * across side, ending last rep before corner at **; then sk 2 dc; (ch 2, dc in next dc) 9 times, ch 2, sk 2 dc; rep from first * and work rem 2 sides and corner as established; end ch 2, sk 2 dc, dc in last dc, ch 2, dc in third ch of ch-5; ch 5, turn.

Row 5: Sk first dc; (dc in next dc, ch 2) 2 times; sk 2 dc; * dc in next 4 dc, 3 dc over ch-5 lp, ch 3, 3 dc over next ch-5 lp, dc in next 4 dc; ** ch 3, sk 3 dc, trc in next dc; (ch 1, trc in next dc) 4 times, ch 3, sk 3 dc; rep from * across side, ending last rep before corner at **; then sk 2 dc; (ch 3, trc in next dc) 11 times, ch 3, sk 2 dc. Start over again at first *; work other 2 sides and corner as before. End with ch 2, sk 2 dc, dc in last st of 7-dc grp, ch 2, dc in next dc, ch 2, dc in third st of turning ch-5; ch 5, turn.

Row 6: Sk first dc; (dc in next dc, ch 2) 3 times; * sk 2 dc, dc in next 4 dc, 2 dc in sp, ch 3, sl st in top of dc just made, dc in same sp, dc in next 4 dc, ch 2, sk 2 dc, dc in next dc; (dc in next trc, **ch 4, sl st in third ch from hook—picot made,** ch 1, dc in same trc) 5 times, dc in next dc, ch 2; rep from * around, having eleven 2-dc picot grps around corner. End with ch 2, sk 2 dc, dc in last st of ch-7 grp; (ch 2, dc in next dc) twice, ch 2, dc in third st of turning ch-5.

Work sc evenly across *top* edge of curtain only; fasten off.

FINISHING: Wash, starch, and steam-press curtain panel; spread out flat over clean sheet on floor or carpet until completely dry. Machine-stitch bias hem facing strip across top of panel on wrong side for rod pocket.

PINEAPPLE ANTIMACASSAR SET

Shown on page 126.

Chair back measures about 10x16 inches. Arm chair pieces measure 7x10 inches.

MATERIALS
Clark's Big Ball 3-cord crochet cotton, Size 10 (200-yard ball): 4 balls of white or ecru
Size 9 steel crochet hook

Abbreviations: See page 186.
Gauge: First 5 rows of pattern = 2 inches along the straight edges.

INSTRUCTIONS
For the chair back
Starting at center, ch 10; join with sl st to form ring.

Row 1: Ch 4, work 16 trc in ring; ch 4, turn.

Row 2: Sk first trc, trc in next 15 trc; trc in top of ch-4; ch 5, turn. (Push trc in ring together so work lies flat.)

Row 3: Sk first trc, trc in next trc; (ch 1, trc in next trc) 14 times; ch 1, trc in top of ch-4; ch 4, turn.

Row 4: Sk first trc; trc in ch-1 sp; * trc in next trc, trc in next ch-1 sp; rep from * across; end trc in last ch-1 turning sp; trc in fourth ch of beg ch-5—33 trc across, counting beg ch-4 as trc; ch 4, turn.

Row 5: Sk first trc; trc in each trc across; trc in top of ch-4; ch 4, turn.

Row 6: Trc in first trc; ch 2, sk trc, 2 trc in next trc; * ch 2, sk 2 trc, 2 trc in next trc; rep from * across; end ch 2, sk 2 trc, 2 trc in top of turning ch-4—12 trc grp across; turn.

Row 7: Sl st in next trc and into ch-sp; ch 4, in same sp make trc, ch 2, and 2 trc; in *each* ch-2 lp across work 2 trc, ch 2, and 2 trc; turn.

Row 8: Sl st in next trc and into ch-2 sp; ch 4, in same sp work trc, ch 2, and 2 trc; * ch 1, in next ch-2 sp make 2 trc, ch 2, and 2 trc; rep from * across; turn.

Rows 9 and 10: Sl st in next trc and into ch-2 sp; ch 4, in same sp work trc, ch 2, and 2 trc; * ch 2, in next ch-2 sp make 2 trc, ch 2, and 2 trc; rep from * across; turn.

Row 11: Sl st in next trc and into ch-2 sp; ch 4, in same sp work trc, ch 2, and 2 trc; * ch 3, in next ch-2 sp make 2 trc, ch 2, and 2 trc; rep from * across; turn.

Row 12: Sl st in next trc and into ch-2 sp; ch 4, in same sp work trc, ch 2, and 2 trc; * ch 4, in next ch-2 sp make 2 trc, ch 2, and 2 trc; rep from * across; turn.

Row 13: Sl st in next trc and into ch-2 sp; ch 4, in same sp work trc, ch 2, and 2 trc; * ch 5, in next ch-2 sp make 2 trc, ch 2, and 2 trc; rep from * across; turn.

Row 14: Sl st in next trc and into ch-2 sp; ch 4, in same sp work trc, ch 2, and 2 trc; * ch 4, in next ch-2 sp make 2 trc, ch 5, and 2 trc; ch 4, in next ch-2 sp make 2 trc, ch 2, and 2 trc; rep from * across; turn.

Note: Hereafter when all rows begin "work beg shell," work sl st in next trc and sl st into ch-2 sp; ch 4, in same sp work trc, ch 2, and 2 trc.

Row 15: Work beg shell; * ch 3, in ch-5 lp work 14 dtr (yo hook 3 times); ch 3, in ch-2 lp work 2 trc, ch 2, and 2 trc; rep from * across; turn.

Row 16: Work beg shell; * ch 4, dtr in next dtr; (ch 1, dtr in next dtr) 13 times; ch 4, in next ch-2 sp work 2 trc, ch 2, and 2 trc; rep from * across; turn.

Row 17: Work beg shell; * ch 4, sc in ch-1 sp; (ch 5, sc in next ch-1 sp) 12 times; ch 4, in next ch-2 sp work 2 trc, ch 2, and 2 trc; rep from * across; turn.

Row 18: Work beg shell; * ch 4, sc in first ch-5 lp of pineapple lp; (ch 5, sc in next ch-5 lp) 11 times; ch 4, in next ch-2 sp work 2 trc, ch 2, 2 trc; rep from * across; turn.

Row 19: Work beg shell; ch 2, in same ch-2 sp work 2 trc; * ch 4, sc in first ch-5 lp of pineapple lp; (ch 6, sc in next ch-5 lp) 10 times; ch 4, in next ch-2 lp work 2 trc, ch 2, 2 trc, ch 2, and 2 trc; rep from * across; turn.

Row 20: Work beg shell; ch 2, in next ch-2 sp work 2 trc, ch 2, and 2 trc; * ch 4, sc in first ch-6 pineapple lp; (ch 6, sc in next ch-6 lp) 9 times; ch 4, in next ch-2 lp work 2 trc, ch 2, and 2 trc; ch 2, in next ch-2 lp work 2 trc, ch 2, and 2 trc; rep from * across; turn.

Row 21: Work beg shell; (work 2 trc, ch 2, and 2 trc in next ch-2 sp) 2 times; * ch 4, sc in first pine-apple lp; (ch 6, sc in next ch-6 lp) 8 times; ch 4; (in next ch-2 lp work 2 trc, ch 2, and 2 trc) 3 times; rep from * across; turn.

Row 22: Work beg shell; (ch 3, in next ch-2 lp work 2 trc, ch 2, and 2 trc) 2 times; * ch 4, sc in first pineapple lp; (ch 6, sc in next ch-6 lp) 7 times; ch 4, (in next ch-2 lp work 2 trc, ch 2, and 2 trc; ch 3) 2 times; in ch-2 lp work 2 trc, ch 2, and 2 trc; rep from * across; turn.

Row 23: Work beg shell; (ch 4, in next ch-2 lp work 2 trc, ch 2,

and 2 trc) 2 times; * ch 4, sc in first pineapple lp; (ch 6, sc in next ch-6 lp) 6 times; (ch 4, in next ch-2 lp work 2 trc, ch 2, and 2 trc) 3 times; rep from * across; turn.

Row 24: Work beg shell; * ch 4, in next ch-2 lp work 2 trc, ch 5, and 2 trc; ch 4, in next ch-2 lp work 2 trc, ch 2, and 2 trc; ch 4, sc in first pineapple lp; (ch 6, sc in next ch-6 lp) 5 times; ch 4, work 2 trc, ch 2, and 2 trc in next ch-2 lp; rep from * across; turn.

Row 25: Work beg shell; * ch 4, in ch-5 lp work 14 dtr; ch 4, in next ch-2 sp work 2 trc, ch 2, and 2 trc; ch 4, sc in first pineapple lp; (ch 6, sc in next ch-6 lp) 4 times; ch 4, in next ch-2 lp work 2 trc, ch 2, and 2 trc; rep from * across; turn.

Row 26: Work beg shell; * ch 4, dtr in first dtr; (ch 1, dtr in next dtr) 13 times; ch 4, in next ch-2 lp work 2 trc, ch 2, and 2 trc; ch 4, sc in first pineapple lp; (ch 6, sc in next ch-6 lp) 3 times; ch 4, in next ch-2 lp work 2 trc, ch 2, and 2 trc; rep from * across; turn.

Row 27: Work beg shell; * ch 4, sc in first ch-1 sp; (ch 4, sc in next ch-1 sp) 12 times; ch 4, in next ch-2 sp work 2 trc, ch 2, and 2 trc; ch 4, sc in first pineapple lp; (ch 6, sc in next ch-6 lp) 2 times; ch 4, in next ch-2 lp work 2 trc, ch 2, and 2 trc; rep from * across; turn.

Row 28: Work beg shell; * ch 4, sc in first pineapple lp; (ch 4, sc in next ch-4 lp) 11 times; ch 4, in next ch-2 sp work 2 trc, ch 2, and 2 trc; ch 4, sc in first pineapple lp; ch 6, sc in next lp; ch 4, in next ch-lp work 2 trc, ch 2, and 2 trc; rep from * across; turn.

Row 29: Work beg shell; * ch 4, sc in first pineapple lp; (ch 4, sc in next ch-4 lp) 10 times; ch 4, in next ch-2 lp work 2 trc, ch 2, and 2 trc; ch 5, sc in ch-6 lp, ch 5, in ch-2 lp work 2 trc, ch 2, and 2 trc; rep from * across; turn.

Row 30: Work beg shell; * ch 4, sc in first pineapple lp; (ch 5, sc in next ch-4 lp) 9 times; ch 4, in next ch-2 lp work 2 trc, ch 2, and 2 trc; ch 2, in next ch-2 lp work 2 trc, ch 2, and 2 trc; rep from * across; turn.

Row 31: Work beg shell; * ch 4, sc in first pineapple lp; (ch 5, sc in next ch-4 lp) 8 times; ch 4, (in next ch-2 sp work 2 trc, ch 2, and 2 trc) 3 times; rep from * across; turn.

Row 32: Work beg shell; * ch 4, sc in first pineapple lp; (ch 6, sc in next ch-5 lp) 7 times; ch 4; (in next ch-2 lp work 2 trc, ch 2, and 2 trc; ch 3) twice; in next ch-2 lp work 2 trc, ch 2, and 2 trc; rep from * across; turn.

Row 33: Work beg shell; * ch 4, sc in first pineapple lp; (ch 6, sc in next ch-6 lp) 6 times; (ch 4, in next ch-2 sp work 2 trc, ch 2, and 2 trc) 3 times; rep from * across; turn.

Row 34: Work beg shell; * ch 4, sc in first pineapple lp; (ch 6, sc in next ch-6 lp) 5 times; ch 4, in next ch-2 lp work 2 trc, ch 2, and 2 trc; ch 4, in next ch-2 lp work 2 trc, ch 5, and 2 trc; ch 4, in next ch-2 lp work 2 trc, ch 2, and 2 trc; rep from * across; turn.

Row 35: Work beg shell; * ch 4, sc in first pineapple lp; (ch 6, sc in next ch-6 lp) 4 times; ch 4, in next ch-2 lp work 2 trc, ch 2, and 2 trc; ch 4, in ch-5 lp work 15 dtr; ch 4, in next ch-2 lp work 2 trc, ch 2, and 2 trc; rep from * across; turn.

Row 36: Work beg shell; * ch 4, sc in first pineapple lp; (ch 6, sc in next ch-6 lp) 3 times; ch 4, in next ch-2 lp work 2 trc, ch 2, and 2 trc; ch 3, dtr in first dtr; (ch 1, dtr in next dtr) 14 times; ch 4, in next ch-2 lp work 2 trc, ch 2, and 2 trc; rep from * across; turn.

continued

135

Row 37: Work beg shell; * ch 4, sc in first pineapple lp; (ch 6, sc in next lp) 2 times; ch 4, in next ch-2 lp work 2 trc, ch 2, and 2 trc; (ch 4, sc in ch-1 lp) 14 times; ch 4, in next ch-2 lp work 2 trc, ch 2, and 2 trc; rep from * across; turn.

Row 38: Work beg shell; * ch 4, sc in pineapple lp, ch 6, sc in next lp; ch 4, in ch-2 lp work 2 trc, ch 2, and 2 trc; ch 4, sc in pineapple lp; (ch 4, sc in next lp) 12 times; ch 4, in next ch-2 lp work 2 trc, ch 2, and 2 trc; rep from * across; turn.

Row 39: Work beg shell; * ch 5, sc in ch-6 lp, ch 5, in ch-2 lp work 2 trc, ch 2, and 2 trc; ch 4, sc in pineapple lp; (ch 5, sc in next lp) 11 times; ch 4, in next ch-2 lp work 2 trc, ch 2, and 2 trc; rep from * across; turn.

Row 40: Work beg shell; in next ch-2 lp work 2 trc, ch 2, and 2 trc; * ch 4, sc in pineapple lp; (ch 5, sc in next lp) 10 times; ch 4, (in next ch-2 lp work 2 trc, ch 2, and 2 trc) 2 times; rep from * across; turn.

Begin to work pineapple tips
Row 41: Sl st across to ch-2 sp, work shell in *next* ch-2 sp; ch 4, work 9 ch-6 lps across pineapple, ch 4, in ch-2 lp work 2 trc, ch 2, and 2 trc; turn.

Rows 42–50: Work in rows to complete first pineapple, working 1 less lp in each pineapple.

Row 51: Work beg shell; in next ch-2 lp work 2 trc, ch 2, and 2 trc; fasten off.

Join thread in next ch-2 sp of Row 40 and complete second pineapple tip.

Work as established to complete rem three pineapples tips.

Note: At end of Row 41 of fifth tip, sl st into ch-2 sp of last shell; turn; work beg shell.

For the edging
Rnd 1: Join thread in starting ring at top of Chair Back, ch 4, in ring work 3 trc, ch 2, and 4 trc; * ch 3,

sk next row; around turning ch of next row, work **2 trc, ch 2, and 2 trc—shell made;** rep from * 24 times more; ch 4, work shell in next ch-sp; ch 3, in next ch-2 sp work shell; ch 3, work shell around turning ch of next row; rep bet first and second * 4 times; ch 3, dtr in sp bet shells, ch 3, sk next row; work shell around turning ch of next row; work as established around; end ch 3, join to top of beg ch-4.

Rnd 2: Sl st to ch-sp, ch 9, sc in fifth ch from hook—picot made; trc in same sp; * ch 4, sc in ch-3 lp, ch 4, in next ch-2 lp work trc, **ch 5, sc in fifth ch from hook—picot made;** trc in same lp; rep from * around; join last ch-4 to fourth ch of beg ch-9; fasten off.

For the arm pieces
Ch 10; join with sl st to form ring.
Row 1: Ch 4, work 10 trc in ring; ch 4, turn.

Row 2: Sk first trc, trc in next 9 trc; trc in top of ch-4; ch 4, turn.

Row 3: Trc in first trc; 2 trc in each trc across, 2 trc in top of ch-4—22 trc across; ch 4, turn.

Row 4: Sk first trc, trc in each trc across; ch 4, turn.

Row 5: Trc in first trc; (ch 2, sk 2 trc, 2 trc in next trc) 6 times; ch 2, sk 2 trc, 2 trc in top of ch-4; turn.

Rows 6–13: Rep rows 7–14 of Chair Back on page 134.

Row 14: **Sl st in next trc and into ch-2 sp; ch 4, in same sp work trc, ch 2, and 2 trc—beg shell made;** * ch 3, in ch-5 lp work 13 dtr; ch 3, **in ch-2 lp work 2 trc, ch 2, and 2 trc—shell over shell;** rep from * across; turn.

Row 15: Work beg shell; * ch 4, dtr in next dtr; (ch 1, dtr in next dtr) 12 times; ch 4, work shell over shell; rep from * across; turn.

Row 16: Work beg shell; * ch 4, sc in ch-1 sp; work 11 ch-4 lps across pineapple; ch 4, shell over

shell; rep from * across; turn.

Row 17: Work beg shell; * ch 4, work 10 ch-5 lps across pineapple; ch 4, in next ch-2 sp work 2 trc, ch 2, 2 trc, ch 2, and 2 trc; rep from * across; work shell over last ch-2 sp; turn.

Row 18: Work beg shell; * ch 4, work 9 ch-5 lps across pineapple; ch 4, work shell over shell; ch 2, work shell over next shell; rep from * across working shell in last ch-2 sp; turn.

Row 19: Work beg shell; * ch 4, work 8 ch-6 lps across pineapple; ch 4; shell over shell, shell in ch-2 sp, shell over shell; rep from *, ending as before; turn.

Row 20: Work beg shell; * ch 4, work 7 ch-6 lps across pineapple; ch 4; (shell over shell, ch 2) 2 times; shell over shell; rep from *, ending as before.

Row 21: Work beg shell; * ch 4, work 6 ch-6 lps across pineapple; (ch 4, shell over next shell) 3 times; rep from *, ending as before; turn.

Row 22: Work beg shell; * ch 4, work 5 ch-6 lps across pineapple; ch 4, shell over next shell; ch 4, in next shell work 2 trc, ch 5, and 2 trc; ch 4, shell over next shell; rep from *, ending as before; turn.

Row 23: Work beg shell; * ch 4, work 4 ch-6 lps across pineapple, ch 4, shell over shell; ch 3, work 14 dtr in ch-5 lp; ch 3, work shell over shell; rep from *, ending as before; turn.

Row 24: Work beg shell; * ch 4, work 3 ch-6 lps across pineapple, ch 4, shell over shell; ch 4, dtr in first dtr; (ch 1, dtr in next dtr) 13 times; ch 4, shell over shell; rep from *, ending as before; turn.

Row 25: Work beg shell; * ch 4, work 2 ch-6 lps across pineapple, ch 4, shell over shell; ch 4, sc in first ch-1 lp; work 12 ch-4 lps across pineapple; ch 4, shell over shell; rep from *, ending as before; turn.

Row 26: Work beg shell; * ch 4, work 1 ch-6 lp across pineapple, ch 4, shell over shell; ch 4, work 11 ch-4 lps across pineapple; ch 4, shell over shell; rep from *, ending as before; turn.

Row 27: Work beg shell; * ch 5, sc in ch-6 lp, ch 5, shell over shell, ch 4, work 10 ch-5 lps across pineapple; ch 4, shell over shell; rep from *, ending as before; turn.

Row 28: Work beg shell, shell over next shell; * ch 4, work 9 ch-5 lps across pineapple; ch 4, shell over shell, ch 2, shell over shell; rep from *, ending as before; turn.

Row 29: Sl st across to ch-2 sp, work shell in *next* shell; * ch 4, work 8 ch-6 lps across pineapple; ch 4, work shell over shell, shell in ch-2 sp, shell over shell; rep from * across, working shells in last 2 shells; turn.

Row 30: Sl st across to ch-2 sp of first shell; work shell in *next* shell; * ch 4, work 7 ch-6 lps across pineapple; ch 4, shell over shell; (ch 3, shell over next shell) 2 times; rep from * across, ending with shell in last shell; turn.

Row 31: Work beg shell; * ch 4, work 6 ch-6 lps across pineapple; (ch 4, shell over shell) 3 times; rep from * across, ending with shell in last shell; turn.

Row 32: Work beg shell; * ch 4, work 5 ch-6 lps across pineapple; ch 4, shell in next shell; ** ch 4, in next shell work 2 trc, ch 5, and 2 trc; ch 4, shell over next shell; rep from * across, ending at **; turn.

Row 33: Work beg shell; * ch 4, work 4 ch 6 lps across pineapple; ch 4, shell over shell; ** ch 4, work 16 dtr in ch-5 lp; ch 4, work shell over shell; rep from * across, ending at **; turn.

Row 34: Work beg shell; * ch 4, work 3 ch-6 lps across pineapple;

ch 4, shell over shell; ** ch 4, dtr in first dtr; (ch 1, dtr in next dtr) 15 times; ch 4, shell over shell; rep from * across, ending at **; turn.

Row 35: Work beg shell; * ch 4, work 2 ch-6 lps across pineapple; ch 4, shell over shell; ** ch 4, sc in first ch-1 lp; (ch 4, sc in next ch-1 lp) 14 times; ch 4, work shell over shell; rep from * across, ending at **; turn.

Row 36: Work beg shell; * ch 4, work 1 lp across pineapple; ch 4, shell over shell; ** ch 4, sc in first pineapple lp; (ch 4, sc in next lp) 13 times; ch 4, shell over shell; rep from * across, ending at **; turn.

Row 37: Work beg shell; * ch 5, sc in ch-6 lp; ch 5, shell over shell; ** ch 4, sc in first pineapple lp; (ch 4, sc in next lp) 12 times; ch 4, work shell over shell; rep from * across, ending at **; turn.

Row 38: Work beg shell; work shell over next shell; ch 4, sc in first pineapple lp; (ch 4, sc in next lp) 11 times; ch 4; (work shell over shell) 2 times; turn.

Row 39: Sl st across to ch-2 sp of first shell; work shell in *next* shell; * ch 4, work 10 ch-5 lps across pineapple; ch 4, (shell over shell) twice; turn.

Row 40: Sl st across to ch-2 sp of first shell, work shell in *next* shell; work across row as established.

Rows 41–48: Work across pineapple lps as established, working 1 less lp in each succeeding row, and changing from ch-5 lps to ch-6 lps in Row 44.

Row 49: Work beg shell; ch 5, sc in ch-6 lp, ch 5, shell in shell; turn.

Row 50: Work beg shell, shell in next shell; fasten off.

For the edging

Rnd 1: Rep Rnd 1 of Chair Back Edging, *opposite.* Work a total of 25 shells with ch-3 lps between each shell along sides. Work shell at tip of point. Rep Rnd 2 of Chair Back Edging; fasten off.

CLUSTER DOILY PILLOW TOP

Shown at right on page 127.

Pillow measures approximately 17 inches in diameter.

MATERIALS

Clark's Big Ball 3-cord crochet cotton, Size 10 (200-yard ball): 5 balls of white or ecru
Size 9 steel crochet hook.
16-inch pillow form

Abbreviations: See page 186.
Gauge: 6 rnds = 3¼ inches.

INSTRUCTIONS

Beg in center, ch 8; join with sl st to form ring.

Rnd 1: Ch 1, in ring work 16 sc; join with sl st to beg sc.

Rnd 2: Ch 1, sc in same st as join; (ch 2, sk sc, sc in next sc) 7 times; ch 2, join with sl st to beg sc—8 ch-2 lps around.

Rnd 3: Sl st into ch-2 lp, **ch 3, work 4 dc in same lp, drop lp from hook, insert hook in top of beg ch-3, and draw dropped lp through—beg popcorn (pc) made;** * ch 7, **work 5 dc in next ch-2 lp, drop lp from hook, insert hook in top of first dc of 5-dc grp and draw dropped lp through—pc made;** rep from * around, end ch 7, join to top of beg pc.

Rnd 4: Sl st into next 3 ch, work beg pc in same ch *except* work 3 dc instead of 4; * ch 5, sk next ch, work 4-dc pc in next ch, ch 3, ** work 4-dc pc in third ch of next ch-7 lp; rep from * around; end last rep at **; join to top of beg pc.

Rnd 5: Sl st into next 2 ch; work beg 4-dc pc in same ch; * ch 5, sk

continued

ch, work 4-dc pc in next ch; in center ch of next ch-5 lp work dc, ch 4, and dc; ** work 4-dc pc in second ch of next ch-5 lp; rep from * around; end last rep at **; join to top of beg pc.

Rnd 6: Sl st in next 3 ch, ch 1, sc in same ch-5 lp; * ch 1, in ch-4 lp work 11 dc; ch 1, ** sc in ch-5 lp; rep from * around; end last rep at **; join to beg sc.

Rnd 7: Sl st in next ch and in first dc of 11-dc grp; ch 1, sc in first dc, * sc in next dc, **ch 3, sl st in third ch from hook—picot made;** sc in next 2 dc, ch 7, sk 3 dc, sc in next 2 dc, work picot, sc in next 2 dc, ch 5; ** sc in first dc of next 11-dc grp; rep from * around; end last rep at **; join last ch-5 to first sc; fasten off.

Rnd 8: Rejoin thread in center ch of any ch-7 lp, ch 1, work 2 sc in same lp; * ch 5, **holding back last lp of next trc on hook, work 2 trc in center ch of next ch-5 lp—trc dec made;** ch 5, ** work 2 sc in next ch-7 lp; rep from * around; end last rep at **; join to first sc.

Rnd 9: Sl st in next sc and into ch-5 lp, ch 1, work 10 sc in same ch-5 lp; * sc in trc cl; 10 sc in next ch-5 lp; ch 2, ** sk 2 sc, 7 sc in next ch-5 lp; (ch 8, turn; sl st in seventh sc of next 10-sc grp, turn; work 15 sc in ch-8 lp); work 3 more sc in rem sp of ch-5 lp below; rep from * around; end last rep at **; sl st in next 7 sc, rep bet ( ); join with sl st to next sc below.

Rnd 10: Sl st into next 3 sc, ch 4, in same st as last sl st work trc, ch 2, and 2 trc; * ch 1, sc in first sc of 15-sc grp; (ch 3, sk sc, sc in next sc) 7 times—7 pineapple lps; ch 1; ** in sc above trc cl work 2 trc, ch 2, and 2 trc; rep from * around; end last rep at **; join to top of beg ch-4.

Rnd 11: Sl st in next st and into ch-2 lp; ch 3, in same lp work dc, ch 2, and 2 dc; * ch 2, sc in first ch-3 pineapple lp; (ch 3, sc in next ch-3 lp) 6 times; ch 2, ** in ch-2 lp bet trc work **2 dc, ch 2, and 2 dc—shell made;** rep from * around; end last rep at **; join to top of beg ch-3.

Rnd 12: Sl st in next st and into ch-2 lp; ch 3, in same lp work dc, ch 2, and 2 dc; * ch 3, sc in first ch-3 pineapple lp; (ch 3, sc in next lp) 5 times; ch 3, ** shell in ch-2 lp of next shell; rep from * around; end last rep at **; join to top of beg ch-3.

Rnd 13: Sl st in next st and into ch-2 lp; ch 3, in same lp work dc, ch 2, 2 dc, ch 2, and 2 dc; * ch 3, sc in first pineapple lp; (ch 3, sc in next lp) 4 times, ch 3, ** in ch-2 lp of shell work 2 dc, ch 2, 2 dc, ch 2, and 2 dc; rep from * around; end last rep at **; join as before.

Rnd 14: Sl st in next st and into ch-2 lp; ch 3, in same lp work dc, ch 2, and 2 dc; ch 3, shell in next ch-2 lp; * ch 3, sc in first pineapple lp, (ch 3, sc in next lp) 3 times; (ch 3, ** shell in next ch-2 lp) 2 times; rep from * around; end last rep at **; join as before.

Rnd 15: Sl st in next st and into ch-2 lp; ch 3, in same lp work dc, ch 2, and 2 dc; * ch 3, sc in ch-3 lp, ch 3, shell in ch-2 lp of next shell; ch 4, sc in first ch-3 pineapple lp; (ch 3, sc in next lp) 2 times; ch 4, ** shell in ch-2 lp of next shell; rep from * around; end last rep at **; join as before.

Rnd 16: Sl st in next st and into ch-2 lp; ch 3, in same lp work dc, ch 2, and 2 dc; * (ch 3, sc in next ch-3 lp) 2 times; ch 3, shell in ch-2 lp of next shell, ch 4, sc in first pineapple lp, ch 3, sc in next ch-3 lp, ch 4, ** shell in ch-2 lp of next shell; rep from * around; end last rep at **; join as before.

Rnd 17: Sl st in next st and into ch-2 lp; ch 3, in same lp work dc, ch 2, and 2 dc; * ch 5, sk next ch-3 lp, in next ch-3 lp work 4-dc pc, ch 3, and 4-dc pc; ch 5, shell in ch-2 lp of shell, ch 5, sc in ch-3 pineapple lp, ch 5, ** shell in ch-2 lp of next shell; rep from * around, end last rep at **; join as before.

Rnd 18: Sl st in next st and into ch-2 lp; ch 3, in same lp work dc, ch 2, and 2 dc; * ch 5, in ch-3 lp bet pc work 4-dc pc, ch 3, 4-dc pc, ch 3, and 4-dc pc; (ch 5, ** shell in ch-2 lp of next shell) 2 times; rep from * around; end last rep at **; join as before.

Rnd 19: Sl st in next st and into ch-2 lp; ch 3, in same lp work dc, ch 2, and 2 dc; * ch 7, in ch-3 lp work 4-dc pc, ch 3, and 4-dc pc; ch 3; in next ch-3 lp work 4-dc pc, ch 3, and 4-dc pc; ch 7, shell in ch-2 lp of next shell, ch 1, ** shell in ch-2 lp of next shell; rep from * around; end last rep at **; join as before.

Rnd 20: Sl st in next st and into ch-2 lp; ch 3, in same lp work dc, ch 2, and 2 dc; * ch 5, (in next ch-3 lp work 4-dc pc, ch 3, and 4-dc pc; ch 3) 2 times; in next ch-3 lp work 4-dc pc, ch 3, and 4-dc pc; ch 5; (shell in ch-2 lp of next shell) ** 2 times; rep from * around; end last rep at **; join to top of beg ch-3.

Rnd 21: Sl st in next st and into ch-2 lp; ch 3, in same lp work dc, ch 2, and 2 dc; * ch 5; (in next ch-3 lp work 4-dc pc, ch 4, and 4-dc pc; ch 4) 4 times; in next ch-3 lp work 4-dc pc, ch 4, and 4-dc pc; ch 5, (shell in ch-2 lp of next shell) 2 times; rep from * around; join as before.

Rnd 22: Sl st in next st and into ch-2 lp; ch 3, in same lp work dc, ch 2, and 2 dc; * ch 5, sc in next ch-4 lp; (ch 4, sc in next ch-4 lp) 8 times; ch 5; (shell in ch-2 lp of next shell) 2 times; rep from * around; join as before.

Rnd 23: Sl st in next st and into ch-2 lp; ch 3, in same lp work dc, ch 2, and 2 dc; * ch 6, sc in next ch-4 lp; (ch 5, sc in next lp) 7 times; ch 6; (shell in ch-2 lp of next shell) 2 times; rep from * around; join as before.

Rnd 24: Sl st in next dc and into ch-2 lp; ch 1, sc in same lp; * ch 5, sc in ch-6 lp; (ch 5, sc in next ch-5 lp) 7 times; (ch 5, sc in next ch-2 lp) 2 times; rep from * around; end ch 2, dc in beg sc.

Rnd 25: Sc in lp just made; * ch 5, sc in next lp; rep from * around; end ch 2, dc in beg sc.

Rnd 26: Sc in lp just made; * ch 6, sc in next lp; rep from * around; end ch 3, dc in beg sc.

Rnds 27–33: Rep Rnd 26.

Rnd 34: Sc in lp just made; * ch 7, sc in next lp; rep from * around; end ch 3, trc in beg sc.

Rnd 35: Sc in lp just made; * ch 7, sc in next lp; in next ch-7 lp work 9 dc; ** sc in next lp; rep from * around; end last rep at **; join to beg sc.

Rnd 36: Sl st in next 3 ch, sc in center ch of ch-7 lp, * ch 1, dc in first dc of 9-dc grp; (ch 1, dc in next dc) 8 times; ch 1, ** sc in center ch of ch-7 lp; rep from * around; end last rep at **; join to beg sc.

Rnd 37: Sc in next ch-1 sp; * ch 3, sc in next ch-1 sp; rep from * around; join to beg sc; fasten off.

Work a second side through Rnd 33. Whipstitch matching rnds 33 together, stretching over 16-inch pillow form.

STAR DAHLIA PILLOW TOP

Shown at left on page 127.

Pillow measures approximately 19 inches in diameter.

―――――MATERIALS―――――
Clark's Big Ball crochet cotton, Size 20 (400-yard ball): 3 balls
Size 11 steel crochet hook
16-inch pillow form

Abbreviations: See page 186.
Gauge: First 6 rnds = 3 inches.

―――――INSTRUCTIONS―――――
Beg in center, ch 8; join with sl st to form ring.

Rnd 1: Ch 1, in ring work 12 sc; join with sl st to beg sc.

Rnd 2: Ch 3, dc in same st as join; work 2 dc in each sc around; join to top of beg ch-3.

Rnd 3: Ch 1, sc in same st as join; * ch 5, sk next dc, sc in next dc; rep from * around; join last ch-5 to beg sc—12 ch-5 lps.

Rnd 4: Sl st in next 3 ch; ch 1, sc in same lp; * ch 7, sc in next ch-5 lp; rep from * around; join last ch-7 to beg sc.

Rnd 5: Sl st in next 4 ch; ch 4, in same ch work trc, ch 1, and 2 trc, ch 3; * in center ch of next ch-7 lp work 2 trc, ch 1, and 2 trc; ch 3; rep from * around; join last ch-3 to top of beg ch-4.

Rnd 6: Ch 4, trc in next trc, * in next ch-1 sp work trc, ch 1, and trc; trc in next 2 trc; ch 3, ** trc in next 2 trc; rep from * around; end last rep at **; join last ch-3 to top of beg ch-4.

Rnd 7: Ch 4, trc in next 2 trc; * in next ch-1 sp work trc, ch 1, and trc; trc in next 3 trc; ch 3, ** trc in next 3 trc; rep from * around; end last rep at **; join as before.

Rnd 8: Ch 4, trc in next 3 trc; * in next ch-1 sp work trc, ch 1, and trc; trc in next 4 trc; ch 3, ** trc in next 4 trc; rep from * around; end last rep at **; join as before.

Rnd 9: Ch 4, trc in next 4 trc, * ch 2, trc in next 5 trc; ch 4, ** trc in next 5 trc; rep from * around; end last rep at **; join as before.

Rnd 10: Ch 4, trc in next 9 trc; * ch 7, trc in next 10 trc; rep from * around; join last ch-7 to top of beg ch-4.

Rnd 11: Ch 4, trc in next 3 trc; **keeping last lp of each trc on hook, work trc in each of next 2 trc, yo, draw through rem 3 lps on hook—trc dec made;** trc in next 4 trc; * ch 3, in center ch of next ch-7 lp work trc, ch 2, and trc; ch 3, ** trc in next 4 trc, work trc dec over next 2 trc, trc in next 4 trc; rep from * around; end last rep at **; join to top of beg ch-4.

Rnd 12: Sl st in next trc, ch 4, trc in next 6 trc; * ch 5, in ch-2 lp work 2 trc, ch 3, and 2 trc; ch 5, ** sk first trc of next 9-trc grp, trc in next 7 trc; rep from * around; end last rep at **; join as before.

Rnd 13: Sl st in next trc, ch 4, trc in next 4 trc; * ch 6, in ch-3 lp work 3 trc, ch 3, and 3 trc; ch 6; ** sk first trc of next 7-trc grp; trc in next 5 trc; rep from * around; end last rep at **; join as before.

Rnd 14: Sl st in next trc, ch 3, work trc dec over next 2 trc; * ch 6, in ch-3 lp work 4 trc, ch 4, and 4 trc; ch 7, ** sk first trc of next 5-trc grp; **holding back last lp of each trc, work trc in each of next 3 trc, yo, draw through all lps on hook—trc cl made;** rep from * around; end last rep at **; join last ch-7 to top of beg trc dec.

Rnd 15: Ch 6, trc in same st as join, * ch 6, in ch-4 lp work 5 trc, ch 6, and 5 trc; ch 6; ** in trc cl work trc, ch 2, and trc; rep from * around; end last rep at **; join last ch-6 in fourth ch of beg ch-6.

Rnd 16: Sl st into ch-2 lp, ch 4, in same lp work trc, ch 3, and 2 trc; * ch 5, in ch-6 lp bet 5-trc grp work (4 trc, ch 3) 3 times; work 4 more trc in same lp; ch 5, ** in next ch-2 lp work 2 trc, ch 3, and 2 trc; rep from * around; end last rep at **; join last ch-5 to top of beg ch-4.

continued

Rnd 17: Sl st in next trc and into ch-3 lp, ch 4, in same lp work 2 trc, ch 3, and 3 trc; * ch 4; (in next ch-3 lp work 4 trc, ch 2, and 4 trc) 3 times; ch 4, ** in next ch-3 lp work 3 trc, ch 3, and 3 trc; rep from * around; end last rep at **; join as before.

Rnd 18: Sl st in next 2 trc and into ch-3 lp, ch 4, in same lp work 3 trc, ch 3, and 4 trc; * ch 3; in next ch-2 lp work **4 trc, ch 2, and 4trc—8-trc shell made;** ch 2, in next ch-2 lp work 4 trc, ch 4, and 4 trc; ch 2, in next ch-2 lp work 8-trc shell; ch 3, ** in next ch-3 lp work 4 trc, ch 3, and 4 trc; rep from * around; end last rep at **; join.

Rnd 19: Sl st in next 3 trc and into ch-3 lp, ch 4, in same lp work 3 trc, ch 3, and 4 trc; * ch 3, in next ch-2 lp work 8-trc shell; ch 3, in ch-4 lp work 11 dtr (yo hook 3 times); ch 3, in next ch-2 lp work 8-trc shell; ch 3, ** sk next ch-3 lp, in next ch-3 lp work 4 trc, ch 3, and 4 trc; rep from * around; end last rep at **; join.

Rnd 20: Sl st in next 3 trc and into ch-3 lp, ch 4, in same lp work 3 trc, ch 3, and 4 trc; * ch 3, in next ch-2 lp work 8-trc shell; ch 3, dtr in next dtr; (ch 1, dtr in next dtr) 10 times; ch 3, in next ch-2 lp work 8-trc shell; ch 3, ** sk ch-3 lp, in next ch-3 lp work 4 trc, ch 3, and 4 trc; rep from * around; end last rep at **; join.

Rnd 21: Sl st in next 3 trc and into ch-3 lp, ch 4, in same lp work 3 trc, ch 3, and 4 trc; * ch 3, in next ch-2 lp work 8-trc shell; ch 2, sc in ch-1 sp; (ch 3, sc in next ch-1 sp) 9 times; ch 2, in ch-2 lp work 8-trc shell; ch 3, ** sk ch-3 lp, in next ch-3 lp work 4 trc, ch 3, and 4 trc; rep from * around; end last rep at **; join.

Rnd 22: Sl st in next 3 trc and into ch-3 lp, ch 4, in same lp work 3 trc, ch 3, and 4 trc; * ch 4, in next ch-2 lp work 8-trc shell; ch 2, sc in first ch-3 lp; (ch 3, sc in next ch-3 lp) 8 times; ch 2, in ch-2 lp work 8-trc shell; ch 3, ** sk ch-3 lp, in next ch-3 lp work 4 trc, ch 3, and 4 trc; rep from * around; end last rep at **; join.

Rnd 23: Sl st in next 3 trc and into ch-3 lp, ch 4, in same lp work 3 trc, ch 2, 4 trc, ch 2, and 4 trc; * ch 4, in ch-2 lp work 8-trc shell; ch 3, sc in ch-3 lp; (ch 3, sc in ch-3 lp) 7 times; ch 3, in next ch-2 lp work 8-trc shell; ch 4, ** sk next ch-3 lp, in next ch-3 lp work 4 trc, ch 2, 4 trc, ch 2, and 4 trc; rep from * around; end last rep at **; join.

Rnd 24: Sl st in next 3 trc and into ch-2 lp; ch 4, in same lp work 3 trc, ch 2, and 4 trc; * in next ch-2 lp work 8-trc shell; ch 4, in next ch-2 lp work 8-trc shell; ch 3, sc in first ch-3 lp of pineapple; (ch 3, sc in next ch-3 lp) 6 times; ch 3, in next ch-2 lp work 8-trc shell; ch 3, ** in next ch-2 lp work 8-trc shell; rep from * around; end last rep at **; join.

Rnd 25: Sl st in next 3 trc and into ch-2 lp; ch 4, in same lp work 3 trc, ch 2, and 4 trc—beg 8-trc shell made; * ch 1, in next ch-2 lp work 8-trc shell; ch 4, in next ch-2 lp work 8-trc shell; ch 3, sc in first ch-3 pineapple lp; (ch 3, sc in next ch-3 lp) 5 times, ch 3, in next ch-2 lp work 8-trc shell; ch 4, ** in next ch-2 lp work 8-trc shell; rep from * around; end last rep at **; join.

Rnd 26: Sl st in next 3 trc and into ch-2 lp; ch 4, in same lp work 3 trc, ch 2, and 4 trc; * in ch-1 st work trc, ch 3, and trc; in next ch-2 lp work 8-trc shell; ch 4, in next ch-2 lp work 8-trc shell; ch 4, sc in first pineapple lp; (ch 3, sc in next ch-3 lp) 4 times; (ch 4, ** work 8-trc shell in next ch-2 lp) 2 times; rep from * around; end last rep at **; join.

Rnd 27: Sl st in next 3 trc and into ch-2 lp; ch 4, in same lp work 3 trc, ch 2, and 4 trc; * work 8-trc shell in next ch-3 lp; work 8-trc shell in next ch-2 lp; ch 5, work 8-trc shell in next ch-2 lp; ch 4; sc in first pineapple lp; (ch 3, sc in next ch-3 lp) 3 times; ch 4, work 8-trc shell in next ch-2 lp, ch 5, ** work 8-trc shell in next ch-2 lp; rep from * around; end last rep at **; join last ch-5 to top of beg ch-4.

Rnd 28: Sl st in next 3 trc and into ch-2 lp; ch 4, in same lp work 3 trc, ch 2, and 4 trc; * (8-trc shell in next ch-2 lp) 2 times; ch 5, 8-trc shell in next ch-2 lp, ch 5, sc in first pineapple lp; (ch 3, sc in next ch-3 lp) 2 times; ch 5, 8-trc shell in next ch-2 lp; ch 5, ** 8-trc shell in next ch-2 lp; rep from * around; end last rep at **; join.

Rnd 29: Sl st in next 3 trc and into ch-2 lp; ch 4, in same lp work 3 trc, ch 2, and 4 trc; * (ch 1, 8-trc shell in next ch-2 lp) 2 times; ch 6, 8-trc shell in next ch-2 lp, ch 6, sc in first pineapple lp, ch 3, sc in next ch-3 lp, ch 6, 8-trc shell in next ch-2 lp, ch 6, ** 8-trc shell in next ch-2 lp; rep from * around; end last rep at **; join.

Rnd 30: Sl st in next 3 trc and into ch-2 lp; ch 4, in same lp work 3 trc, ch 2, and 4 trc; * (ch 1, 8-trc shell in next ch-2 lp) 2 times; ch 6, 8-trc shell in next ch-2 lp; in next ch-2 lp work 4 trc, ch 1, sl st back in ch-2 lp of previous 8-trc shell, ch 1, work 4 trc in same ch-2 lp to complete 8-trc shell; ch 6, ** 8-trc shell in next ch-2 lp; rep from * around; end last rep at **; join; fasten off.

PILLOW ASSEMBLY: Cut two circles of fabric to fit pillow form. With right sides together, sew circles together, leaving opening for turning and inserting pillow form. Clip curves; turn and press. Insert pillow form into opening and stitch opening closed. Center crochet piece on top of form and tack Rnd 30 along outside edge of pillow seam.

ROUND DRESSER DOILY

Shown on page 128.

Doily measures approximately 9 inches in diameter.

MATERIALS

J. & P. Coats Knit-Cro-Sheen (225-yard ball): 1 ball makes 1 doily
Size 8 steel crochet hook

Abbreviations: See page 186.
Gauge: First 3 rnds = 2 inches.

INSTRUCTIONS

Beg in center, ch 8, join with sl st to form ring.

Rnd 1: Ch 3, work 19 dc in ring; join with sl st to top of beg ch-3.

Rnd 2: Ch 3, dc in same st as join; * ch 2, sk dc, 2 dc in next dc; rep from * around; end ch 2, join with sl st to top of beg ch-3.

Rnd 3: Sl st in next dc and into ch-2 sp; ch 3, in same sp work dc, ch 2, and 2 dc; * ch 2, in next ch-2 sp work **2 dc, ch 2, and 2 dc—shell made;** rep from * around; end ch 2, join to top of beg ch-3.

Rnd 4: Sl st in next dc and into ch-2 sp; ch 3, in same sp work dc, ch 5, and 2 dc; * ch 3, **shell in ch-2 sp of next shell—shell over shell made;** ch 3, in ch-2 sp of next shell work 2 dc, ch 5, and 2 dc; rep from * around; end ch 3, join to top of beg ch-3.

Rnd 5: Sl st in next dc and into ch-5 lp; ch 4, work 10 trc in same ch-5 lp, * ch 3, shell over shell, ch 3, 11 trc in next ch-5 lp; rep from * around; end ch 3, join to top of beg ch-4.

Rnd 6: Ch 5, trc in next trc; (ch 1, trc in next trc) 9 times; * ch 3, shell over shell, ch 3, trc in next trc; (ch 1, trc in next trc) 10 times; rep from * around; end ch 3, join to fourth ch of beg ch-5.

Rnd 7: Sl st into next ch-1 sp, sc in same sp; * (ch 3, sc into next ch-1 sp) 9 times, ch 3, shell over shell, ch 3, sc in next ch-1 sp; rep from * around; end ch 3, sc in first ch-3 lp of first pineapple.

Rnd 8: (Ch 3, sc in next lp) 8 times; * ch 3, shell over next shell; (ch 3, sc in next pineapple lp) 9 times; rep from * around; end ch 3, sl st in sc at beg of rnd; fasten off.

Tips of pineapples: Work now begins to work in rows.

Row 9: Join thread in ch-2 sp of next shell of previous rnd; ch 3, in same sp make dc, ch 2, and 2 dc; (ch 3, sc in next lp) 8 times; ch 3, shell in shell; ch 3, turn.

Rows 10–14: Shell in shell; (ch 3, sc in next pineapple lp) 7 times; ch 3, shell in next shell; ch 3, turn. Continue in this manner, having 1 less ch-3 lp in each pineapple.

Row 15: Shell in shell; (ch 3, sc in next pineapple lp) twice; ch 3, shell in next shell—1 lp rem at point; ch 3, turn. Work shell over shell, ch 4, sc in rem pineapple lp, ch 4, 2 dc in next shell, ch 1, sl st back in ch-2 sp of last shell; ch 1, 2 dc in same lp as last 2 dc; fasten off.

Join thread in same ch-2 lp of the same shell used for end of Row 9 on previous pineapple tip, and complete the next tip in the same way. Continue in this manner until all five tips are worked.

EDGING: *Rnd 1:* Attach thread to point of any pineapple tip where shells were joined, ch 3; in same place make dc, ch 2, and 2 dc; * (ch 3, shell in next turning ch) 3 times, ch 2, **holding back last lp of next 2 dc, dc in turning ch before next shell, dc around side of dc of next shell, yo, draw through all lps on hook—dc-dec made;** (ch 3, shell in next turning ch) 3 times, ch 3, shell in point of tip where shells meet; rep from * around; join.

Rnd 2: Sl st in next dc and into ch-2 sp, ch 6 (to count as dc and ch-3 for a picot), sc in third ch from hook; dc in same ch-2 sp as sl st; * ch 3, sc in next ch-3 lp, ch 3; in ch-2 sp of next shell make dc, **ch 3, sc in third ch from hook—picot made,** and dc, rep from * twice more; ch 3, sc in top of dc-dec, ch 3; in ch-2 sp of next shell make dc, picot, and dc; ch 3, sc in next ch-3 lp. Cont around in this manner; join and fasten off; block.

PINEAPPLE DIAMOND DRESSER DOILY

Shown on page 128.

Doily measures 17 inches long and 11½ inches wide.

MATERIALS

J. & P. Coats Knit-Cro-Sheen (225-yard ball): 1 ball
Size 8 steel crochet hook

Abbreviations: See page 186.
Gauge: First 4 rnds = 2¾ inches.

INSTRUCTIONS

Ch 8, join with sl st to form ring.

Rnd 1: Ch 3, work 23 dc in ring; join with sl st to top of beg ch-3.

Rnd 2: Ch 3, dc in same st as sl st; * ch 2, sk dc, 2 dc in next dc; rep from * around; end ch 2, join with sl st to top of beg ch-3.

Rnd 3: Sl st in next dc and into ch-2 sp, ch 3, in same sp work dc, ch 2, and 2 dc; in *each* ch-2 sp around work **2 dc, ch 2, and 2 dc—shell made;** join to top of beg ch-3—12 shells around.

continued

Rnd 4: **Sl st in next dc and into ch-2 sp, ch 3, in same sp work dc, ch 2, and 2 dc—beg shell made;** * ch 2, work shell in ch-2 sp of next shell; rep from * around; end ch 2; join to top of beg ch-3.

Rnd 5: Work beg shell; * ch 4, in ch-2 sp of next shell work 2 dc, ch 5, and 2 dc; ch 4, ** work shell in ch-2 sp of next shell; rep from * around; end last rep at **; join.

Rnd 6: Work beg shell; * ch 3, in ch-5 lp work 13 trc; ch 3, ** work shell in ch-2 sp of next shell; rep from * around; end last rep at **; join.

Rnd 7: Work beg shell; * ch 3, trc in next trc; (ch 1, trc in next trc) 12 times; ch 3, ** work shell in ch-2 sp of next shell; rep from * around; end last rep at **; join.

Rnd 8: Work beg shell; * (ch 3, sc in next ch-1 sp) 12 times; ch 3, work shell in ch-2 sp of next shell; (ch 3, sc in next ch-1 sp) 12 times, ch 3; in ch-2 sp of next shell work 2 dc, ch 2, 2 dc, ch 2, and 2 dc; (ch 3, sc in next ch-1 sp) 12 times; ch 3, ** work shell in ch-2 sp of shell; rep from * once more; end last rep at **; join.

Rnd 9: Work beg shell; * ch 3, sk next ch-3 lp, sc in next ch-3 lp; (ch 3, sc in next ch-3 lp) 10 times; ch 3, work shell in ch-2 lp of shell; rep from * once more; ch 2, work shell in next ch-2 lp, ch 3, sk next ch-3 lp, sc in next lp; (ch 3, sc in next ch-3 lp) 10 times; ch 3, work shell in ch-2 lp of shell; rep from first * once more; join last ch-3 to top of beg ch-3.

Rnd 10: Work beg shell; * ch 3, sc in first ch-3 pineapple lp; (ch 3, sc in next lp) 9 times; ch 3, shell in ch-2 lp of shell; rep from * once more; ch 2, shell in ch-2 lp bet shells, ch 2, shell in ch-2 lp of next shell, ch 3, sc in first pineapple lp; (ch 3, sc in next lp) 9 times; ch 3, shell in ch-2 lp of next shell; rep

from first * once more; join last ch-3 to top of beg ch-3.

Rnd 11: Work beg shell; * ch 3, sc in first pineapple lp; (ch 3, sc in next lp) 8 times; ch 3, shell in ch-2 lp of shell; rep from * once more; (ch 3, shell over shell) 2 times; ch 3, sc in first pineapple lp; (ch 3, sc in next lp) 8 times; ch 3, shell in ch-2 lp of shell; rep from first * once more; join last ch-3 to top of beg ch-3.

Rnd 12: Work beg shell; * ch 3, sc in first pineapple lp; (ch 3, sc in next lp) 7 times; ch 3, in sp of next shell work 2 dc, ch 2, 2 dc, ch 2, and 2 dc; ch 3, sc in first pineapple lp; (ch 3, sc in next lp) 7 times; ch 3, shell in shell, ch 4, in sp of next shell work 2 dc, ch 5, and 2 dc; ch 4, shell in shell, ch 3, sc in first pineapple lp; (ch 3, sc in next lp) 7 times; ** ch 3; in ch-2 sp of next shell work 2 dc, ch 2, 2 dc, ch 2, and 2 dc; rep from * and work to **; then ch 3, 2 dc in same sp as beg shell, ch 2, join to beg ch-3.

For the first pineapple tip: Row 1: Work beg shell; ch 3, work 6 lps across pineapple, ch 3, shell in next shell; ch 4, turn.

Row 2: Shell in shell, ch 3, work 5 lps across pineapple; ch 3, shell in next shell; ch 4, turn.

Rep Row 2 making 1 lp less on each row until 1 lp rem; ch 4, turn.

Next row: Shell in shell, ch 4, sc in lp, ch 4, 2 dc in next shell, ch 1, sl st in sp of last completed shell, ch 1, 2 dc in same place as last 2 dc, ch 4, turn, sc in joining of shells; fasten off.

For the next 3 pineapple tips: Row 1: Join thread in next ch-2 sp of Rnd 12 and work beg shell; ch 3, work 6 lps across pineapple, ch 3, shell in shell, ch 3, 13 trc in ch-5 lp, ch 3, shell in shell, ch 3, work 6 lps across pineapple, ch 3, shell in shell; ch 4, turn.

Row 2: Shell in shell, ch 3, work 5 lps across pineapple, ch 3, shell in shell, ch 3, trc in next trc; (ch 1, trc in next trc) 12 times; ch 3, shell in shell, ch 3, work 5 lps across pineapple, ch 3, shell in shell; ch 4, turn.

Row 3: Shell in shell, ch 3, work 4 lps across pineapple, ch 3, shell in shell, ch 3, sc in first ch-1 sp; (ch 3, sc in next ch-1 sp) 11 times; ch 3, shell in shell, ch 3, work 4 lps across pineapple, ch 3, shell in shell; ch 4, turn.

Row 4: Shell in shell, ch 3, work 3 lps across pineapple, ch 3, in next ch-2 sp of shell work 2 dc, ch 2, 2 dc, ch 2, and 2 dc; ch 3, sc in first ch-3 pineapple lp; (ch 3, sc in next ch-3 lp) 10 times; ch 3, in ch-2 lp of next shell work 2 dc, ch 2, 2 dc, ch 2, and 2 dc; ch 3, work 3 lps across pineapple, ch 3, shell in shell; ch 4, turn.

Rows 5–7: Complete first pineapple tip separately; fasten off.

Rejoin thread in next ch-2 sp of Row 4 and complete next pineapple tip; fasten off.

Rejoin thread in next ch-2 sp of Row 4 and complete next pineapple tip; fasten off.

Complete opposite half of doily to correspond, working instructions for First Pineapple Tip, *above left;* follow instructions for Next 3 Pineapple Tips, *below left.*

DOILY EDGING: *Rnd 1:* Join thread to any ch-4 lp at tip of any pineapple and work beg shell; * ch 3, shell in next ch-4 lp; rep from * around; end ch 3, join with sl st to top of beg ch-3.

Rnd 2: Sl st in next dc and into ch-2 sp, ch 6 (to count as dc and ch-3 for a picot), sc in third ch from hook; dc in same ch-2 sp as sl st; * ch 3, sc in next ch-3 lp, ch 3; in next shell make dc, **ch 3, sc in third ch from hook—picot made,** and dc; rep from * around; join and fasten off; block.

SCALLOPED DOILY

Shown on page 129.

Doily measures 22 inches across the diameter.

MATERIALS

J. & P. Coats Knit-Cro-Sheen (225-yard ball): 2 balls
Size 11 steel crochet hook

Abbreviations: See page 186.
Gauge: First 6 rnds = 3¼ inches.

INSTRUCTIONS

Ch 10, join with sl st to form ring.

Rnd 1: Ch 3, work 31 dc in ring; join with sl st to top of beg ch-3—32 dc counting beg ch-3 as dc.

Rnd 2: Ch 1, sc in same st as join, sc in each dc around; join with sl st to beg sc—32 sc around.

Rnd 3: Ch 1, sc in each sc around; join to beg sc.

Rnd 4: Ch 4, * dc in next sc, ch 1; rep from * around; join last ch-1 to third ch of beg ch-4—32 ch-2 sps.

Rnd 5: Sl st into next ch-1 sp, ch 6; * trc in next ch-1 sp, ch 2; rep from * around; join last ch-2 to fourth ch of beg ch-6.

Rnd 6: Sl st into ch-2 sp; ch 6, trc in same sp; * ch 3, sk next sp, in next sp work trc, ch 2, and trc; rep from * around; join last ch-3 to fourth ch of beg ch-6.

Rnd 7: Sl st into ch-2 sp; ch 4, in same sp make trc, ch 2, and 2 trc; * ch 1, trc in next ch-3 sp, ch 1, ** in next ch-2 sp make 2 trc, ch 2, and 2 trc; rep from * around ; end last rep at **; join to beg ch-4.

Rnd 8: Sl st in next trc and into ch-2 sp; ch 4, in same sp make trc, ch 2, and 2 trc; * ch 2, sk 2 trc, trc in next trc, ch 2; ** in ch-2 sp of next shell work 2 trc, ch 2, and 2 trc; rep from * around; end last rep at **; join to top of beg ch-4.

Rnd 9: Sl st in next trc and into ch-2 sp; ch 4, in same sp make 2 trc, ch 3, and 3 trc; * ch 2, sk 2 trc, trc in next trc, ch 2, ** in sp of next shell work 3 trc, ch 3, and 3 trc, rep from * around; end last rep at **; join as before.

Rnd 10: Rep Rnd 9, except work ch-3 bet trc in lieu of ch-2; join as before.

Rnd 11: Sl st in next 2 trc and into ch-2 sp; ch 4, in same sp work 3 trc, ch 5, and 4 trc; * ch 3, sk 3 trc, 3 trc in next trc, ch 3, ** in ch-3 sp of next shell work 4 trc, ch 5, and 4 trc; rep from * around; end last rep at **; join as before.

Rnd 12: Sl st in next 3 trc and into ch-5 lp, ch 4, in same sp work 7 trc, ch 3, and 8 trc; * ch 3, trc in center st of 3-trc grp, ch 3, ** in ch-5 lp work 8 trc, ch 3, and 8 trc; rep from * around; end last rep at **; join.

Rnd 13: Ch 4, trc in next 3 trc; * ch 2, in next ch-3 lp make 4 trc, ch 2, and 4 trc; ch 2, sk 4 trc, trc in next 4 trc; ch 2, ** sk next 2 ch-3 lps, trc in next 4 trc; rep from * around; end last rep at **; join as before.

Rnd 14: Sl st in each of next 3 trc, 2 ch, 4 trc and into ch-2 lp; ch 4, in same lp make 3 trc, ch 2, and 4 trc; * ch 6, sk next ch-2 sp and next 2 trc; trc in next 2 trc, trc in next 2 ch, trc in next 2 trc, ch 6, ** sk next ch-2 lp, work 4 trc, ch 2, and 4 trc in ch-2 lp of next shell; rep from * around; end last rep at **; join.

Rnd 15: Sl st in next 3 trc and into ch-2 lp, ch 4, in same lp make 3 trc, ch 3, and 4 trc; * ch 7, sk first trc of 6-trc grp, trc in next 4 trc; ch 7, ** work 4 trc, ch 3, and 4 trc in ch-2 lp of next shell; rep from * around; end last rep at **; join.

Rnd 16: Ch 4, trc in next 3 trc; * in ch-2 lp make 4 trc, ch 3, and 4 trc; trc in next 4 trc, ch 6, sk next sp and next trc, trc in next 2 trc; sk trc, ch 6, ** trc in next 4 trc; rep from * around; end last rep at **; join.

Rnd 17: Ch 4, trc in next 3 trc, * ch 2, work 4 trc, ch 3, and 4 trc in ch-3 lp of next shell, ch 2, sk 4 trc, trc in next 4 trc; ch 6, ** sk next two ch-6 lps, trc in next 4 trc; rep from * around; end last rep at **; join.

Rnd 18: Ch 4, trc in next 3 trc, * trc in next ch, ch 3, work 4 trc, ch 3, and 4 trc in ch-3 lp of next shell, ch 3, sk first ch of ch-2 lp, trc in next ch, trc in next 4 trc; ch 5, ** trc in next 4 trc; rep from * around; end last rep at **; join.

Rnd 19: Ch 4, trc in next 4 trc; * ch 6, in ch-3 lp of next shell work 4 trc, ch 3, and 4 trc; ch 6, sk 4 trc, trc in next 5 trc, ch 3, ** trc in next 5 trc; rep from * around; end last rep at **; join.

Rnd 20: Ch 4, trc in next 3 trc, *ch 9, in ch-3 lp of shell work 4 trc, ch 3, and 4 trc; ch 9, sk first trc of 5-trc grp, trc in next 4 trc; ch 2, ** trc in next 4 trc; rep from * around; end last rep at **; join.

Rnd 21: Ch 4, trc in next 2 trc; * ch 10, in ch-3 lp of shell work 4 trc, ch 3, and 4 trc; ch 10, sk first trc of 4-trc grp, trc in next 3 trc, ch 2, ** trc in next 3 trc; rep from * around; end last rep at **; join.

Rnd 22: Ch 4, trc in next 2 trc; * ch 12, in ch-3 lp of shell work 4 trc, ch 3, and 4 trc; ch 12, sk next ch-10 lp, trc in next 3 trc; ch 2, ** trc in next 3 trc; rep from * around; end last rep at **; join.

Rnd 23: Ch 4, trc in next 2 trc; * ch 8, trc in next 4 trc, in ch-3 sp work 4 trc, ch 3, and 4 trc; trc in next 4 trc, ch 8, trc in next 3 trc, ch 2, ** trc in next 3 trc; rep from * around; end last rep at **; join.

Rnd 24: Sl st in next trc, ch 9, sk ch-8 lp, trc in next trc; * (ch 1, trc in next trc) 7 times; ch 1, in ch-3 sp work trc, ch 1, and trc; ch 1, trc

continued

in next trc; (ch 1, trc in next trc) 7 times; ch 5, trc in center trc of 3-trc grp, ch 2, ** trc in center trc of next 3-trc grp, ch 5, sk ch-8 lp, trc in next trc; rep from * around; end last rep at **; join last ch-2 to fourth ch of beg ch-9.

Rnd 25: Sl st in next 2 ch; * ch 4, trc in next trc; (ch 1, trc in next ch-1 sp) 8 times; ch 1, in next ch-1 sp work trc, ch 1, and trc; (ch 1, trc in next ch-1 sp) 8 times; ch 1; trc in next trc; ** (ch 4, sc in next lp) 3 times; rep from * around; end last rep at **; then (ch 4, sc in next lp) 2 times, ch 4, join to first ch of beg ch-4.

Rnd 26: Sl st in next 3 ch and first trc; ch 5, * (trc in next ch-1 sp, ch 1) 9 times; in next ch-1 sp work trc, ch 1, and trc; (ch 1, trc in next ch-1 sp) 9 times; ch 1, trc in next trc; ch 3, sk next ch-4 lp, 2 trc in next lp, ch 1, 2 trc in next lp, ch 3, ** trc in next trc, ch 1; rep from * around; end last rep at **; join last ch-3 to fourth ch of beg ch-5.

Rnd 27: Sl st into ch-1 sp, ch 1, sc in same sp; * (ch 3, sc in next ch-1 sp) 20 times; ch 4, sc in next ch-1 sp, ch 4, ** sc in next ch-1 sp; rep from * around; end last rep at **; join last ch-4 to beg sc.

Rnd 28: Sl st into ch-3 lp, ch 1, sc in same lp; * (ch 3, sc in next ch-3 lp) 19 times; ch 3, sc in next sc, ch 3, sk ch-4 lp, sc in next lp; rep from * around; join to beg sc.

Rnd 29: Sl st into ch-3 lp, sc in same lp; * (ch 3, sc in next ch-3 lp) 18 times; ch 2, sc in next sc, ch 2, sk next ch-3 lp, sc in next lp; rep from * around; join to beg sc.

Rnd 30: Sl st into ch-3 lp, ch 1, sc in same lp; * (ch 3, sc in next lp) 17 times; ch 1, sc in next sc, ch 1, sc in next lp; rep from * around; join to beg sc.

Rnd 31: Sl st into ch-3 lp, ch 1, sc in same lp; * (ch 4, sc in next lp) 16 times; sc in next sc, sc in next ch-3 lp; rep from * around; join to beg sc; fasten off.

ROSY-SQUARE AFGHAN

Shown on pages 130 and 131.

Afghan measures 66x50 inches, including border.

MATERIALS
Unger Utopia worsted-weight yarn (240-yard ball): 10 balls *each* of light pink (No. 181) and medium pink (No. 182); and 4 balls of rose (No. 293)
Size G aluminum crochet hook
Large-eye, blunt-end needle

Abbreviations: See page 186.
Gauge: Each block measures 6¼ inches square.

INSTRUCTIONS
Note: The afghan shown on pages 130 and 131 consists of 63 blocks—31 light pink and 32 medium pink. The blocks are arranged in checkerboard fashion into 9 rows, each row consisting of 7 blocks. The last row of each block is bordered with a round of rose single crochets.

BLOCK MOTIF: Beg at center, ch 5, join with sl st to form ring.

Rnd 1: Ch 3, 2 dc in ring; * ch 1, 3 dc in ring; rep from * 2 times more; ch 1, join to top of beg ch-3—12 dc in ring.

Rnd 2: Sl st in next dc, ch 3, in same st work dc, ch 1, and 2 dc; * ch 1, dc in ch-1 sp, ch 1, sk dc, in next dc work 2 dc, ch 1, and 2 dc—corner made; rep from * 2 times more; end ch 1, dc in ch-1 sp, ch 1, join to top of beg ch-3.

Rnd 3: Ch 3, dc in next dc; * in ch-1 corner sp work 2 dc, ch 1, 2 dc; dc in next 2 dc, ch 1, dc in next dc, ch 1, dc in next 2 dc; rep from * 3 times more; end ch 1, dc in next dc, ch 1; join to top of beg ch-3.

Rnd 4: Ch 3, dc in next 3 dc; * in ch-1 corner sp work 2 dc, ch 1, and 2 dc; dc in next 4 dc, ch 1, dc in next dc, ch 1, dc in next 4 dc; rep from * 3 times more; end ch 1, dc in next dc, ch 1; join to top of beg ch-3.

Rnd 5: Ch 3, dc in next 5 dc; * in ch-1 corner sp work 2 dc, ch 1, and 2 dc; dc in next 6 dc, ch 1, dc in next dc, ch 1, dc in next 6 dc; rep from * 3 times more; end ch 1, dc in next dc, ch 1; join to top of beg ch-3.

Rnd 6: Ch 3, dc in next 7 dc; * in ch-1 corner sp work 2 dc, ch 1, 2 dc; dc in next 8 dc, ch 1, dc in next dc, ch 1, dc in next 8 dc; rep from * 3 times more; end ch 1, dc in next dc, ch 1; join to top of beg ch-3.

Rnd 7: Ch 3, dc in next 9 dc; * in ch-1 corner sp work 2 dc, ch 1, and 2 dc; dc in next 10 dc; ch 1, dc in next dc, ch 1, dc in next 10 dc; rep from * 3 times more; end ch 1, dc in next dc, ch 1; join to top of beg ch-3; fasten off.

Rnd 8: Join rose in top of join at end of last rnd; ch 1, sc in same st as join and in next 11 dc; * work 3 sc in corner; sc in next 12 dc; (sc in ch-1 sp, sc in next dc) 2 times; sc in next 11 dc; rep from * around; join to first sc; fasten off.

ASSEMBLY: Use blunt-end needle and rose yarn to whip-stitch blocks together in the *back lps* of each sc.

BORDER: *Rnd 1:* Join medium pink in any corner sc, ch 5, dc in same sc; * ch 2, sk 2 sc, dc in next sc; rep from * to next corner; in corner sc work dc, ch 2, and dc; work rem 3 sides as established; join to third ch of beg ch-5.

Rnd 2: Sl st into ch-2 sp, ch 3, in same sp work dc, ch 2, and 2 dc; work 3 dc in each ch-2 lp around working 2 dc, ch 2, and 2 dc in each corner; join to beg ch-3.

Rnds 3 and 4: Sl st in next dc and into ch-2 lp; ch 3, in same lp work dc, ch 2, and 2 dc; dc in each dc around working 2 dc, ch 2, and 2 dc in each corner; join to top of beg ch-3; fasten off.

Rnd 5: Join light pink in any corner ch-2 lp, ch 1, work 3 sc in same lp, sc in each dc around working 3 sc in each corner; join to first sc.

Rnds 6–9: Sc in each sc around working 3 sc in corner sc; join to first sc; fasten off at end of Rnd 9.

Rnd 10: Join rose in any sc, working *clockwise,* sc in each sc around working ch 1 bet each sc; join to first sc; fasten off.

RIBBONS AND LACE BEDSPREAD

Shown on pages 130 and 131.

Bedspread shown measures approximately 84x102 inches.

————MATERIALS————
Lily 18th-Century mercerized crochet and bedspread cotton (500-yard skein): 21 skeins of white or ecru
Tubular satin strapping or ¼-inch-wide ribbons: 200 yards in color of choice
Sewing thread to match satin strapping or ribbon
Size 6 steel crochet hook or size to obtain gauge

Abbreviations: See page 186.
Gauge: The large motif measures 6 inches from point to point across center.

————INSTRUCTIONS————
Note: Bedspread consists of 238 large motifs and is arranged in 17 rows, each row having 14 motifs. The First Large Motif is worked once. All successive Large Motifs are joined to the existing work on Rnd 11. If you desire, you can make all the Large Motifs separately and then sew them together at three-picot groupings.

FIRST LARGE MOTIF: Beg at center, ch 6, join with sl st to form ring.

Rnd 1: Ch 3, work 23 dc in ring, join with sl st to top of beg ch-3.

Rnd 2: Ch 6, * sk dc, dc in next dc, ch 3, rep from * around; join with sl st to third ch of beg ch-6.

Rnd 3: * Ch 8, sc in third ch from hook, hdc in next ch, dc in next 2 ch, trc in next 2 ch, sk ch-3 lp, sl st in next dc, rep from * around; join with sl st in first ch of beg ch-8—12 triangles around.

Rnd 4: Sl st along the side of first triangle to point, sc in point; * ch 7, sl st in next point, rep from * around; join with sl st to beg sc.

Rnd 5: (Work 8 sc in next ch-7 lp) 12 times—96 sc around; do not join; place marker to mark beg of rnd.

Rnds 6–9: Sc in each sc around; do not join; place marker to mark beg of rnds.

Rnd 10: Ch 6, * sk sc, dc in next sc, ch 3; rep from * around; join with sl st in third ch of beg ch-6—48 dc around.

Rnd 11: * Ch 3, dc in next dc, **(ch 3, sc in top of last dc made— picot made)** 3 times, ch 3, sc in next dc, rep from * around; end ch 3; join to top of beg ch-3; fasten off.

SECOND LARGE MOTIF: Work as for First Large Motif through Rnd 10.

Rnd 11: * Ch 3, dc in next dc, work picot, ch 1, sl st in center picot of any corresponding picot of first motif, ch 1, complete picot, work another picot, ch 3, sc in next dc of motif in progress; rep from * twice more; complete second motif as for first motif with no more joining.

Join third motif to second motif in same way, leaving 3 picot grps free bet joinings; join fourth motif to first and third motifs.

Continue to make and assemble 10 more motifs to complete first row.

At the beginning of the second row, join the first motif to the top 3 picot grps of the first motif. Join the second motif of this row to the first motif of the second row and to the second motif of the first row, having three picot grps between the joinings. Continue in this manner to complete the second row and all remaining rows. After all motifs are made and assembled, you are ready to make and join the Filler Motifs to complete the spread.

FILLER MOTIF (Make 208): Work as for Large Motif through Rnd 2.

Rnd 3 (joining rnd): * Ch 3, dc in ch-3 lp, work picot, ch 1, sl st in center picot of corresponding grp of first (or any) motif, ch 1, complete picot, work another picot; ch 3, sc in next dc of Filler Motif; rep from * twice more, join in same way for second, third, and fourth motifs, sc in first dc, fasten off.

RIBBON TRIM: Cut 30-inch pieces of tubular satin or ribbon and weave these strands through Rnd 10 of Large Motif, under one dc and over one dc. Tie in bow; tack knot with matching thread. Tie overhand knot at each end of satin or ribbon.

A Showcase Of Afghans

TIME-HONORED DESIGNS

Fancywork patterns stitched in fine cotton threads were favored by crocheters in the mid-1800s. But by the turn of the century, lush woolen afghans had become the rage. Frequent contests were held by women's magazines and needlework societies to honor noteworthy designs.

A trail of single cross-stitch violets and a trio of bouquets embellish the textured coverlet, *opposite.* According to the book *Language of Flowers,* violets symbolize faithfulness and modesty—both highly prized virtues in Victorian times. See page 156 for instructions to make this afghan.

Here are two updated versions of the enduring favorites, the ripple and granny-square afghans. *Above,* granny-square motifs are assembled into panels that are bordered with strips using the afghan-stitch technique. Cross-stitch embroidery on these five panels is reminiscent of wallpaper patterns of an earlier time.

The airy ripple afghan, *opposite,* features scalloped ruffles that run through the peaks and add interesting texture to this old-fashioned classic. Ribbons are intermittently laced through open spaces and tied in bows for a wonderfully romantic touch.

Instructions for these two afghans begin on page 158.

Originally known on the Continent as crocheted quilts, traveling rugs, or "couvrepieds" (French for foot covers), these useful coverlets came to be called afghans in America after the simple, flat, dense stitch first used to create them. Today, every stitch in the crochet repertoire appears in one afghan pattern or another.

Strikingly different in design, weight, and texture, each of the coverlets pictured here is composed of 6½-inch squares—a format reminiscent of the stitched quilt block designs that also were vying for the needleworker's interest at the turn of the century.

At *left,* a popcorn-stitch granny-square afghan is worked in rich shades of rose, peach, mauve, butterscotch, and taupe worsted-weight yarns. *Opposite,* a lacy-square afghan is stitched using brushed off-white yarn. See pages 160–162 for the instructions for these two projects.

There's an afghan for every season. Some are made for snuggling on a cold winter's night; others, such as the trio pictured here, are as light and airy as a springtime morning.

Stitch the granny-square coverlet, *above*, in bright sherbet colors, or crochet the lacy white throw beside it to take the chill off those first sunny-but-cool days of May. The luxurious Ruby Glow afghan, *opposite*, boasts a garden bouquet of scarlet blossoms, each framed in a block of white—like June roses nestled amid beds of sweet alyssum. The instructions for these three afghans begin on page 162.

When women began to move out of the home and into the work force during World War I, they began to realize the therapeutic value of handwork. A 1915 ad for Ardern's crochet cotton declared: "A New Army—the Army of Women Workers—has arisen, who find that the weariness of manual and clerical labor is appreciably relieved by a change to the restful pastime of 'doing a bit of crochet.'"

Each of the afghans pictured here involves just the sort of simple but satisfying repeat pattern that tempts even a novice crocheter to relax and visit while stitching. After all, as an ad—printed in Lead's *Home Needlework* in 1928—reminded readers: "There's nothing more pleasant than the happy hour or two spent in friendly chatter and restful crocheting."

A smattering of embroidered daisies adds a fanciful finish to the border of the lacy shell-stitch afghan, at *left*. The afghan-stitch coverlet, *opposite*, with a diamond pattern and arrowhead border, is worked in five separate panels. The panels are then joined and bordered with a combination of basic stitches to form a slightly scalloped edge.

See pages 166 and 167 for the instructions for these afghans.

VIOLET BOUQUET AFGHAN

Shown on pages 146 and 147.

Afghan measures 53x67 inches.

MATERIALS

Brunswick Germantown knitting worsted yarn (100-gram skein): 15 skeins ecru (No. 4000)

DMC Floralia 3-ply Persian wool (5.4-yard skein) in the following amounts and colors: 10 skeins red violet (No. 7553), 10 skeins periwinkle (No. 7810), 12 skeins dark periwinkle (No. 7245), 16 skeins dark green (No. 7897), 12 skeins green (No. 7904), 6 skeins light green (No. 7955), and 1 skein *each* yellow (No. 7973) and orange (No. 7436)

Size J afghan hook or size to obtain gauge cited below

Size I crochet hook

1½ yards 1-inch-wide lavender ribbon

Tapestry needle

Abbreviations: See page 186.
Gauge: With J hook in afghan st: 4 sts = 1 inch; 3 rows = 1 inch.

INSTRUCTIONS

This afghan is made up of five panels. Three panels are worked using the afghan-stitch technique; two panels are worked using crochet stitches. Borders are crocheted around the panels, then the violet motifs are cross-stitched atop the afghan stitches. See page 188 for step-by-step instructions for working the afghan stitch.

OUTSIDE PANEL (make 2): With afghan hook, ch 35.

Row 1 (first half): Keeping all lps on hook, insert hook in top lp of second ch from hook, yo, draw up lp; * insert hook in top lp of next ch, yo, draw up lp; rep from * across row—35 lps on hook.

Row 1 (second half): Yo, draw through first lp on hook; * yo, draw through 2 lps on hook; rep from * across row until 1 lp rem on hook.

Row 2 (first half): Sk first 2 bars, insert hook under next bar, yo, draw up lp; draw up lp in first skipped bar to right; draw up lp in next unworked bar; (**sk next bar, insert hook under next bar, yo, draw up lp; draw up lp in skipped bar to right—cross-stitch [cs] made;** draw up lp in next bar), draw up lp in next 22 bars; rep bet ( )s twice—35 lps on hook.

Row 2 (second half): Rep second half of Row 1.

Rep first and second halves of Row 2 until 183 rows have been worked.

Last row (bind-off row): Sk the first bar, * **insert hook under next bar, yo, draw the yarn through the bar and through the lp on the hook—sl st made and 1 lp on hook;** rep from * across the row; fasten off.

LACY SHELL PANEL (make 2): With Size I crochet hook, ch 19.

Row 1: Work 2 dc in fourth ch from hook; (sk 2 ch, dc in next ch, sk 2 ch, 5 dc in next ch) twice; sk 2 ch, dc in last ch; ch 3, turn.

Row 2: Work 2 dc in base of turning ch; (sk 2 dc, dc in third dc of 5-dc grp, sk 2 dc, 5 dc in next dc) twice; sk 2 dc, dc in top of turning ch; ch 3, turn.

Rep Row 2 until the length of the panels is the same as that of the outside panels (approximately 100 rows); fasten off.

CENTER PANEL (make 1): With afghan hook, ch 64.

Row 1 (first half): Keeping all lps on hook, insert hook in top lp of second ch from hook, yo, draw up lp; * insert hook in top lp of next ch, yo, draw up lp; rep from * across row—64 lps on hook.

Row 1 (second half): Yo, draw through first lp on hook; * yo, draw through 2 lps on hook; rep from * across row until 1 lp rem on hook.

Row 2 (first half): Keeping all lps on hook, sk first 2 bars, insert hook under next bar, yo, draw up lp; draw up lp in skipped bar to right; * draw up lp in next unworked bar; **sk next bar, insert hook under next bar, yo, draw up lp; draw up lp in skipped bar—cross-stitch (cs) made;** rep from * across row; draw up lp in last bar—64 lps.

Row 2 (second half): Rep second half of Row 1.

Rows 3–5: Rep first and second halves of Row 2.

Row 6 (first half): Sk first bar, (cs over next 2 bars, draw up lp in next bar) 6 times—cs pat; cs over next 2 bars, * **pull up lp in next bar, (yo and pull up lp in same bar) 3 times, yo and draw through 7 lps—bobble made;** cs over next 2 bars, rep from * 7 times more—8 bobbles made; (draw up lp in next bar, cs over next 2 bars) 6 times; draw up lp in last bar.

Row 6 (second half): Rep second half of Row 1.

Row 7 (first half): Sk first bar, keep to cs pat as established over next 18 bars; cs over next 2 bars, draw up lp in next 22 bars; work cs pat over next 20 bars; draw up lp in last bar.

Row 7 (second half): Rep second half of Row 1.

Row 8 (first half): Sk first bar, (cs over next 2 bars, draw up lp in next bar) 6 times; bobble in next bar, draw up lp in next 24 bars, bobble in next bar; (draw up lp in

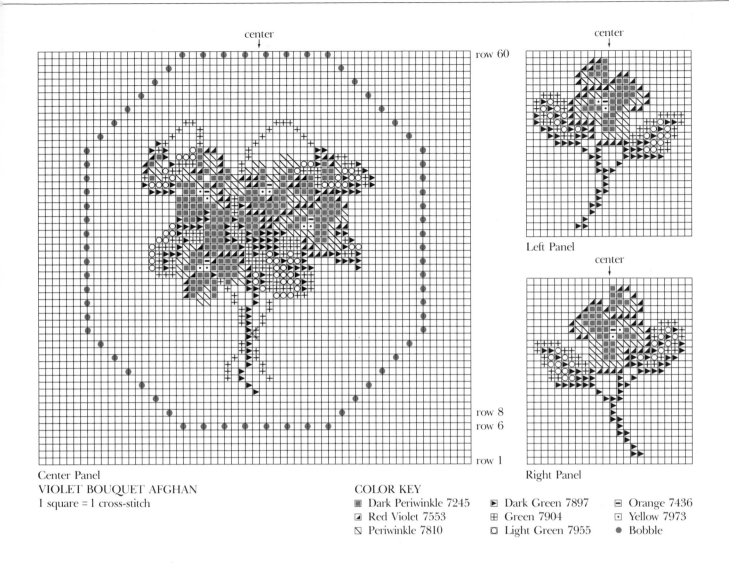

center ↓ row 60

Center Panel
VIOLET BOUQUET AFGHAN
1 square = 1 cross-stitch

Left Panel

center ↓

Right Panel

row 8
row 6

row 1

COLOR KEY

▣ Dark Periwinkle 7245   ▶ Dark Green 7897   ⊟ Orange 7436
◩ Red Violet 7553   ⊞ Green 7904   ⊡ Yellow 7973
◺ Periwinkle 7810   ▫ Light Green 7955   ● Bobble

next bar, cs over next 2 bars) 6 times; draw up lp in last bar.

Row 8 (second half): Rep second half of Row 1.

Rows 9–60: Referring to chart *above left* for bobble placement, work in cross-stitch, bobble, and basic afghan stitch as established.

Rep rows 2–60 two times more. Rep Row 2 five times to complete 183 rows.

Last row (bind-off row): Sk first bar, *** insert hook in next bar, yo, draw the yarn through the bar and through the lp on the hook—sl st made and 1 lp on hook;** rep from * across row; fasten off.

PANEL BORDERS: *Note:* If necessary, adjust hook size to make work lie flat.

Using Size I crochet hook, join yarn at any corner. Sc around all four sides of each panel; work 43 sc along each of the short sides; 183 sc along each long side; work 3 sc in each corner; join with sl st to first sc.

Rnd 1: Ch 2; pull up lp in second ch from hook and next 3 sc, yo, draw through all 5 lps on hook, ch 1 for eye; *** pull up lp in center of eye, pull up lp in back of last picked-up st of star, pull up lp in next 2 sc; yo and draw**

through all 5 lps on hook, ch 1 for eye—star st made; rep from * to within 1 st of corner—21 stars made; **(pull up lp in center of eye, pull up lp in back lp of last picked-up st of star, pull up lp in same st as last star st, pull up lp in next sc, yo, draw through all 5 lps on hook; ch 1 for eye) 4 times—corner made;** rep bet *'s for each side—91 star sts on each long side; end with sl st in top of beg ch-2; ch 2, turn.

Rnd 2: * Work 2 hdc in eye of each star stitch; rep from * to corner; 3 hdc in eye of corner star st; rep from first * for each side; sl st to top of turning st; fasten off.

continued

ASSEMBLY: Arrange panels as follows from left to right: Outside panel, lacy shell panel, center panel, lacy shell panel, and outside panel. Whipstitch panels together with ecru yarn, matching stitches and making sure that corner stars match.

CROSS-STITCHING THE PANELS: Sk 4 rows from the top of the right outside panel; locate the center st in the next row. Referring to the Right Panel Chart on page 157, work cross-stitch embroidery on the panel using tapestry needle and all three strands of Persian yarn. (See photo on page 160 for working cross-stitches on top of the basic afghan stitch.) Begin stitching the flower at the center arrow. Complete the flower and stem, then start the next flower in the row directly below. Stitch seven flowers.

Cross-stitch the left outside panel in the same manner, referring to the Left Panel Chart on page 157.

Cross-stitch the center panel following the Center Panel Chart on page 157, stitching a violet bouquet inside each oval. When stitching is complete, cut three 18-inch lengths of ribbon; tie three bows; and sew one bow to each bouquet at the "X" marking on the stems.

SHELL BORDER: Join yarn in center hdc of top right corner star st; ch 1.

Rnd 1: Work 3 sc in same st as join; work 189 sc along first short side; work 3 sc in center hdc of next corner star st; work 195 sc along first long side; work 3 sc in center hdc of next corner star st; work rem two sides to match; join with sl st to first sc.

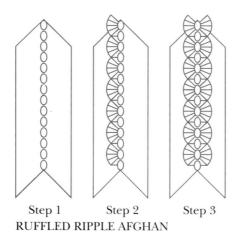

Step 1   Step 2   Step 3

RUFFLED RIPPLE AFGHAN

Rnd 2: Sl st in next sc, ch 3; in same st work 2 dc, ch 3, and 3 dc; * ch 3, sk 2 sc, sc in next sc, ch 3; ** sk 2 sc, **work 3 dc, ch 3, and 3 dc in next sc—shell made,** rep from * across short side; end last rep of side at **; work shell in corner sc, continue as established, working a shell in each corner; join with sl st to top of beg ch-3; fasten off and block afghan.

RUFFLED RIPPLE AFGHAN

Shown on page 149.

Afghan measures approximately 52x65 inches.

MATERIALS

Unger Fluffy yarn (50-gram ball): 13 balls *each* teal blue (No. 420) and soft teal blue (No. 499)
50 yards of ecru ¼-inch satin ribbon
Size H aluminum crochet hook or size to obtain gauge cited below
Sewing needle; thread to match ribbon

Abbreviations: See page 186.
Gauge: 9 sts = 2 inches over ripple pattern.

INSTRUCTIONS

With teal blue yarn, ch 238.

Row 1: Sc in third ch from hook; sc in next 6 ch, 3 sc in next ch; * sc in next 8 ch, draw up lp in next ch, sk ch, draw up lp in next ch, yo, and draw through all lps on hook; sc in next 8 ch, 3 sc in next ch, rep from * across; sc in last 8 ch, ch 1; turn.

Row 2: Sc in first sc, **draw up lp in next 2 st, yo, draw through all lps on hook—sc-dec made;** sc in next 6 sc, 3 sc in next sc, * sc in next 8 sc, draw up lp in next sc, sk st, draw up lp in next st, yo and draw through all lps on hook, sc in next 8 sc, 3 sc in next sc, rep from * across; sc in next 6 sc, work sc-dec; sc in top of turning ch, ch 1; turn.

Row 3: Rep Row 2; ch 4 to turn at end of row.

Row 4 (eyelet row): Sk first sc, sk next st, dc in next sc, (ch 1, sk sc, dc in next sc) 3 times; dc in next sc—top of ripple point; * dc in next sc, (ch 1, sk sc, dc in next sc) 4 times; sk st, dc in next st, (ch 1, sk sc, dc in next sc) 4 times; dc in next sc—ripple point; rep from * across; end with dc in next st, (ch 1, sk sc, dc in next sc) 4 times; ch 1, turn.

Row 5: Sc in first st, draw up lp in next ch-1 sp, draw up lp in top of next dc, yo and draw through all lps on hook; (sc in next ch-1 sp, sc in next dc) 3 times, 3 sc in next dc—ripple point; * (sc in next dc, sc in next ch-1 sp) 4 times; draw up lp in next 2 dc, yo and draw through all lps on hook; (sc in next ch-1 sp, sc in next dc) 4 times; 3 sc in next dc—ripple point; rep from * across; end with (sc in next dc, sc in next ch-1 sp) 3 times, draw up lp in next dc, draw up lp in next ch-1 sp, yo and draw through all lps on hook, sc in third ch of ch-4; ch 1, turn.

Rep rows 2–5 for pat. Change yarn to soft teal blue at end of third teal blue eyelet row (Row 4).

Continue changing colors at end of Row 4 of each pat rep; work until there are seven teal blue sections alternating with seven soft teal blue sections. End the seventh soft teal blue section after the second eyelet row (Row 4) by working Row 5, Row 2, and Row 3; fasten off.

SIDE EDGINGS: Work left side with teal blue yarn and work right side with soft teal blue yarn.

Row 1: With right side facing, join yarn and sc evenly along side of the afghan, ch 1, turn.

Row 2: Sc in first sc, * sk sc, work 5 dc in next sc, sk sc, sc in next sc, repeat from * along side; fasten off. Rep rows 1–2 on opposite side.

RUFFLES: The ruffles are worked into slip stitches that are stitched to the afghan in vertical rows atop the *center point stitches* of alternating ripples. Alternate the yarn colors of the slip-stitch rows using the side edgings to determine the next color.

Referring to the diagram *opposite*, follow the three steps to crochet the ruffles as follows: Beginning at the bottom edge of the afghan and referring to Step 1, sl st in every row to the top of the afghan. This creates a surface ch upon which to work the ruffles.

Working down the side of the sl st row and referring to Step 2, ch 1, sc in back lp of first sl st; (5 dc in next front lp, sc in next back lp); rep bet ( )s down the row; sl st in beg ch.

Referring to Step 3, work ruffle on opposite side of lps as established on previous side; end with sl st to beg sc; fasten off.

Continue to work ruffles across afghan in alternating ripples.

Weave ribbons in only the eyelet rows of the teal blue sections. Fold and miter ribbon at all ripple Vs across rows, securing with sewing thread; tack ends of ribbon in place along side edges.

Make 39 small bows. Referring to photo on page 149 as a guide, randomly tack bows in place.

GRANNY–SQUARE AND PANEL AFGHAN

Shown on 148.

Afghan measures approximately 48x58 inches.

MATERIALS

Brunswick Windrush yarn (100-gram skein): 9 skeins off-white (No. 90020), 4 skeins medium jade (No. 90592), 1 skein banana (No. 90015), and 3 skeins *each* of powder blue (No. 90111) and sugar plum (No. 90025)
Size J aluminum afghan hook
Size I crochet hook or size to obtain gauge cited below
Size H crochet hook for edging
Tapestry needle

Abbreviations: See page 186.
Gauge: 5 sts = 1 inch in afghan st. One granny square measures 4¾ inches square.

INSTRUCTIONS

Note: This afghan is made up of nine panels—five afghan-stitch panels alternating with four granny-square panels.

AFGHAN-STITCH PANEL (make 5):

With Size J afghan hook and off-white yarn, ch 24.

Row 1 (first half): Leaving all lps

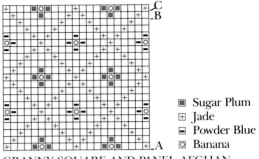

GRANNY SQUARE AND PANEL AFGHAN
1 Square = 1 Cross-Stitch

■ Sugar Plum
⊞ Jade
⊟ Powder Blue
◎ Banana

on hook, sk first ch, * insert hook in next ch, yo, draw up lp; rep from * in each ch across—24 lps on hook.

Row 1 (second half): Yo and draw yarn through first lp on hook, * yo, draw yarn through next 2 lps on hook; rep from * until 1 lp rem on hook.

Row 2 (first half): Insert hook under second vertical bar of Row 1, yo, draw up lp and leave on hook; * insert hook in next vertical bar, yo, draw up lp and leave on hook; rep from * across row to within 1 bar of end; insert hook under last bar and thread behind it, yo, draw up lp—24 lps on hook.

Row 2 (second half): Rep second half of Row 1. Rep Row 2 (first and second halves) until 211 rows are completed.

Last row (bind-off row): Sk the first upright bar, *** insert the hook in next bar, yo, draw through the bar and through the lp on the hook—sl st made and 1 lp on hook;** rep from * across row; change to jade yarn in last st; fasten off off-white yarn.

EDGING FOR AFGHAN-STITCH PANELS: Place Size H hook in jade lp, ch 1, make 3 sc in corner, sc in each vertical lp along side, 3 sc in corner, sc in opposite side of ch along next side; work
continued

remaining 2 sides to correspond, always working 3 sc in each corner; join with sl st to first jade st; fasten off.

FOR THE CROSS-STITCH EMBROIDERY: Referring to chart on page 159, work cross-stitch embroidery on each panel, using tapestry needle and 1 strand of yarn. The photo, *right,* shows how the cross-stitches are worked on top of the afghan-stitch panel. Begin stitching over the second bar from the right edge. Work from A to B 10 times; work from A to C once.

GRANNY-SQUARE PANEL (make 52 squares): Crochet 24 squares with powder blue for Rnd 2, and 28 squares with sugar plum for Rnd 2.

With Size I hook and banana yarn, ch 3; join with sl st to form ring.

Rnd 1: Ch 3; work 11 dc into ring; join with sl st to top of beg ch-3; fasten off.

Rnd 2: Attach powder blue or sugar plum (depending on the square) in any sp between 2 dc; ch 3, make 4 more dc in same sp; * (hdc in sp between next 2 dc) twice, **work 5 dc in next sp—corner grp made,** rep from * around; end with hdc in each of last 2 sp; join with sl st to top of beg ch-3; fasten off.

Rnd 3: Attach jade in sp between last dc of corner grp and first hdc; ch 3, dc in same sp; * sk 2 hdc, make 2 dc in sp before first dc of next corner grp, ch 1, sk 2 dc, make 3 dc in sp between second and third dc of same corner grp, ch 3, sk dc, make 3 dc in sp between third and fourth dc of same corner grp; ch 1, sk 2 dc, ** make 2 dc in sp between last dc and first hdc, rep from * around; end last rep at **; join with sl st to top of beg ch-3; fasten off.

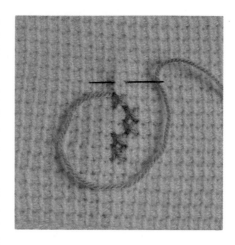

Rnd 4: Attach off-white yarn in any ch-3 corner sp; ch 3, in same sp work 2 dc, ch 3, and 3 dc; * (ch 1, 3 dc in next ch-1 sp) twice; ch 1, ** in corner ch-3 sp work 3 dc, ch 3, and 3 dc, rep from * around; end last rep at **; join to top of beg ch-3; fasten off.

Whipstitch squares together to make 4 panels, *each* panel with 13 squares. Begin and end each panel with sugar plum squares (Rnd 2), alternating colors accordingly.

EDGING FOR THE GRANNY PANELS: With Size H hook, attach jade yarn at any top corner of panel; 3 sc in corner, sc in each st around panel, always working 3 sc in corners; join with sl st to beg sc; fasten off.

Note: The cluster edging is worked only along the *long sides of each* panel. This edging is worked with two colors. Always carry the unused yarn under the cluster of the color in use.

With right side facing and Size H hook, attach sugar plum at corner st of panel; working in same st as join, **(yo, draw up a lp) 3 times, yo, draw yarn through all lps on hook—cluster (cl) made;** sc in next sc with sugar plum, attach powder blue, * cl in next sc with powder blue, sc in next sc with powder blue, cl in next sc with sugar plum, sc in next sc with sugar plum; rep from * to corner; fasten off.

Rep cluster edging on opposite side of panel. Work edging on opposite sides of rem three panels.

ASSEMBLY: Sew panels together with afghan-st panels along the outside edges and alternating the granny-square panels in between.

AFGHAN EDGING: With right side facing and Size H hook, refer to the Edging for the Granny Panels to work edging around afghan using sugar plum and powder blue yarn; sl st to join; fasten off both colors. Join jade, work sc in each st around, working 2 sc in each corner; join with sl st to beg sc; fasten off.

POPCORN GRANNY AFGHAN

Shown on page 150.

Afghan measures 48x64 inches, including border.

MATERIALS

Unger Utopia yarn (3½-ounce skein): 2 skeins *each* of rose pink (No. 293), peachy pink (No. 182), and deep mauve (No. 173); 3 skeins of butterscotch (No. 156); and 5 skeins of taupe (No. 114)

Size H aluminum crochet hook or size to obtain gauge cited below

Yarn needle

Abbreviations: See page 186.
Gauge: Finished block = 6¼ inches square.

INSTRUCTIONS

Our afghan is worked with the yarn colors cited in the materials list. Rounds 1 and 2 are always worked with the same yarn color. Rounds 3 and 4 are each worked with different yarn colors. Round 5 is always worked with taupe yarn. The specific yarn colors for the border rounds are given in the instructions.

SQUARE MOTIF (make 63): With any color, ch 8, join with sl st to form ring.

Rnd 1: Ch 3, in ring work 3 dc, drop lp from hook, insert hook in top of beg ch-3 and draw dropped lp through—beg popcorn (pc) made; * ch 3, **in ring work 4 dc, drop lp from hook, insert hook in top of first dc of 4-dc grp and pull dropped lp through—pc made;** rep from * 6 times more; ch 3, join with sl st to top of first pc—8 pc around.

Rnd 2: Sl st into ch-3 lp; ch 3, in same lp work 2 dc, ch 2, and 3 dc; * 3 dc in next lp; in next lp work 3 dc, ch 2, and 3 dc—corner made; rep from * 2 times more; 3 dc in last lp; join with sl st to top of beg ch-3; fasten off.

Rnd 3: Join any yarn color in ch-2 lp of any corner, ch 3, in same lp work 2 dc, ch 2, and 3 dc; * dc in next 9 dc; in next ch-2 lp work 3 dc, ch 2, and 3 dc; rep from * 2 times more; dc in next 9 dc; join with sl st to top of beg ch-3; fasten off.

Rnd 4: Join any yarn color in ch-2 lp of any corner, ch 5, dc in same lp, * (ch 1, sk dc, dc in next dc) 7 times; ch 1, in corner lp work dc, ch 2, and dc; rep from * 2 times more; (ch 1, sk dc, dc in next dc) 7 times; ch 1, join to third ch of beg ch-5; fasten off.

Rnd 5: Join taupe in any ch-2 corner lp; ch 3, in same lp work 2 dc, ch 2, and 3 dc; * dc in next dc; (dc in ch-1 sp, dc in next dc) 8

times; in ch-2 corner sp work 3 dc, ch 2, and 3 dc; rep from * 2 times more; end (dc in ch-1 sp, dc in next dc) 8 times; join with sl st to top of beg ch-3; fasten off.

ASSEMBLY: Sew squares together with taupe yarn, sewing through back lps of matching dcs. Sew blocks in horizontal rows, each row with seven blocks; make nine rows; sew rows together.

BORDER: *Rnd 1:* With mauve, sc around entire afghan, working 3 sc in each corner st; join with sl st to first sc; fasten off.

Rnd 2: Join butterscotch in any sc, ch 4, sk sc, hdc in next sc; * ch 1, sk sc, hdc in next sc; rep from * around; join with sl st to third ch of beg ch-4; fasten off.

Rnd 3: Join taupe in any hdc, ch 1, sc in each hdc and ch-1 sp around; join with sl st to beg ch-1.

Rnd 4: Working alternately with peachy pink and rose pink, join first color in any sc, sc in next 3 sc; join second color and sc in next 3 sc (carry the unused color under the 3-sc grp of the color in use); work 3 sc of each color alternately around the entire afghan; do not join; mark the last st in each rnd.

Rnds 5 and 6: Rep Rnd 4, working the same color above each 3-sc grp in the previous rnd. At end of Rnd 6 join with sl st to sc following the marked st; fasten off both colors.

Rnd 7: Join taupe in any sc; ch 1, sc in each sc around, working 3 sc in each corner to keep work flat; join with sl st to beg sc.

Rnd 8: Join butterscotch in any sc, ch 1; * sc in each of next 2 sc, **ch 3, sl st in last sc made—picot made;** rep from * around; join to first sc; fasten off. Weave in all ends, and block.

Shown on page 151.

LACY–SQUARE AFGHAN

Afghan measures approximately 47½ x 60½ inches.

MATERIALS

Caron Bulky Boucle yarn (3.5-ounce ball): 15 balls of off-white (No. 4802)
Size H aluminum crochet hook or size to obtain gauge cited below

Abbreviations: See page 186.
Gauge: Finished block = 6½ inches square.

INSTRUCTIONS

Note: Afghan is made of 63 blocks joined in nine rows; each row contains seven blocks. Blocks are assembled together while working Rnd 5. When all blocks are assembled, work filler motifs in all opening centers between blocks.

FIRST BLOCK: Beg in center, ch 5, join with sl st to form ring.

Rnd 1: Ch 4, dc in ring; (ch 1, dc in ring) 6 times, ch 1; join with sl st to third ch of beg ch-4—8 ch-1 sps around.

Rnd 2: Sl st into next ch-1 sp, ch 1, sc in same sp; (ch 5, sc in next ch-1 sp) 7 times; ch 5, join with sl st to sc at beg of rnd—8 ch-5 lps around.

Rnd 3: Sl st into next ch-5 lp, ch 3, in same lp work 3 dc, ch 2, and 4 dc; (3 sc in next ch-5 lp; in next ch-5 lp work 4 dc, ch 2, and 4 dc) 3 times; 3 sc in last ch-5 lp; join to top of ch-3 at beg of rnd.

continued

161

Rnd 4: Ch 4, sk next dc, dc in next dc, ch 1; * in ch-2 sp work (dc, ch 1) twice, dc in same sp; (ch 1, sk next st, dc in next st) 5 times, ch 1; rep from * 3 times more; on last rep, work between second set of ( )s 3 times instead of 5; join last ch-1 to third ch of beg ch-4.

Rnd 5: Sl st into next ch-1 sp, ch 1, sc in same sp, ch 3, sc in same sp; (in next ch-1 sp work sc, ch 3, and sc) twice; * ch 1, (in next ch-1 sp work sc, ch 3, and sc) 8 times, rep from * twice more; (in next ch-1 sp work sc, ch 3, and sc) 5 times; join to sc at beg of rnd—1 ch-1 st at each corner; fasten off.

SECOND BLOCK: Work same as First Block through Rnd 4.

Rnd 5: Work through Rnd 5 of the First Block until the instructions in ( )s are worked 8 times; ch 1, * sc in next ch-1 sp, ch 2, drop hook from work, insert hook into corresponding ch-3 lp on side of First Block, draw dropped lp through, ch 2, sc in same lp on block in progress; rep from * in rem 7 lps on side of block; ch 1, then work rem sides as for First Block without joining sides; fasten off when rnd completed.

Join 5 more blocks following instructions for Second Block to complete the first row; always join the block in progress to the one you just completed.

EIGHTH BLOCK: Work as for Second Block, except join to top of First Block to begin second row of afghan. Work all the blocks that begin a new row in this manner.

NINTH BLOCK: Work as for Second Block except join 2 *sides* of block in progress; join 1 side to the adjacent block of the same row and join the next side to the block in the previous row. Continue to work and join all blocks within a row in this manner.

FILLER MOTIF: For ease in working, cut a 36-inch strand of yarn for each filler motif. Make slipknot in one end of strand. With right side facing, insert hook in any ch-1 corner st and draw slipknot up to top of work from underside; ch 7, drop hook from work, twist work and insert hook into opposite ch-1 st (diagonally) so hook points to center of opening, and draw dropped lp through; ch 4, drop hook from work and insert hook in ch-1 st of block to right and draw dropped lp through; ch 4, drop hook from work, insert hook in center of first ch-7 lp, draw dropped lp through, ch 3, drop hook from work, insert hook in ch-1 st of block (diagonal) and draw dropped lp through; ch 4, drop hook from work, insert hook in same ch-1 st at beg of filler motif, draw dropped lp through; fasten off.

Rep Filler Motif in all open spaces. Weave in all ends.

BORDER: *Rnd 1:* Join yarn in any ch-1 st of afghan corner, ch 3, 2 dc in same st; * (in next ch-3 lp work 2 dc) 8 times; (2 dc in next weaving ch-lp bet blocks) twice; rep from * to corner; work 3 dc in corner ch-1 st; work rem 3 sides to correspond; join to top of ch-3.

Rnd 2: Sc around post of ch-3 (just below the join), ch 3, sc in top lps of next dc, ch 3, sc around post of same dc, ch 3, sc in top lps of next dc; * sc around post of next dc, ch 3, sc in top lps of next dc; rep from * to next 3 corner sts. Sc around post of first corner st, ch 3, sc in top lps of center corner st, ch 3, sc around post of center corner st, ch 3, sc in top lps of next corner st; rep from first * to complete next side. Work rem 2 sides to correspond; join to first sc; fasten off. Weave in all yarn ends, and block.

RUBY GLOW AFGHAN

Shown on page 152.

Afghan measures 52x68 inches; each block is 8 inches across.

MATERIALS
Coats & Clark Red Heart Super Sport yarn (3-ounce ball): 14 balls ecru (No. 109), 4 balls ruby glow (No. 768)
Size E aluminum crochet hook, or size to obtain gauge given below
Tapestry needle

Abbreviations: See page 186.
Gauge: 5 dc = 1 inch; 2½ rows = 1 inch.

INSTRUCTIONS
Note: In the instructions that follow, the ** indicates where the last rep ends in the rnd; then join with sl st to the beg ch-3 unless stated otherwise.

SQUARE MOTIF (Make 48): With ruby glow, ch 6, join with sl st to form ring.

Rnd 1: Ch 4, (dc in ring, ch 1) 11 times, join with sl st to third ch of beg ch-4—12 ch-1 sps made.

Rnd 2: Sl st in first sp; **ch 3, 4 dc in same sp, drop lp from hook, insert hook in top of beg ch-3, pull dropped lp through—beg popcorn (pc) made;** * ch 3, **5 dc in next sp, drop lp from hook, insert hook in first dc of 5-dc grp, pull dropped lp through— pc made;** rep from * around; end ch 3, join with sl st to first pc; fasten off—12 pc around.

Rnd 3: Attach ecru with sl st in any ch-3 sp, ch 6, dc in same sp; * ch 2, hdc in next pc, ch 2, sc in next pc, ch 2, hdc in next pc, ch 2, ** make dc, ch 3, and dc in next ch-3 sp—corner made; rep from * around; join last ch-2 with sl st to third ch of beg ch-6.

Rnd 4: Ch 3; * 2 dc, ch 3, and 2 dc in corner ch-3 sp; dc in next dc, ch 2, dc in hdc, ch 2, dc in sc, ch 2, dc in hdc, ch 2, ** dc in dc; rep from * around; join last ch-2 to top of beg ch-3.

Rnd 5: Sl st in next 2 dc, ch 3; * 2 dc, ch 3, and 2 dc in corner ch-3 sp; dc in next dc, ch 2, sk dc, dc in next dc; (ch 2, dc in next dc) 4 times, ch 2; ** sk dc, dc in next dc; rep from * around; join last ch-2 to top of beg ch-3.

Rnd 6: Sl st in next 2 dc, ch 3; * 2 dc, ch 3, and 2 dc in corner ch-3 sp; dc in next dc, ch 2, sk dc, dc in next dc; (ch 2, dc in next dc) 6 times, ch 2; ** sk dc, dc in next dc; rep from * around; join last ch-2 to top of beg ch-3.

Rnd 7: Sl st in next 2 dc, ch 3; * 2 dc, ch 3, and 2 dc in corner ch-3 sp; dc in next dc, ch 2, sk dc, dc in next dc; (ch 2, dc in next dc) 3 times; (dc in next ch-2 sp, dc in next dc) twice; (ch 2, dc in next dc) 3 times, ch 2; ** sk dc, dc in next dc; rep from * around; join last ch-2 to top of beg ch-3.

Rnd 8: Sl st in next 2 dc, ch 3; * 2 dc, ch 3, and 2 dc in corner ch-3 sp; dc in next dc, ch 2, sk dc, dc in next dc; (ch 2, dc in next dc) twice; (dc in next ch-2 sp, dc in next dc) twice; dc in next 4 dc; (dc in next ch-2 sp, dc in next dc) twice; (ch 2, dc in next dc) twice, ch 2; ** sk dc, dc in next dc; rep from * around; join last ch-2 to top of beg ch-3.

Rnd 9: Sl st in next 2 dc, ch 3; * 2 dc, ch 3, and 2 dc in corner ch-3 sp; dc in next dc, ch 2, sk dc, dc in next dc, ch 2, dc in next dc; (dc in next ch-2 sp, dc in next dc) twice; dc in next 12 dc; (dc in next ch-2 sp, dc in next dc) twice; ch 2, dc in next dc, ch 2; ** sk dc, dc in next dc; rep from * around; join last ch-2 to top of beg ch-3.

Rnd 10: Sl st in next 2 dc, ch 3; * 2 dc, ch 3, and 2 dc in corner ch-3 sp; dc in next dc, ch 2, sk dc, dc in next dc, ch 2, dc in next dc, dc in next ch-2 sp, dc in next 21 dc, dc in next ch-2 sp, dc in next dc, ch 2, dc in next dc, ch 2; ** sk dc, dc in next dc; rep from * around; join last ch-2 to top of beg ch-3.

Rnd 11: Ch 3, * dc in next 2 dc, make 2 dc, ch 2, and 2 dc in corner ch-3 sp; dc in next 3 dc; (dc in next ch-2 sp, dc in next dc) twice; dc in next 24 dc; (dc in next ch-2 sp, dc in next dc) twice; rep from * around; join to top of beg ch-3; fasten off—41 dc on each side.

Rnd 12: Join ruby glow with sc in any corner ch-2 sp, ch 2, sc in same sp, * sc in 41 dc across side, work sc, ch 2, and sc in next corner ch-2 sp, rep from * around; join with sl st in first sc; fasten off.

BLOCK ASSEMBLY: With right sides up, using the tapestry needle sew blocks together with ruby glow yarn. Line up blocks and sew through lps of matching sc. Sew six rows with eight squares in each; then sew the rows together.

BORDER: *Rnd 1:* Join ecru with sl st in any ch-2 corner sp, ch 3, make dc, ch 3, and 2 dc in same sp; * dc in next sc, ch 5, sk 4 sc, sc in next 11 sc, ch 5, sk 4 sc, dc in next 3 sc, ch 5, sk 4 sc, sc in next 11 sc, ch 5, sk 4 sc; ** dc in next sc, dc in joining sts between blocks; rep from * across side of afghan, ending each side at **; then work dc in last sc of last block, make 2 dc, ch 3, and 2 dc in corner sp. Continue to rep from first * as established, working remaining three sides and corners in same manner; join to top of beg ch-3.

Rnd 2: Sl st in next dc and corner ch-3 sp, ch 3; make dc, ch 3, and 2 dc in same sp; * dc in next dc, make dc, ch 3, and dc in next dc; ** dc in next dc, ch 5, sk sc, sc in next 9 sc, ch 5; rep from * across side of afghan; then work dc in next dc; make dc, ch 3, and dc in next dc; dc in next dc, then work 2 dc, ch 3, and 2 dc in next corner ch-3 sp. Continue to rep from first * as established, working remaining three sides and corners in same manner; end last rep at **; then work dc in last dc, join.

Rnd 3: Sl st in next dc and corner ch-3 sp, ch 6, dc in same sp; * ch 3, dc in next dc, ch 3, sk dc, dc in next dc; (ch 3, dc in ch-3 sp, ch 3, dc in next 2 dc, ch 5, sk sc, sc in next 7 sc, ch 5, dc in next 2 dc); rep bet ( )s across side, ending with dc in first 2 dc of corner scallop; ch 3, dc in sp; (ch 3, sk dc, dc in next dc) twice, ch 3; ** make dc, ch 3, and dc in corner sp; rep from * around; end last rep at **; join to third ch of beg ch-6.

Rnd 4: Sl st into ch-3 sp, ch 6, dc in same sp; ** (ch 3, dc in next sp) 4 times; * ch 3, dc in next 2 dc, ch 5, sk sc, sc in 5 sc, ch 5, dc in next 2 dc; (ch 3, dc in next sp) twice; rep from * across side, ending with dc in 2 dc at beg of corner scallop; (ch 3, dc in next sp) 4 times; ch 3, make dc, ch 3, and dc in corner sp; rep from ** around; join as for Rnd 3.

Rnd 5: Sl st in corner ch-3 sp, ch 6, dc in same sp; ** (ch 3, dc in next ch-3 sp) 5 times; * ch 3, dc in

continued

next 2 dc, ch 5, sk sc, sc in 3 sc, ch 5, dc in next 2 dc, ch 3, dc in next ch-3 sp, ch 3; make dc, ch 3, and dc in next ch-3 sp; ch 3, dc in next sp; rep from * across side, ending with dc in 2 dc at start of corner scallop; (ch 3, dc in next ch-3 sp) 5 times; ch 3, make dc, ch 3, and dc in corner sp; rep from ** around; join as for Rnd 3.

Rnd 6: Sl st in corner ch-3 sp, ch 6, dc in same sp; ** (ch 3, dc in next ch-3 sp) 6 times; * ch 3, dc in next 2 dc, ch 5, sk sc, sc in next sc, ch 5, dc in next 2 dc; (ch 3, dc in next sp) twice, ch 3, make dc, ch 3, dc in next ch-3 sp; (ch 3, dc in next sp) twice; rep from * across side, ending with dc in 2 dc at start of corner scallop; (ch 3, dc in next ch-3 sp) 6 times; ch 3, make dc, ch 3, and dc in corner sp; rep from ** around; join as for Rnd 3.

Rnd 7: Sl st in corner ch-3 sp, ch 6, dc in same sp; ** (ch 3, dc in next ch-3 sp) 7 times; * ch 3, dc in next 4 dc; (ch 3, dc in next ch-3 sp) 3 times; ch 3, make dc, ch 3, and dc in center ch-3 sp; (ch 3, dc in next sp) 3 times; rep from * across side, ending with dc in 4 dc at start of corner scallop; (ch 3, dc in next sp) 7 times, ch 3, make dc, ch 3, and dc in corner sp; rep from ** around; join as for Rnd 3; fasten off ecru.

Rnd 8: With wrong side of afghan facing, join ruby glow with sc in fourth dc of 4-dc grp before any corner scallop; * (2 sc in next ch-3 sp, sc in next dc, **ch 3, sl st in top of last sc made—picot made**) 16 times, 2 sc in last ch-3 sp on scallop, sc in dc, sk dc, sc in next dc, work picot, sc in next dc; rep from * around; rep between ( )s 8 times across each side scallop and 16 times for corner scallops; end with sc and picot in last dc; join to first sc; fasten off.

PASTEL GRANNY–SQUARE AFGHAN

Shown on page 153.

Afghan measures 49x63½ inches, including border.

MATERIALS
Unger Roly Sport (1.75-ounce skein): 3 skeins *each* of lavender (No. 4074), pink (No. 4208), yellow (No. 4277), blue (No. 4584), green (No. 4537), and salmon (No. 4310)
Unger Fluffy (1.75-ounce skein): 9 skeins of white (No. 460)
Size G aluminum crochet hook or size to obtain gauge cited below

Abbreviations: See page 186.
Gauge: Each block = 7 inches square.

INSTRUCTIONS
Note: In the instructions that follow, the ** indicate the point where the last repeat ends in the round. Then complete the round as directed in the instructions.

BLOCK: Ch 5, join with sl st to form ring.

Rnd 1: Ch 3, 4 dc in ring; drop hook from work and insert hook in top of beg ch-3 and draw dropped lp through—beg popcorn (pc) made; ch 3; * **make 5 dc in ring, drop hook from work and insert hook in top of first dc of 5-dc grp and draw dropped lp through—popcorn (pc) made;** ch 3; rep from * 2 times more; join with sl st to beg pc.

Rnd 2: Sl st into ch-3 lp, ch 3, in same lp work 2 dc, ch 2, and 3 dc; * in next ch-3 lp work 3 dc, ch 2, and 3 dc; rep from * 2 times more; join with sl st to beg ch-3.

Rnd 3: Ch 3, dc in next 2 dc; * in ch-2 corner lp work 3 dc, ch 2, and 3 dc; ** dc in next 6 dc; rep from * 3 times more; then dc in next 3 dc; join to top of beg ch-3.

Rnd 4: Sl st in next dc, ch 4, (sk dc, dc in next dc, ch 1) twice; * in ch-2 lp work dc, ch 2, and dc; ** (ch 1, sk dc, dc in next dc) 6 times; ch 1, rep from * 3 times more; then (ch 1, sk dc, dc in next dc) 3 times; ch 1, join with sl st to third ch of beg ch-4.

Rnd 5: Ch 4, dc in next dc, ch 1, dc in next dc; * 2 dc in ch-1 sp; dc in next dc; in ch-2 corner lp work 2 dc, ch 2, and 2 dc; dc in next dc, 2 dc in ch-1 sp, dc in next dc; ** (ch 1, dc in next dc) 5 times; rep from * 3 times more; then (ch 1, dc in next dc) 2 times; ch 1, join to third ch of beg ch-4.

Rnd 6: Ch 4, dc in next dc, dc in ch-1 sp; * dc in next 6 dc; in ch-2 corner lp work 2 dc, ch 2, and 2 dc; dc in next 6 dc, dc in ch-1 sp, dc in next dc; ** (ch 1, dc in next dc) 3 times; dc in ch-1 sp; rep from * 3 times more; ch 1, dc in next dc, ch 1, join to third ch of beg ch-4.

Rnd 7: Ch 3; * dc in ch-1 sp; dc in next 10 dc; in ch-2 corner lp work 2 dc, ch 2, and 2 dc; dc in next 10 dc; dc in ch-1 sp, dc in next dc, ch 1, ** dc in next dc; rep from * 3 times more; join last ch-1 to top of beg ch-3.

Rnd 8: Ch 1, sc in same st as join; sc in each dc and ch-1 sp around, working 3 sc in each corner; join to first sc; fasten off.

Make eight blocks from each yarn color. Arrange blocks in pleasing color pattern, placing six blocks in each of eight rows.

Blocks are edged with two rounds of white. After the first block is completed, all successive blocks are joined to the previous block as you work the second round of edging.

FIRST BLOCK EDGING: *Rnd 1:* Beginning with block in lower left-hand corner, join white and work 3 sc in center sc of any corner; * (ch 1, sk sc, sc in next sc) 15 times; ch 1, sk sc, 3 sc in next sc; rep from * 3 times more; end ch 1, join to first sc.

Rnd 2: In next sc work sc, ch 2, and sc; * ch 2, sk sc, sc in next ch-1 sp; (ch 2, sc in next ch-1 sp) 15 times; ch 2, sk sc, in next sc work sc, ch 2, and sc; rep from * around; join last ch-2 with sl st to first sc; fasten off.

SECOND BLOCK EDGING: Rep Rnd 1 of edging for First Block.

Rnd 2: Complete first side of Rnd 2 of edging for First Block up to second corner; in corner sc work sc, ch 1, drop hook from work, insert hook in corresponding ch-2 corner lp of first block, draw dropped lp through, ch 1, sc in same corner sc; (ch 1, drop hook from work, insert hook in corresponding ch-2 lp of first block, draw dropped lp through, ch 1, sc in next ch-1 sp of block in progress) 16 times, ch 1, drop hook from work, insert hook in corresponding lp of first block, draw dropped lp through, ch 1, sk sc, sc in next sc, ch 1, drop hook from work, insert hook in corner ch-2 lp, draw dropped lp through, ch 1, sc in same corner sc; rep bet *s of Rnd 2 of First Block Edging to complete rem sides with no more joinings.

Join third to sixth blocks to each preceding block to make one row. Join seventh block to top of first block to begin second row.

Join eighth block to seventh block and second block of Row 1. When joining eighth block at corner, join to corner of *first* (diagonally opposite) block only; then work joinings along next side.

Continue to join remaining blocks as established.

AFGHAN BORDER: *Rnd 1:* Join white in any ch-2 corner lp, ch 1; in same lp work sc, ch 1, and sc; * ch 2, sc in next lp; rep from * around, working sc, ch 2, and sc in *each* corner lp; join to first sc.

Rnd 2: Sl st to corner lp, ch 1; in same lp work sc, ch 2, and sc; rep from * of Rnd 1 *above;* join.

Rnd 3: Sl st to corner lp, ch 1; in same lp work sc, ch 2, and sc; in *each* ch-2 lp around work sc, hdc, and sc, working sc, ch 2, and sc in *each* corner lp; join to first sc; fasten off. Weave in all ends; block.

LACY WHITE AFGHAN

Shown on page 153.

Afghan measures 56x74 inches.

———MATERIALS———
Bernat Berella 4 (100-gram ball): 13 balls of white (No. 8942)
Size I aluminum crochet hook or size to obtain gauge cited below

Abbreviations: See page 186.
Gauge: 3 dc = 1 inch.

———INSTRUCTIONS———
RIGHT SIDE PANEL (worked over 18 sts): *Row 1* (wrong side): (Ch 1, sk ch, 3 dc in next ch, ch 3, sk 3 ch, sc in next ch, ch 3, sk 3 ch, 3 dc in next ch; ch 1, sk ch), dc in next 5 ch, ch 1, sk ch, 3 dc in next ch; ch 3, turn.

Row 2: Sk 2 dc, 3 dc in next dc, ch 1, * dc in 2 dc, **work 5 dc in next dc, remove hook from lp, insert hook in first dc of 5-dc grp from front to back on right-side row or from back to front**

on wrong-side row, pick up dropped lp and draw through st—popcorn (pc) made; dc in next 2 dc, * (ch 1, 3 dc in next dc; sc in ch-3 lp, ch 3, sc in next ch-3 lp, sk 2 dc, 3 dc in next dc; ch 1).

Row 3: (Ch 1, 3 dc in next dc, ch 3, sc in ch-3 lp, ch 3, sk next 2 dc, 3 dc in next dc; ch 1), * dc in next 2 dc, dc in pc, dc in next 2 dc, * ch 1, 3 dc in next dc, ch 3, turn.

Rep rows 2 and 3 for pat.

LEFT SIDE PANEL (worked over 18 sts): *Row 1* (wrong side): 2 dc in fourth ch from hook; ch 1, sk ch, dc in next 5 ch; rep bet ( )s of Row 1 of Right Side Panel.

Row 2: Rep bet ( )s of Row 2 of Right Side Panel; rep bet *s of Row 2 of Right Side Panel; ch 1, 3 dc in next dc, ch 3, turn.

Row 3: Sk 2 dc, 3 dc in next dc, ch 1, rep bet *s of Row 3 of Right Side Panel; rep bet ( )s of Row 3 of Right Side Panel.

Rep rows 2 and 3 for pat.

LACE PANEL (worked over 20 sts): *Row 1* (wrong side): Ch 1, sk ch, 3 dc in next ch, ch 3, sk 3 ch, sc in next ch, ch 3, sk 3 ch, work 3 dc in next ch, ch 1, 3 dc in next ch; ch 3, sk 3 ch, sc in next ch, ch 3, sk 3 ch, 3 dc in next ch, ch 1, sk ch.

Row 2: Ch 1, 3 dc in next dc, sc in ch-3 lp, ch 3, sc in next ch-3 lp; 3 dc, ch 2, and 3 dc in next ch-1 sp; sc in ch-3 lp, ch 3, sc in ch-3 lp, sk 2 dc, 3 dc in next dc, ch 1.

Row 3: Ch 1, 3 dc in next dc, ch 3, sc in ch-3 lp, ch 3, work 3 dc, ch 1, 3 dc in next ch-2 sp; ch 3, sc in ch-3 lp, ch 3, sk 2 dc, 3 dc in next dc, ch 1.

Rep rows 2 and 3 for pat.

DIAMOND PANEL (worked over 15 sts): *Row 1* (wrong side): Dc in next 15 ch.

continued

Row 2: Dc in 7 dc, pc in next dc, dc in next 7 dc.

Row 3: Dc in next 6 dc, (pc in next dc, dc in top of pc, pc in next dc), dc in next 6 dc.

Row 4: Dc in next 5 dc, (pc in next dc, dc in pc, dc in dc, dc in pc, pc in dc), dc in next 5 dc.

Row 5: Dc in next 4 dc, (pc in dc, dc in pc, dc in dc, ch 1, sk dc, dc in next dc, dc in pc, pc in dc), dc in next 4 dc.

Row 6: Dc in 3 dc, (pc in next dc, dc in pc, dc in dc, ch 3, sc in ch-1 sp, ch 3, sk dc, dc in next dc, dc in pc, pc in next dc), dc in next 3 dc.

Row 7: Dc in next 2 dc, pc in next dc, * dc in pc, dc in dc, (ch 3, sc in next ch-3 lp) twice, ch 3, sk dc, dc in dc, dc in pc, pc in dc *; dc in next 2 dc.

Row 8: Dc in 2 dc, dc in pc, (pc in dc, dc in dc, dc in ch-3 lp, ch 3, sc in ch-3 lp, ch 3, dc in next ch-3 lp, dc in dc, pc in dc, dc in pc), dc in next 2 dc.

Row 9: Dc in 3 dc, (dc in pc, pc in dc, dc in dc, dc in ch-3 lp, ch 1, dc in next ch-3 lp, dc in dc, pc in next dc, dc in pc), dc in next 3 dc.

Row 10: Dc in 4 dc, (dc in pc, pc in dc, dc in dc, dc in ch-1 sp, dc in dc, pc in next dc, dc in pc), dc in next 4 dc.

Row 11: Dc in 5 dc, (dc in pc, pc in dc, dc in dc, pc in dc, dc in pc), dc in next 5 dc.

Row 12: Dc in 6 dc, dc in pc, pc in dc, dc in pc, dc in next 6 dc. Rep rows 3–12 for pat.

CENTER DIAMOND PANEL (worked over 45 sts): *Row 1* (wrong side): Dc in next 45 ch.

Row 2: Dc in 7 dc, pc in dc, * dc in 9 dc, pc in dc; rep from * twice, dc in next 7 dc.

Row 3: Dc in 6 dc, * rep bet ( )s of Row 3 of Diamond Panel *above;* dc in 7 sts; rep from * twice; rep bet ( )s once, dc in next 6 dc.

Row 4: Dc in 5 dc, * rep bet ( )s of Row 4 of Diamond Panel; dc in 5 dc; rep from * twice, rep bet ( )s once more; dc in next 5 dc.

Row 5: Dc in 4 dc, * rep bet ( )s of Row 5 of Diamond Panel; dc in 3 dc; rep from * twice, rep bet ( )s once more; dc in next 4 dc.

Row 6: Dc in 3 dc, * rep bet ( )s of Row 6 of Diamond Panel; dc in dc; rep from * twice, rep bet ( )s once more; dc in next 3 dc.

Row 7: Dc in 2 dc, pc in dc, rep bet *s of Row 7 of Diamond Panel 4 times; dc in next 2 dc.

Row 8: Dc in 2 dc, dc in pc; rep bet ( )s of Row 8 of Diamond Panel 4 times; dc in next 2 dc.

Row 9: Dc in 3 dc, * rep bet ( )s of Row 9 of Diamond Panel; dc in dc; rep from * twice, rep bet ( )s once more; dc in next 3 dc.

Row 10: Dc in 4 dc, * rep bet ( )s of Row 10 of Diamond Panel; dc in 3 dc; rep from * twice, rep bet ( )s once more; dc in next 4 dc.

Row 11: Dc in 5 dc, * rep bet ( )s of Row 11 of Diamond Panel; dc in next 5 dc; rep from * 3 times.

Row 12: Dc in 6 dc, * dc in pc, pc in dc, dc in pc, dc in 3 dc, pc in dc, dc in 3 dc; rep from * twice; dc in pc, pc in dc, dc in pc, dc in next 6 dc.

Rep rows 3–12 for pat.

For the afghan

With white, ch 154.

Row 1 (wrong side): Work Row 1 of each pat in the following sequence: Left Side Panel over first 21 sts (includes beg turning ch), Diamond Panel over next 15 sts, Lace Panel over next 20 sts, Center Diamond Panel over next 45 sts, Lace Panel over next 20 sts, Diamond Panel over next 15 sts, and Right Side Panel over last 18 sts. Continue pats as established until there are 11 diamonds.

Last row (wrong side): Continue in pats as established over Left and Right Side Panels and Lace Panels; work 15 dc over each Diamond Panel and 45 dc over Center Diamond Panel. Fasten off.

FRINGE: Double three 22-inch-long strands of yarn in half, and knot in each corner of the short ends of afghan. Repeat with six 22-inch-long strands in every fourth st across both short ends. Take six strands from each adjacent 12-strand group; tie an overhand knot about 2 inches below first knot. Trim evenly.

EMBROIDERED SHELL-STITCH AFGHAN

Shown on page 154.

Afghan measures approximately 48x60 inches.

MATERIALS
Brunswick Windmist yarn (50-gram ball): 18 balls peach ice (No. 2822); 1 ball *each* of bay green (No. 2810) and faded rose (No. 2824)
Sizes J and K aluminum crochet hooks or sizes to obtain gauge cited below
Tapestry needle

Abbreviations: See page 186.
Gauge: 4 sts = 1 inch with the smaller hook in pattern st.

INSTRUCTIONS
With Size J hook and peach ice, ch 172.

Row 1: Dc in fourth ch from hook; * ch 2, sk 2 ch, **in next ch work 6 dc—shell made;** sk 4 ch, sc in next ch, ch 2, sk 2 ch, dc in next 2 ch; rep from * to end of row; ch 3, turn.

Row 2: Dc in next dc; * ch 2, 6 dc in next sc, sc in sixth dc of shell, ch 2, ** dc in next 2 dc; rep from * to end of row, end last rep at **; then dc in next dc and in top of turning ch; ch 3, turn.

Rep Row 2 for pattern until 56 inches or the desired length is completed; do not fasten off.

BORDER: *Note:* The border is worked in rnds.

Rnd 1: With Size K hook and peach ice, ch 1, work sc evenly around, working 3 sc in corners (make sure opposite sides of the border have the same number of sts); end with 2 sc in last corner, sl st to beg ch-1. Work eight more rnds in sc, working 3 sc in each corner sc and ending with sl st to beg ch-1; fasten off.

EMBROIDERY: Following the embroidery diagram, *below,* use the tapestry needle and faded rose yarn to work one lazy daisy flower (colored in red) in each corner of the border. Add the bay green straight stitches (marked in blue). Spacing evenly, work the remaining flowers approximately 4 inches apart (from flower center to flower center) along each side of the border.

1 Square = 1 Stitch

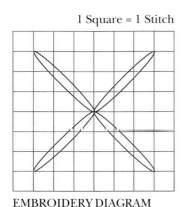

EMBROIDERY DIAGRAM

AFGHAN WITH ARROWHEAD BORDER

Shown on page 155.

Afghan measures approximately 45x62 inches.

MATERIALS

Red Heart Classic 4-ply yarn (3.5-ounce skein): 12 skeins of blue gray (No. 807) and 4 skeins of off-white (No. 003)
Size J afghan hook or size to obtain gauge cited below
Size J aluminum crochet hook

Abbreviations: See page 186.
Gauge: With size J afghan hook, 4 sts = 1 inch; 7 rows = 2 inches.

INSTRUCTIONS

PANEL (make 6): With blue gray and afghan hook, ch 27.

Row 1 (first half): Leaving all lps on hook, sk first ch, * insert hook in next ch, yo, draw up lp; rep from * in each ch across—27 lps on hook.

Row 1 (second half): Yo and draw through first lp on hook, * yo, draw through next 2 lps on hook; rep from * until 1 lp rem on hook.

Row 2 (first half): Insert hook under *second* vertical bar of Row 1, yo, draw up lp and leave on hook; * insert hook in next bar and draw up lp; rep from * across row to within 1 bar of end; insert hook under last bar and thread behind it, yo, draw up lp—27 lps on hook.

Row 2 (second half): Rep second half of Row 1.

Rep Row 2 (first and second halves) until 192 rows or any multiple of eight rows (approximately 60 inches) are completed.

Last row: Draw up lp under second bar and draw through lp on hook—1 lp on hook; * draw up lp in next bar and draw through lp on hook; rep from * across to within 1 bar of end; insert hook under last bar and thread behind it, draw up lp and draw through lp on hook; fasten off.

PANEL EDGING (worked around each strip): With off-white yarn, Size J crochet hook, and right side facing, attach yarn at top of left side; working along the long side of the afghan, ch 1, * hdc in first bar of next row; dc in second bar *below* next row; trc in third bar *below* next row; dtr (yo hook 3 times) in fourth bar *below* next row; trc in third bar *below* next row; dc in second bar *below* next row; hdc in first bar *below* next row; sc in edge st of next row; rep from * to corner; ch 1.

Working across short edge, work sc in first 5 sts, rep from first * twice, sc in last 5 sts, ch 1. Sc in first st of next long side; rep from first * to corner; work remaining sides to correspond; join with sl st to beg ch-1; fasten off. Work rem five strips in same manner.

Sew strips together, matching sts as you sew.

OUTSIDE EDGING: *Note:* Work around the posts of each stitch instead of in the top lps for a smoother appearance.

With right side facing, off-white yarn, and Size J crochet hook, join yarn in first sc at top of long edge; ch 1, * hdc in next st, dc in next st, trc in next 3 st, dc in next st, hdc in next st, sc in next st, rep from * to corner. Work 2 sc in ch-1 sp at corner; sc in next 5 sc, then rep from first * twice, sc in next 5 sc. Continue in this manner around afghan; work 1 row sc around entire afghan, working 3 sc in each corner; fasten off and block.

167

An Old-Fashioned Christmas

A STITCHING CELEBRATION

❧

Christmas has long been a star-spangled holiday for Americans. From the close of the Civil War to the turn of the century, flags and patriotic mementos blossomed on Christmas trees and tables across the nation. They served as talismans betokening the end of strife and the blessed advent of peace.

A golden shower of crocheted stars twinkles on the table wreath, *left.* The crisp star-patterned doily, *opposite,* offers a stunning backdrop for a favorite holiday or year-round centerpiece.

A tree flocked with angels and starlike snowflakes recalls these beautiful lines of Longfellow:
"Silently one by one, in the infinite meadows of heaven,
Blossomed the lovely stars, the forget-me-nots of the angels." (From Evangeline, 1847)

Stars and angels are among the most familiar and beloved of all Christmas motifs. Pictured here are imaginative variations on these two celestial themes.

The quaint little centerpiece angel, *left,* complete with halo, lofty wings, and a Christmas bouquet, is destined to become a family favorite. Her dress is fashioned separately and is worn over a crocheted cone-shaped base.

Opposite, airy crocheted snowflakes (in round, pineapple, and spiderweb designs) hang like radiant heavenly stars among the branches of a tabletop tree. Mixed in with old-fashioned cardboard angels, curls of shiny tinsel, paper robins, and yellow Christmas roses, these elegant creations turn simple boughs of pine into a lush Victorian fantasy.

Instructions for these trims and decorations begin on page 176.

*M*ore than a century ago
Charles Dickens wrote, "There seems a magic in the
very name of Christmas." The magic is with us still—all
of us, at least, who pledge along with Dickens' dear
enlightened Mr. Scrooge, who promised to keep alive the
spirit of this season when he said, "I will honor
Christmas in my heart and try to keep it all the year."

This collection of dainty designs in pastel shades will spark the Christmas spirit as you stitch them up for holiday gifts and will keep it glowing year-round.

The crocheted stocking *opposite* is hung by the chimney (with the requisite care) above a matching Christmas afghan (perfect for that "long winter's nap"). Both are embellished with embroidered rows of hearts and trees worked in simple cross-stitch.

At *right*, companion ornaments—stocking, angel, and an old-fashioned cornucopia—make appealing pick-up projects to stash in your workbasket and stitch up in spare moments throughout the year.

Instructions for these projects begin on page 181.

STAR DOILY

Shown on page 168.

Doily measures approximately 17¼ inches in diameter.

MATERIALS

J. & P. Coats Knit-Cro-Sheen (225-yard ball): 2 balls ecru (No. 61)
Size 10 steel crochet hook

Abbreviations: See page 186.

INSTRUCTIONS

Beg at center, ch 6; join with sl st to form ring.

Rnd 1: Ch 3, work 23 dc in ring—24 dc counting ch-3 as st; join with sl st to top of beg ch-3.

Note: The ** in the following instructions indicate the place where the last repeat ends in the round. Then join the rnd by slip-stitching to the top of the beginning ch-3 unless specified otherwise.

Rnd 2: Ch 3, dc in same ch as join, dc in next dc, 2 dc in next dc, ch 1; * 2 dc in next dc, dc in next dc, 2 dc in next dc, ch 1; rep from * around; join—8 ch-1 sp around.

Rnd 3: Ch 3, dc in same ch as join; * dc in 3 dc, 2 dc in next dc, ch 2, ** 2 dc in next dc; rep from * around; join.

Rnd 4: Ch 3, dc in same ch as join; * dc in each dc to last dc of this grp; 2 dc in last dc, ch 3, ** 2 dc in next dc; rep from * around; join.

Rnds 5–6: Work as for Rnd 3, *except* work ch-4 lps between grps on Rnd 5; work ch-5 lps between grps on Rnd 6—13 dc in each grp at end of Rnd 6.

Rnds 7–8: Work as for Rnd 3, working ch-6 lps bet grps on each rnd—17 dc in each grp at end of Rnd 8.

Rnd 9: Ch 3, dc in same ch as join; * dc in 7 dc, ch 2, sk next dc, dc in next 7 dc, 2 dc in next dc, ch 6, ** 2 dc in next dc; rep from * around; join.

Rnd 10: Ch 3, dc in next 7 dc, * ch 2, 3 dc in ch-2 sp, ch 2, sk next dc, dc in 8 dc, ch 6, ** dc in next 8 dc; rep from * around; join.

Rnd 11: Ch 3, dc in same ch as join, * dc in next 6 dc; (ch 2, 3 dc in next ch-2 sp) twice; ch 2, sk next dc, dc in 6 dc, 2 dc in next dc, ch 6, ** 2 dc in next dc; rep from * around; join.

Rnd 12: Ch 3, dc in next 6 dc, * ch 2, 3 dc in ch-2 sp, ch 8; **yo hook 6 times, insert hook in next ch-2 sp and draw up lp—8 lps on hook; (yo, draw through 2 lps) 7 times—long st made;** ch 8, 3 dc in next ch-2 sp, ch 2, sk next dc, dc in 7 dc, ch 6, ** dc in next 7 dc; rep from * around; join.

Rnd 13: Ch 3, dc in next 5 dc, * ch 2, 3 dc in next ch-2 sp, ch 8, sc in eighth ch of ch-8 lp, sc in top of long st, sc in first ch of next ch-8 lp, ch 8, 3 dc in next ch-2 sp, ch 2, sk next dc, dc in 6 dc, ch 6, ** dc in next 6 dc; rep from * around; join.

Rnd 14: Ch 3, dc in next 4 dc, * ch 2, 3 dc in next ch-2 sp, ch 8, sc in eighth ch of ch-8 lp, sc in 3 sc, sc in first ch of next ch-8 lp, ch 8, 3 dc in next ch-2 sp, ch 2, sk next dc, dc in 5 dc, ch 6, ** dc in next 5 dc; rep from * around; join.

Rnd 15: Ch 3, dc in next 3 dc, * ch 2, 3 dc in next ch-2 sp, ch 8, sc in eighth ch of ch-8 lp, sc in 5 sc, sc in first ch of next ch-8 lp, ch 8, 3 dc in next ch-2 sp, ch 2, sk next dc, dc in 4 dc, ch 6, ** dc in 4 dc; rep from * around; join.

Rnd 16: Ch 3, dc in next 2 dc, * ch 2, 3 dc in next ch-2 sp, ch 8, sc in 7 sc, ch 8, 3 dc in next ch-2 sp, ch 2, sk next dc, dc in 3 dc, ch 6, ** dc in 3 dc; rep from * around; join.

Rnd 17: Ch 3, dc in next 2 dc, * 3 dc in ch-2 sp, ch 2, 3 dc in next ch-8 lp, ch 8, sc in 7 sc, ch 8, 3 dc at end of next ch-8 lp, ch 2, 3 dc in ch-2 sp, dc in 3 dc, ch 6, ** dc in 3 dc; rep from * around; join.

Rnd 18: Ch 3, dc in next 5 dc, * 3 dc in next ch-2 sp, ch 2, 3 dc in next ch-8 lp, ch 8, sk next sc, sc in 5 sc, ch 8, 3 dc at end of next ch-8 lp, ch 2, 3 dc in next ch-2 sp, dc in 6 dc, ch 6, ** dc in 6 dc; rep from * around; join.

Rnd 19: Ch 3, dc in next 8 dc, * 3 dc in next ch-2 sp, ch 2, 3 dc in next ch-8 lp, ch 8, sk next sc, sc in 3 sc, ch 8, 3 dc at end of next ch-8 lp, ch 2, 3 dc in ch-2 sp, dc in 9 dc, ch 6, ** dc in 9 dc; rep from * around; join.

Rnd 20: Ch 3, dc in next 11 dc, * 3 dc in next ch-2 sp, ch 2, 3 dc in next ch-8 lp, ch 5; **yo hook 4 times, draw up lp in center sc— 6 lps on hook, (yo and draw through 2 lps) 5 times—another long st made;** ch 5, 3 dc at end of next ch-8 lp, ch 2, 3 dc in ch-2 sp, dc in 12 dc, ch 6, ** dc in 12 dc; rep from * around; join.

Rnd 21: Ch 3, dc in 14 dc, * 3 dc in next ch-2 sp, ch 2, 3 dc in next ch-5 lp, ch 3, sk long st, 3 dc at end of next ch-5 lp, ch 2, 3 dc in next ch-2 sp, dc in 15 dc, ch 6, ** dc in 15 dc; rep from * around; join.

Rnd 22: Ch 3, dc in same ch as join, * dc in 17 dc, 3 dc in next ch-2 sp; (ch 2, 3 dc in next sp) twice; dc in 17 dc, 2 dc in next dc, ch 6, ** 2 dc in next dc; rep from * around; join.

FIRST STAR POINT: *Row 1:* Ch 3, **draw up lp in each of next 2 dc, (yo and draw through 2 lps** on hook) twice—dec made; dc in 17 dc; (ch 2, 3 dc in ch-2 sp) twice; ch 2, sk 2 dc, dc in 19 dc; ch 3, turn.

Row 2: Work dec over next 2 dc, dc in 14 dc, ch 2, 3 dc in next ch-2 sp, ch 6, dtr (yo hook 3 times) in next ch-2 sp, ch 6, 3 dc in next ch-2 sp, ch 2, sk 2 dc, dc in 16 dc; ch 3, turn.

Row 3: Work dec over next 2 dc, dc in 11 dc, ch 2, 3 dc in ch-2 sp, ch 6, sc in ch-6 lp, sc in dtr, sc in ch-6 lp, ch 6, 3 dc in ch-2 sp, ch 2, sk 2 dc, dc in 13 dc; ch 3, turn.

Row 4: Work dec over next 2 dc, dc in 8 dc, ch 2, 3 dc in ch-2 sp, ch 6, sc in ch-6 lp, sc in 3 sc, sc in ch-6 lp, ch 6, 3 dc in ch-2 sp, ch 2, sk 2 dc, dc in 10 dc; ch 3, turn.

Row 5: Work dec over next 2 dc, dc in 5 dc, ch 2, 3 dc in ch-2 sp, ch 6, sc in ch-6 lp, sc in 5 sc, sc in ch-6 lp, ch 6, 3 dc in ch-2 sp, ch 2, sk 2 dc, dc in 7 dc; ch 3, turn.

Row 6: Work dec over next 2 dc, dc in 2 dc, 3 dc in ch-2 sp, ch 8, sc in 7 sc, ch 8, 3 dc in ch-2 sp, sk 2 dc, dc in 4 dc; ch 3, turn.

Row 7: Work dec over next 2 dc, dc in next dc, ch 3, sk 3 dc, 3 dc in ch-8 lp, ch 8, sk next sc, sc in 5 sc, ch 8, 3 dc in ch-8 lp, ch 3, sk 3 dc, dc in next 3 dc; ch 4, turn.

Row 8: 3 dc in ch-3 sp, ch 3, 3 dc in ch-8 lp, ch 8, sk next sc, sc in 3 sc, ch 8, 3 dc in ch-8 lp, ch 3, 3 dc in ch-3 sp, trc in last dc; ch 4, turn.

Row 9: 3 dc in ch-3 sp, ch 3, 3 dc in ch-8 lp, ch 8, sk sc, sc in center sc, ch 8, 3 dc in ch-8 lp, ch 3, 3 dc in ch-3 sp, trc in last dc; ch 4, turn.

Row 10: 3 dc in ch-3 sp, ch 3, 3 dc in ch-8 lp, ch 4, dtr (yo hook 3 times) in sc, ch 4, 3 dc in ch-8 lp, ch 3, 3 dc in ch-3 sp, trc in last dc; ch 4, turn.

Row 11: 3 dc in ch-3 sp; (ch 3, 3 dc in ch-4 lp) twice; ch 3, 3 dc in ch-3 sp, trc in last dc; ch 4, turn.

Row 12: 3 dc in ch-3 sp; (ch 3, 3 dc in ch-3 sp) twice; trc in last dc; ch 4, turn.

Row 13: 3 dc in ch-3 sp, dc in 3 dc, 3 dc in ch-3 sp, trc in last dc; ch 3, turn.

Row 14: Dec over next 2 dc, dc in 4 dc, dec over next 2 dc; ch 3, turn.

Row 15: Work dec over next 2 dc, dc in 3 dc; ch 3, turn.

Row 16: Work dec over next 2 dc, dc in last dc; fasten off.

REMAINING STAR POINTS: ** Sk next ch-6 on Rnd 22 of doily center; rep rows 1–16 of First Star Point to make the second point; rep from ** around doily to complete all the points.

BORDER: Join thread to first ch of any ch-6 of Rnd 22, ch 1, 2 sc in same ch, ** ch 5, * sk next row, in end of next row make dc, **ch 3, sc in third ch from hook—picot made,** dc in same sp; ch 5, sk next row, sc in end of next row, ch 5; rep from * around entire point; ch 5, 2 sc in next ch-6 lp bet points; rep from ** around doily; join to beg ch-1, fasten off.

STAR ORNAMENTS

Shown on pages 168 and 169.

Large star measures 4⅞ inches across; small star measures 3½ inches across.

MATERIALS

J & P. Coats Metallic Knit-Cro-Sheen (100-yard ball): Two balls of gold (No. 90G) make six stars of each size
Size 8 steel crochet hook

Abbreviations: See page 186.

INSTRUCTIONS

For the large star

Beg in center, ch 5, join with sl st to form ring.

Rnd 1: Ch 3, dc in ring; (ch 2, 2 dc in ring) 4 times; ch 2, join with sl st to top of beg ch-3.

Rnd 2: Sl st in next dc and into ch-2 sp; **ch 3, dc in same sp, ch 2, 2 dc in same sp—beg shell made;** ch 1, **in next ch-2 sp work 2 dc, ch 2, and 2 dc—shell made;** (ch 1, shell in next ch-2 sp) 3 times more; ch 1, join with sl st to top of beg ch-3.

Rnd 3: Sl st in next dc and into ch-2 sp; work beg shell in same sp; ch 1, 2 dc in next ch-1 sp, ch 1, (shell in next ch-2 sp, ch 1, 2 dc in next ch-1 sp, ch 1) 4 times; join with sl st to top of beg ch-3.

Rnd 4: Sl st in next dc and into ch-2 sp; work beg shell in same sp, (ch 1, 2 dc in next ch-1 sp) twice; ch 1, (shell in next ch-2 sp, ch 1, 2 dc in next ch-1 sp, ch 1, 2 dc in next ch-1 sp, ch 1) 4 times; join with sl st to top of beg ch-3; fasten off.

STAR POINTS: *Row 1:* Attach thread in any ch-2 sp of shell, ch 1, sc in same sp; (sc in next 2 dc and ch-sp) 4 times; **ch 3, sl st in third ch from hook—picot made;** turn—13 sc.

Row 2: Sk first sc, sc across row; work picot; turn—12 sc.

Rows 3–11: Rep Row 2, dec 1 st at beg of each row—3 sc rem at end of Row 11.

Row 12: Sc in second sc, sl st in next sc; fasten off.

For next star point, join thread in same ch-2 sp of corner shell where Row 1 of first point began; rep rows 1–12 to complete next point.

Rep rows 1–12 for rem points.

continued

For the small star

Beg at center, ch 5, join with sl st to form ring.

Rnd 1: Ch 3, dc in ring; (ch 2, 2 dc in ring) 4 times; ch 2, join with sl st to top of beg ch-3.

Rnd 2: Sl st in next dc and into ch-2 sp; **ch 3, dc in same sp, ch 2, 2 dc in same sp—beg shell made;** ch 1, **in next ch-2 sp make 2 dc, ch 2, and 2 dc—shell made;** (ch 1, work shell in next ch-2 sp) 3 times; ch 1; join with sl st to top of beg ch-3.

Rnd 3: Sl st in next dc and into ch-2 sp; work beg shell in same sp; ch 1, 2 dc in next ch-1 sp, ch 1; (shell in next ch-2 sp, ch 1, 2 dc in next ch-1 sp, ch 1) 4 times; join to top of beg ch-3; fasten off.

STAR POINTS: *Row 1:* Attach thread in any ch-2 sp of any shell, ch 1, sc in same sp, (sc in next 2 dc and ch-sp) 3 times; **ch 3, sl st in third ch from hook—picot made;** turn—10 sc.

Row 2: Sk first sc, sc across row; work picot; turn—9 sc.

Rows 3–8: Rep Row 2, dec 1 st at beg of each row—3 sc at end of Row 8.

Row 9: Sc in second sc, sl st in next sc; fasten off.

For next star point, join thread in same ch-2 sp of shell where Row 1 of first point began; rep rows 1–9 to complete next point.

Rep rows 1–9 for rem points.

CHRISTMAS ANGEL

Shown on page 170.

Angel measures 13 inches tall.

MATERIALS

DMC Cebelia cotton thread, Size 10 (282-yard ball): 4 balls ecru; 1 ball camel (No. 437)

Size 7 steel crochet hook
12-inch-long dowel measuring $\frac{3}{16}$ inch in diameter
5-inch square of foam-core board for base
1 bag (12 oz.) polyester fiberfill
3 yards *each* of ⅛-inch-wide burgundy and forest green ribbon
Miniature grapevine wreath for halo
Assorted dried flowers for bouquet
Ecru sewing thread; needle
45-inch piece of ecru nylon netting
Seed pearls (optional)
Hot-glue gun or crafts glue

Abbreviations: See page 186.
Gauge: 8 dc = 1 inch; 4½ rows = 1 inch.

INSTRUCTIONS

The angel is made up of a crocheted cone-shaped body, a dress, arms, head, and wig.

CONE BASE: With ecru, ch 10; join with sl st to form ring.

Note: When working the base, always join with a sl st to top of beg ch-3 unless otherwise stated.

Rnd 1: Ch 3, work 13 dc in ring; join with sl st to top of beg ch-3.

Rnd 2: Ch 3, dc in joining, 2 dc in each dc around; join—28 sts.

Rnd 3: Rep Rnd 2—56 sts.

Rnd 4: Ch 3, dc in joining; * dc in next 3 dc, 2 dc in next dc; rep from * around; dc in last 3 dc; join—70 sts.

Rnd 5: Ch 3, dc in joining; * dc in next 6 dc, 2 dc in next dc; rep from * around; dc in last 6 dc; join—80 sts.

Rnd 6: Rep Rnd 5 *except* work 7 dc bet inc—90 sts.

Rnd 7: Rep Rnd 5 *except* work 8 dc bet inc—100 sts.

Rnd 8: Rep Rnd 5 *except* work 9 dc bet inc—110 sts.

Rnd 9: Rep Rnd 5 *except* work 10 dc bet inc; fasten off—120 sts.

Draw around crochet circle on foam-core board; cut out circle. Punch a small hole in the center of the board; set circle aside.

CONE BODY: Ch 6, join with sl st to form ring. Rep rnds 1–9 of Cone Base; do not fasten off.

Rnd 10: Note: On this rnd, the base piece and this piece are crocheted together. Place circles together right sides up with piece in progress on top. Ch 1, sc in joining of top circle *and at same time* through any dc of inside base circle. Work sc in each pair of dc until 60 sts are worked. Slip foam-core board between layers, making sure punched hole is beneath larger hole in the center of the crocheted base cover. Finish rnd to enclose board completely; join with sl st in first st.

Rnds 11–16: Ch 3, dc in each st around; join—120 sts. As work progresses, let side facing you be the outside of the body.

Rnd 17: Ch 3, dc in 21 dc, * **holding back last lp of each st on hook, dc in next 2 dc, yo, and draw through all lps on hook—dc-dec made;** dc in next 22 dc; rep from * around; dec over last 2 dc; join—115 sts.

Rnd 18: Ch 3, dc in each dc around.

Rnd 19: Ch 3, dc in 20 dc; * dec over next 2 dc, dc in next 21 dc; rep from * around; dec over last 2 dc, join—110 sts.

Rnd 20: Ch 3, dc in each dc around.

Rnds 21–45: Continue to dec 5 sts evenly spaced in each odd-numbered row as before. Work dc in each dc on even-numbered rows—45 sts at end of Rnd 45.

Rnds 46–51: Ch 3, dc in each dc around.

Before proceeding further, add hot glue to end of dowel rod and insert the glued end through center hole in crocheted base and into small hole in board. Stuff body firmly almost to top of work.

Rnd 52: Ch 3, (dec over next 2 dc) 22 times; join.

Rnd 53: Ch 3, (dec over next 2 dc) 11 times; join—12 sts; fasten off, leaving a 12-inch tail. Weave tail through top of all dc on this row. Insert additional stuffing as needed; draw up thread and knot securely.

BASE FOR HEAD: *Note:* These two rnds form the base for the head and the shoulder stitches for the arms.

Ch 6, join with sl st to form ring.

Rnd 1: Ch 1, (sc, ch 3) 8 times in ring; join last ch-3 with sl st in first sc.

Rnd 2: Ch 3, 2 dc in joining; (3 dc in next sc) 7 times; join to top of beg ch-3; do not fasten off.

FIRST ARM: *Note:* Next 2 steps are worked in rows.

Row 1: Ch 3, dc in 6 dc, ch 3; turn.

Row 2: Sk first dc, dc in 6 sts, ch 7, turn; join to top of ch-3.

Note: Work now begins to work in rnds.

Rnd 3: With right side of work as outside of the arm tube, ch 3, dc in 6 dc, 8 dc over ch-7 lp; join to top of beg ch-3—15 sts.

Rnds 4–23: Ch 3, dc in 14 dc; join to top of beg ch-3.

Row 24: Fold arm in half with joining at side, ch 1, make 7 sc across, catching in top lps of sts on both sides; turn.

Row 25 (hand): Sk 3 sc, work 8 dc in center sc; join with sl st in last sc; fasten off.

SECOND ARM: With top sides of rnds 1 and 2 of Base for Head facing, sk next 5 dc on base for head, join thread with sl st in sixth st, ch 3, dc in next 6 dc; ch 3, turn. Beg with Row 2, work Second Arm same as First Arm.

HEAD: *Note:* At ends of following rnds, join to top of beg ch-3 unless otherwise stated.

Rnd 1: Hold Base for Head so arm openings are facing down. Join thread with sl st in any ch-3 lp of Base for Head on Rnd 1; ch 3, dc in same lp, (2 dc in next ch-3 lp) 7 times; join—16 sts.

Rnd 2: Ch 3, dc in joining; * dc in next dc, 2 dc in next dc; rep from * around; dc in last dc; join—24 sts.

Rnd 3: Rep Rnd 2—36 sts.

Rnd 4: Ch 3, dc in joining; * dc in next 2 dc, 2 dc in next dc; rep from * around; dc in last 2 dc; join—48 sts.

Rnd 5: Ch 3, dc in joining; * dc in next 3 dc, 2 dc in next dc; rep from * around; dc in last 3 dc; join—60 sts.

Rnds 6–9: Ch 3, dc in each dc around.

Rnd 10: Ch 3, dc in next 2 dc; * dec over 2 dc, dc in next 3 dc; rep from * around; dec over last 2 dc; join—48 sts.

Rnd 11: Ch 3, dc in next dc, * dec over 2 dc, dc in next 2 dc; rep from * around; dec in last 2 dc; join—36 sts.

Rnd 12: Ch 3, * dec over 2 dc, dc in next dc; rep from * around; dec over last 2 dc; join—24 sts.

Rnd 13: Rep Rnd 12—16 sts.

Stuff head firmly before working next rnd.

Rnd 14: Ch 3, dc in next dc, (dec over next 2 dc) 7 times; join; fasten off.

Stuff arms so they are firm but still flexible. Sew arm top openings closed. Place flat section of the arm and head pieces over top of the dowel rod and body; sew down securely.

WIG: *Rnd 1:* With camel thread ch 4, work 7 dc in fourth ch from hook; join with sl st in top of ch.

Rnd 2: **Ch 3, work 4 dc in same st as join, drop lp from hook, insert hook in top of beg ch-3, draw dropped lp through, ch 1 tightly—beg popcorn (pc) made;** (ch 1, **in next dc work 5 dc, drop lp from hook, insert hook in top of first dc of 5-dc grp, draw dropped lp through, ch 1 tightly—pc made**) 7 times; end ch 1; join to top of beg pc.

Rnd 3: Ch 1, sc in joining; (2 sc in ch-1 sp, sc in next pc) 7 times, 2 sc in last ch-1 sp; join—24 sc.

Rnd 4: Work beg pc in joining; * dc in next sc, pc in next sc; rep from * around; dc in last sc; join to top of beg ch-3—12 pc.

Rnd 5: Ch 1, sc in joining; * 2 sc in dc, sc in pc; rep from * around; 2 sc in last dc; join to first sc—36 sc around.

Rnd 6: Rep Rnd 4—18 pc.

Rnd 7: Ch 1, sc in joining; * 2 sc in next st, sc in each of next 2 sts; rep from * around; sc in last st; join to first sc—48 sts.

Rnd 8: Rep Rnd 4—24 pc.

Rnd 9: Ch 1, sc in each st around; join—48 sts.

Rnd 10: Rep Rnd 4; ch 1, turn—24 pc.

Note: The sides of the wig will now be worked in rows.

continued

Row 11: (Sc in dc, sc in pc) 17 times, sc in next dc, leave rem 13 sts unworked; ch 3, turn—35 sc.

Row 12: Sk first sc; (pc in next sc, dc in next sc) 17 times; ch 1, turn—17 pc.

Row 13: Sc in each dc and pc across, sc in top of beg ch-3; ch 3, turn—35 sc.

Rows 14–16: Rep rows 12 and 13; then rep Row 12.

Row 17: Sk first dc, sc in next 5 sts; (**draw up lp in each of next 2 sts, yo, draw yarn through all 3 lps on hook—sc-dec made;** sc in next 5 sts) 4 times, do not sc in turning ch at end of row; ch 3, turn—29 sc.

Row 18: Sk first sc; (pc in next sc, dc in next sc) 14 times; ch 1, turn—14 pc.

Row 19: Sc in first dc; (sk pc, 7 dc in next dc, sk pc, sc in next dc) 7 times, making last sc in top of turning ch; fasten off.

Place wig on angel head and adjust for straightness. Sew by hand with thread, only around face.

DRESS: Beginning at neck edge with ecru, loosely ch 33.

Row 1: 2 dc in fourth ch from hook; (2 dc in next ch) 29 times more; ch 3, turn.

Row 2: Sk first dc, dc in each dc across row, dc in top of ch-3 at end; ch 3, turn—61 sts.

Note: Beg ch-3 counts as dc when working next row.

Row 3: Sk first dc, dc in next 2 dc, 2 dc in next dc; (dc in next 4 dc, 2 dc in next dc) 11 times, dc in last 2 sts. Drop ecru from hook, but do not fasten off—73 sts.

Row 4: Join second ball of ecru in top of ch-3 at beg of Row 3. Working in back lps (sk 2 dc, 7 dc in next dc, sk 2 dc, sc in next dc) 12 times; fasten off.

Row 5 (right side of dress): With first ball of ecru, ch 3, sk first dc; working across in both lps of unworked sts of Row 3 and in back lps of those already worked in Row 3, dc in next 9 dc, ch 12 loosely, sk 17 dc, dc in 19 dc, ch 12, sk 17 dc, dc in last 10 sts; ch 3, turn—2 ch-12 lps form sleeve openings.

Row 6: Ch 3, sk first dc, dc in next 2 dc. Working in each dc and in each ch of the ch-12 lp under each arm, * 2 dc in next st, dc in next 3 sts; rep from * across; end dc in last 2 dc and top of turning ch; ch 3, turn—78 sts.

Row 7: Sk first dc, dc in each dc across; ch 4, turn—78 sts.

Row 8: Dc in next dc; * ch 1, sk dc, dc in next st; rep from * across; ch 3, turn—39 ch-1 sp.

Row 9: Sk first sp; * in next sp work dc, ch 1, and dc, dc in next sp; rep from * across; do not work dc in last sp, instead sk ch, dc in next ch; ch 3, turn.

Row 10: * Sk next dc, **work 2 dc, ch 2, and 2 dc in next ch-1 sp—shell made;** sk dc, dc in next dc; rep from * across; ch 3, turn.

Rows 11–16: * Shell in sp of next shell, dc in dc bet shells; rep from * across; dc at end; ch 3, turn.

Row 17: (Shell in shell, dc in dc) twice; * dc in same st as last dc; (shell in shell, dc in dc) 3 times; rep from * across; end (shell in shell, dc in dc) twice; ch 3, turn.

Row 18: (Shell in shell, dc in next dc) twice; * ch 1, dc in next dc; (shell in shell, dc in dc) 3 times; rep from * across, end as for Row 17; ch 3, turn.

Row 19: (Shell in shell, dc in dc) twice; * in ch-1 sp work dc, ch 1, and dc; dc in next dc; (shell in shell, dc in dc) 3 times; rep from * across, end as before; ch 3, turn.

Row 20: Shell in shell, dc in dc, shell in shell, * dc bet second dc

of shell and next dc, shell in ch-1 sp, dc bet second dc and next shell; (shell in shell, dc in dc) twice, shell in shell; rep from * across; end (shell in shell, dc in dc) twice; ch 3, turn.

Rows 21–26: Rep rows 11–16.

Rows 27–36: Rep rows 17–26. Ch 5 to turn at end of Row 36.

Row 37: * Dc in sp of shell, ch 2, dc in dc bet shells, ch 2; rep from * across; dc in last st; ch 1, turn—66 sps.

Row 38: * Sk sp, 9 trc in next sp, sk sp, sc in next dc; rep from * across; end with sc in third ch of turning ch-5; fasten off—22 scallops across.

Row 39: With right side of dress facing, attach ecru with sl st in first trc on first scallop of Row 38; ch 3, dc in second trc, * (dc in next trc, ch 3, sl st in top of dc just made, dc in same trc) 5 times; **holding back last lp of each st, work dc in next 2 trc, dc in next sc, dc in first 2 trc of next scallop, yo, draw through all lps on hook—cluster (cl) made;** rep from * across; end dc-dec over last 2 trc; fasten off.

SLEEVES: Hold dress with the right side out and work around each armhole as follows:

Rnd 1: Sk first 6 ch of underarm, attach ecru with sc in seventh ch; work sc in rem 5 ch, 3 sc around post of dc of Row 5 of Dress, sc in first 8 dc under ruffle at top of armhole, 2 sc in center dc, sc in rem 8 dc, 3 sc around post of dc of Row 5, sc in last 6 underarm ch; join with sl st in first sc—36 sc.

Rnd 2: Ch 3, * sk sc, in next sc work dc, ch 1, and dc; sk sc, dc in next sc; rep from * around; join with sl st in top of beg ch-3.

Rnd 3: Sl st in dc, ch-1 sp, 3 dc, ch-1 sp, and 2 dc; * (sk dc, shell in next ch-1 sp, sk dc, dc in next dc)

4 times, sk dc, shell in ch-1 sp, sk dc, sl st in rem dc and ch-1 sp of rnd; sl st in joining.

Rnd 4: Ch 3; working over sl st of Rnd 3, (shell in ch-1 sp, dc in center dc) twice; (shell in shell, dc in dc bet shells) 5 times; shell in ch-1 sp, dc in center dc, shell in ch-1 sp; join—9 shells.

Rnds 5–10: Ch 3, (shell in shell, dc in dc bet shells) 8 times; shell in last shell; join.

Rnd 11: Ch 3, (dc in sp of next shell, dc in dc bet shells) 8 times; dc in last shell; join.

Rnd 12: Ch 1, sc in joining, sc in each dc around, join in first sc—18 sc.

Rnds 13–32: Ch 1, sc in each sc around; join in first sc.

Rnd 33: Ch 1, sc in first sc; * **ch 3, sl st in top of sc just made— picot made;** sc in next 2 sc; rep from * around; end with sc in last sc; join, fasten off.

Work second sleeve in same manner as first sleeve.

FINISHING: Place dress on figure. If necessary, use crochet hook to carefully pull arm through lower part of sleeve. Starting at lower edge of skirt, hand-sew back opening.

Trim the dress around the waist and hemline with ribbons. Hand-sew seed pearls or other beads to the dress, if desired.

For the halo, hot-glue some dried flowers to the miniature wreath; sew the wreath to the top of the wig.

Make a miniature bouquet or fill a miniature basket with dried flowers. Bring the hands together and sew or hot-glue one of these items to the angel's hands. Make the wings using the length of netting. Cut the netting into an 18x45-inch piece. Tie netting into a bow and tack onto the back of the angel.

MEDALLION SNOWFLAKES

Shown on page 171.

Medallions measure 5 inches in diameter.

MATERIALS
For several ornaments
DMC Cebelia crochet cotton, Size 30 (50-gram ball): One ball of white
Size 10 steel crochet hook

Abbreviations: See page 186.
Gauge: 14 dc = 1 inch; 7 rows = 1 inch.

INSTRUCTIONS
ROUND SNOWFLAKE: Ch 8, join with sl st to form ring.

Rnd 1: Ch 3, work 19 dc in ring; join with sl st in top of beg ch-3.

Rnd 2: Ch 3, (2 dc in next dc, dc in next dc) 9 times, 2 dc in last dc; join with sl st in top of beg ch-3— 30 dc counting beg ch-3 as dc.

Rnd 3: Ch 3, (2 dc in next dc, dc in each of next 2 dc) 9 times, 2 dc in next dc, dc in last dc; join with sl st in top of beg ch-3—40 sts.

Rnd 4: Ch 1, sc in same place as joining; (ch 10, sk 3 dc, sc in next dc) 9 times; ch 4, dtr (yo hook 3 times) in first sc.

Rnd 5: Ch 3, work 2 dc in lp just made; (ch 10, 3 dc in next lp) 9 times; ch 4, dtr in top of beg ch-3.

Rnd 6: Sc in lp just made, (ch 12, sc in next lp) 9 times; ch 12, join with sl st in first sc.

Rnd 7: Work 15 sc over each ch-12 lp; join with sl st in first sc.

Rnd 8: Sl st in next sc, (sc in next 11 sc, ch 5, sk next 4 sc) 10 times; join with sl st in first sc.

Rnd 9: (Sc in next 9 sc, ch 5, sc in next lp, ch 5, sk next sc) 10 times; join with sl st in first sc.

Rnd 10: * Sc in next 7 sc; (ch 5, sc in next lp) twice, ch 5, sk next sc; rep from * around; join with sl st in first sc.

Rnd 11: * Sc in next 5 sc; (ch 5, sc in next lp) 3 times, ch 5, sk next sc; rep from * around; join with sl st in first sc.

Rnd 12: * Sc in next 3 sc; (ch 5, sc in next lp) 4 times, ch 5, sk next sc; rep from * around; end ch 2, dc in first sc.

Rnd 13: Sc in lp just made, * ch 3, sc in next lp; (ch 5, sc in next lp) 4 times; rep from * around; end ch 2, dc in first sc.

Rnd 14: Sc in lp just made; (ch 5, sc in next ch-5 lp) around, skipping all ch-3 sp; end with sl st in first sc.

Rnd 15: Sl st in next lp, ch 3, 2 dc in same lp, **ch 5, sl st in top of last dc—picot made,** 3 dc in same lp; * ch 3, sc in next lp, ch 3; work 3 dc, picot, and 3 dc in next lp; rep from * around; end ch 3, sl st in top of beg ch-3; fasten off.

PINEAPPLE SNOWFLAKE: Ch 7, join with sl st to form ring.

Rnd 1: Ch 3, dc in ring, (ch 2, 2 dc in ring) 5 times; ch 2, join with sl st in top of beg ch-3.

Rnd 2: **Sl st in next dc and into ch-2 sp; ch 3, work dc, ch 2, and 2 dc in same sp—beg shell made;** * ch 2, in next sp make **2 dc, ch 2, and 2 dc—shell made;** rep from * around; end ch 2, join with sl st in top of beg ch-3.

Rnd 3: Sl st in next dc and into ch-2 sp, work beg shell in same sp; * ch 2, dc in ch-2 sp bet shells; ch 2, shell in ch-2 sp of next shell; rep from * 4 times more; ch 2, dc in ch-2 sp, ch 2; join with sl st in top of beg ch-3.

Note: Hereafter all rnds start with beg shell in first shell; all rnds end with joining of sl st in top of beg ch-3.

continued

Rnd 4: * Shell in shell, ch 2, sk 2 dc of shell, work dc, ch 3, and dc in next dc, ch 2; rep from * around; join.

Rnd 5: * Shell in shell, ch 1, 10 trc in ch-3 sp, ch 1; rep from * around; join.

Rnd 6: * Shell in shell, ch 3, sk first trc, sc in 9 trc, ch 3; rep from * around; join.

Rnd 7: * Shell in shell, ch 4, sk first sc, sc in 8 sc, ch 4; rep from * around; join.

Rnd 8: * Shell in shell, ch 2, 2 dc in same shell sp, ch 5, sk first sc, sc in 7 sc, ch 5; rep from * around; join.

Rnd 9: * Shell in first ch-2 sp, ch 5, shell in next ch-2 sp, ch 5, sk first sc, sc in 6 sc, ch 5; rep from * around; join.

Rnd 10: * Shell in shell, ch 5; work dc, ch 3, and dc in third ch of ch-5 lp; ch 5, shell in shell, ch 5, sk first sc, sc in 5 sc, ch 5; rep from * around; join.

Rnd 11: * Shell in shell, ch 3, sc in ch-5 lp, ch 3, 10 trc in ch-3 sp, ch 3, sc in next ch-5 lp, ch 3, shell in shell; ch 5, **holding back last lp of each dc on hook, work dc in each of next 5 sc, yo, and draw through all lps on hook—cluster (cl) made;** ch 5; rep from * around; join.

Rnd 12: * Shell in shell, ch 5, trc in first trc, **(ch 5, sl st in top of last trc—picot made;** ch 1, trc in next trc) 9 times, ch 5, shell in shell, ch 3, trc in top of cl, ch 3; rep from * around; join; fasten off.

SPIDERWEB SNOWFLAKE:
Ch 7, join with sl st to form ring.

Rnd 1: Ch 3, dc in ring; (ch 2, 2 dc in ring) 5 times; ch 2, join with sl st in top of beg ch-3.

Rnd 2: Sl st in next dc and into ch-2 sp, ch 5, dc in same sp; (dc in next 2 dc, work dc, ch 2, and dc in next sp) 5 times; dc in last 2 dc; join in third ch of beg ch-5.

Rnd 3: Sl st into ch-2 sp, ch 5, dc in same sp; (dc in next 4 dc, work dc, ch 2, and dc in next sp) 5 times; dc in last 4 dc; join with sl st in third ch of beg ch-5.

Rnd 4: Sl st into ch-2 sp, ch 5, dc in same sp; * dc in next 3 dc, ch 10, dc in next 3 dc; work dc, ch 2, and dc in next sp; rep from * around; end dc in last 3 dc; join with sl st in third ch of beg ch-5.

Rnd 5: Sl st into ch-2 sp, ch 5, dc in same sp; * dc in next 2 dc, ch 5, sk 2 dc, sc in ch-10 lp, ch 5, sk 2 dc, dc in next 2 dc; work dc, ch 2, and dc in next sp; rep from * around; end dc in last 2 dc; join with sl st in third ch of beg ch-5.

Rnd 6: Sl st into ch-2 sp, ch 5, dc in same sp; * dc in next dc, ch 6, sc in ch-5 lp, sc in sc, sc in next ch-5 lp; ch 6, sk 2 dc, dc in next dc; work dc, ch 2, and dc in next sp; rep from * around; end with dc in last dc; join with sl st in third ch of beg ch-5.

Rnd 7: Ch 3, * 2 dc in next ch-2 sp, dc in next dc, ch 7, sc in ch-6 lp, sc in 3 sc, sc in next ch-6 lp, ch 7, sk dc, dc in next dc; rep from * around; end ch 7; join with sl st in top of beg ch-3.

Rnd 8: Sl st in next 3 dc, ch 3, * 3 dc in ch-7 lp, ch 6, sk sc, sc in 3 sc, ch 6, 3 dc in next ch-7 lp, dc in next dc, ch 8, sk 2 dc, dc in next dc; rep from * around; end ch 8; join with sl st in top of beg ch-3.

Rnd 9: Sl st in next 3 dc, ch 3, * 3 dc in ch-6 lp, ch 2, sk sc, trc in center sc, ch 2, 3 dc in next ch-6 lp, dc in next dc, ch 6, sc in ch-8 lp, ch 6, sk 3 dc, dc in next dc; rep from * around; end with ch 6; join with sl st in top of beg ch-3.

Rnd 10: Sl st in next 2 dc, ch 3, dc in next dc, * 2 dc in sp, 2 dc in trc, 2 dc in next sp, dc in next 2 dc, ch 7, sc in ch-6 lp, sc in sc, sc in next ch-6 lp, ch 7, sk 2 dc, dc in next 2 dc; rep from * around; end with ch 7; join with sl st in top of beg ch-3.

Rnd 11: Sl st in next 5 dc, ch 3, dc in next 3 dc, * ch 8, sc in ch-7 lp, sc in 3 sc, sc in next ch-7 lp, ch 8, dc in next 4 dc, ch 2, dc in next 4 dc; rep from * around; end with ch 2; join with sl st in beg ch-3.

Rnd 12: Sl st in next 2 dc, ch 3, dc in next dc, * 2 dc in ch-8 lp, ch 7, sk sc, sc in 3 sc, ch 7, 2 dc in next ch-8 lp, dc in first 2 dc, ch 5, sc in ch-2 sp, ch 5, sk 2 dc, dc in next 2 dc; rep from * around; end with ch 5; join with sl st in top of beg ch-3.

Rnd 13: Sl st in next 2 dc, ch 3, dc in next dc, * 2 dc in ch-7 lp, ch 7, sk sc, sc in next sc, ch 7, 2 dc in next ch-7 lp, dc in next 2 dc, ch 7, sc in ch-5 lp, sc in sc, sc in next ch-5 lp, ch 7, sk 2 dc, dc in next 2 dc; rep from * around; end with ch 7, join with sl st in top of beg ch-3.

Rnd 14: Sl st in next 2 dc, ch 3, dc in next dc, * 2 dc in ch-7 lp, ch 12, 2 dc in next ch-7 lp, dc in next 2 dc, ch 8, sc in ch-7 lp, sc in 3 sc, sc in next ch-7 lp, ch 8, sk 2 dc, dc in next 2 dc; rep from * around; end ch 8; sc in top of beg ch-3.

Rnd 15: Sc in next 3 dc, * (2 sc in ch-12 lp, **ch 5, sl st in top of last sc—picot made)** 5 times, 2 sc in same lp; sc in 4 dc, 8 sc in ch-8 lp, sc in next 5 sc; 8 sc in ch-8 lp; sc in 4 dc; rep from * around; join with sl st in first sc; fasten off.

VICTORIAN ORNAMENTS

Shown on page 173.

The stocking measures 6 inches long, the angel measures 4 inches high, and the cornucopia measures 5½ inches long.

MATERIALS

J. & P. Coats Knit-Cro-Sheen (150-yard ball) in the following colors to make six *each* of the three ornament designs: 6 balls of cream (No. 42); 1 ball *each* jade (No. 50) and pink (No. 35)
Size 2 steel crochet hook
Pipe cleaners
⅛ yard unbleached muslin
Polyester fiberfill
Fabric stiffener

Abbreviations: See page 186.
Gauge: 7 sc = 1 inch.

INSTRUCTIONS
For the sock
Beg along the top edge of the stocking, ch 38 with cream.

Row 1: Sc in second ch from hook; * sk ch, 5 dc in next ch, sk ch, sc in next ch; rep from * across; ch 3, turn.

Row 2: Sk first sc; * sk next dc, hdc in next dc, sc in next dc, hdc in next dc, sk dc, dc in next sc; rep from * across; ch 1, turn.

Row 3 (right side): Work sc in first dc; (sk hdc, **5 dc in next sc—shell made,** sk hdc, sc in next dc) 8 times; sk hdc, shell in next sc, sk hdc, sc in top of turning ch; ch 3, turn.

Rep rows 2 and 3 for pattern. Work evenly until there are 14 rows total (ending with Row 2); fasten off.

HEEL: With wrong side facing, fold stocking top in half so back seam is together, count back 9 sts on right-hand side of work, and join yarn; sc across to seam opening; sc across first 10 sts of left-hand side of work (this joins back-seam opening to make heel); ch 1, turn. Work 5 more rows of sc over these 19 sts—18 sts rem for front part of stocking for instep.

TURNING THE HEEL: Sc across 13 sts, ch 1, turn. Sc across 7 sts, ch 1, turn. Sc across 7 sts; sc in first unworked st 2 rows below, ch 1, turn. Sc across 8 sts; sc in first unworked st 2 rows below, ch 1, turn.

Continue in this manner, increasing one st at the end of each row until there are 19 sts across; fasten off.

FOOT: With wrong side facing, count back to the 10th sc of the 19 sc sts just completed and join cream; ch 1, sc in same st as join; (sk st, shell in next st, sk next st, sc in next st) twice; sk next row.

Working in the rows along the side of heel, shell in next row, sk next row, sc in next row, sk next row, shell in next row, sk next row; sc in next row; shell in first sc of instep sts, sc in next dc; rep shell pat across instep sts, ending with shell in last sc.

Working along rows of heel sts, sc in first row, sk next row, shell in next row, sk next row, sc in next row, sk next row, shell in next row.

Working along rem heel sts, sk first sc, sc in next sc, sk next sc, shell in next sc, sk next sc, sc in next sc, sk next sc, shell in next sc; ch 3, turn—13 shells across.

Next row: * Hdc in next dc, sc in next dc, hdc in next dc, dc in sc, sk next dc; rep from * across row; end with dc in last sc, ch 1, turn.

Dec row 1: Sc in first dc; (shell in next sc, sc in next dc) 5 times; sk 5 sts, shell in next sc, sk 5 sts, sc in dc; (shell in next sc, sc in next dc) 5 times; ch 3, turn.

Next row: Rep Row 2 of sock.

Dec row 2: Sc in first dc; (shell in next sc, sc in next dc) 4 times; shell in next sc, sk 3 sts, sc in sc, sk 3 sts; (shell in next sc, sc in next dc) 5 times; ch 3, turn.

Next row: Rep Row 2 of sock.

Dec row 3: Sc in first dc; (shell in next sc, sc in next dc) 4 times; shell in next dc, sc in next dc; rep bet ( )s 4 times; ch 3, turn.

Next row: Rep Row 2 of sock—37 sts across.

Next row: Rep Row 3 of sock.
Next row: Rep Row 2 of sock.

TOE: *Row 1:* **Draw up lp in first 2 sc, yo, draw through 3 lps on hook—sc-dec made;** sc in next 3 sts, work sc-dec over next 2 sts, sc in next 23 sts, sc-dec over next 2 sts, sc in next 3 sts; sc-dec over last 2 sts; ch 1, turn—33 sc.

Row 2: Work sc-dec; (sc in next 2 sc, sc-dec over next 2 sc) across row; sc in last sc; ch 1, turn—25 sc across.

Row 3: (Work sc-dec over 2 sts, sc in next st) across; sc in last st—17 sc.

Row 4: (Sc-dec) across; sc in last sc—9 sc; fasten off.

continued

Sew bottom of foot and toe seam; leave back seam open.

CUFF: (Make three jade cuffs and three pink cuffs for six ornaments.) With the appropriate color, ch 40.

Row 1: Sc in second ch from hook and each ch across; ch 1, turn—39 sc.

Row 2: Sc in each sc across; ch 1, turn.

Rows 3–6: Rep Row 2.

JOINING CUFF: Join alternate contrasting color (jade or pink); ch 1, work sc in first st of cuff, insert hook through second st of cuff and first ch of stocking top; sc through both cuff and stocking in this and every st of both pieces across, ending with sc through last st of cuff only; fasten off color in use; join cream, ch 1, turn.

Sc in first st, (sk st, shell in next st, sk st, sc in next st) across, ending with sc in last 2 sts, ch 10 for hanging loop, sl st to second-to-last sc; fasten off.

BOTTOM OF CUFF EDGING: With right side facing, join alternate contrasting color with ch 1 at bottom of cuff; work 1 row sc along edge, change to cream, ch 1, turn.

Sc in first 3 sts; * sk st, shell in next st, sk st, sc in next st; rep from * across; fasten off.

FINISHING: Referring to Chart 3 on page 184, cross-stitch jade cuffs with pink hearts and pink cuffs with jade trees.

Sew back seam of stocking closed. Sew back seam of cuff.

Use fabric stiffener to stiffen stocking; stuff with plastic wrap to retain shape. Let dry and remove plastic wrap.

For the angel ornament

SKIRT: Begin skirt same as stocking top. Work even in pattern until there are 10 rows total, ending with Row 2; fasten off cream; join pink; ch 1, turn.

Work 2 rows of sc with pink; change to cream, ch 1, turn.

EDGING: Sc in first st; * sk st, shell in next st, sk st, sc in next st; rep from * across; end with sc in last st; fasten off.

Sew back seam of skirt; gather top. Dip in fabric stiffener and dry over an inverted small paper cup so that skirt is puffed out.

HEAD: With cream, ch 3; join with sl st to form ring.

Rnd 1: Work 7 sc in ring; join with sl st to beg sc.

Rnd 2: Work 2 sc in every sc around; sl st to join—14 sc.

Rnd 3: * Sc in next sc, 2 sc in next sc; rep from * around; sl st to join—21 sc.

Rnds 4–8: Sc in each st around; sl st to join.

Rnd 9: * Sc in next sc, **draw up lp in next 2 sts, yo, draw through all lps on hook—sc-dec made;** rep from * around; sl st to join—14 sc.

Stuff head with a small amount of fiberfill.

Rnd 10: (Sc-dec) around; sl st to join—7 sc.

Rnd 11: Sc in each st around; sl st to join. Gather all sts at bottom of head, leaving tail of yarn to sew head onto body.

Dip head into stiffener, leaving yarn tail dry. Allow to dry.

SLEEVES: With cream, ch 17. Sc in second ch from hook and in each ch across—16 sts; ch 1, turn. Work even in sc for 3¼ inches from beginning. Fasten off cream.

Join pink, ch 1. Work 2 rows of sc; fasten off. Join cream, ch 1, sc in same st as join; * sk next st, shell in next st, sk next st, sc in next st; rep from * across; end with sc in last st; fasten off.

Join pink at beg edge of ch-17 sleeve, ch 1. Work sleeve edging with pink and cream as before. Fold sleeve in half lengthwise and sew sleeve seam closed.

ARMS: Fold both ends of pipe cleaner down. Cut 2-inch strips of unbleached muslin, and wrap around ends of pipe cleaner to form covered hands. Sew ends of muslin securely with needle and thread. Thread arms through sleeves. Dip in stiffener and mold covered arms into a wide U shape to dry.

WINGS: (Make 2 for each angel.) With cream, ch 5.

Row 1: Dc in fourth ch from hook, dc in last ch; ch 5, turn.

Row 2: Dc in first dc, ch 2, sk dc, dc in top of beg ch, ch 2, dc in same st; ch 6, turn.

Row 3: Dc in ch-2 sp, ch 2, dc in top of next dc, ch 2, dc in top of next dc, ch 2; work dc, ch 2, and dc in turning ch-5 lp; ch 5, turn.

Row 4: Dc in next dc; (ch 3, dc in next dc) 3 times; ch 3, sk 2 ch, dc in fourth ch of turning ch; ch 6, turn.

Row 5: Dc in next dc; (ch 4, dc in next dc) 3 times; ch 4, sk 3 ch, dc in fourth ch of turning ch; ch 7, turn.

Row 6: Dc in next dc; (ch 5, dc in next dc) 3 times; ch 5, sk 4 ch, dc in fifth ch of turning ch; ch 1, turn.

Row 7: Sc in first st; (sk 2 ch, shell in next ch, sk 2 ch, sc in next dc) 4 times; sk 2 ch, shell in next ch, sk 2 ch, sc in next ch; fasten off. Stiffen wings on plastic-covered flat surface to dry.

When dry, sew head on top of skirt. With arms facing forward, tack them on back of skirt; tack wings in center of arms.

To make a hanging loop, ch a 3-inch length with cream; form a loop and sew it to the back of the angel above the wings.

For the cornucopia
With cream, ch 7.

Row 1: Sc in second ch from hook, sc in next 5 ch; ch 1, turn—6 sc.

Row 2: * 2 sc in next st, sc in next st; rep from * across; ch 1, turn—9 sc.

Row 3: Sc in each sc; ch 1, turn.

Row 4: * 2 sc in next st, sc in next st; rep from * across; end 2 sc in last st, ch 1, turn—14 sc.

Row 5: Sc in each sc; ch 1, turn.

Row 6: Rep Row 2—21 sc.

Row 7: Sc in each sc; ch 1, turn.

Row 8: Sc in first st; * sk sc, 3 dc in next sc, sk sc, sc in next st; rep from * across; ch 3, turn.

Row 9: * Hdc in next dc, sc in next dc, hdc in next dc, dc in sc; rep from * across; ch 1, turn.

Row 10: Sc in first st; * sk hdc, **5 dc in next sc—shell made;** sk hdc, sc in dc; rep from * across; end sc in top of turning ch-3; ch 3, turn.

Row 11: * Sk next dc, hdc in next dc, sc in next dc, hdc in next dc, sk dc, dc in next sc; rep from * across; ch 1, turn.

Row 12: 2 sc in first dc; * sk hdc, shell in next sc, sk hdc, 2 sc in next dc; rep from * across; end 2 sc in top of turning ch-3; ch 3, turn.

Row 13: Dc in next sc; * sk next dc, hdc in next dc, sc in next dc, hdc in next dc, sk dc, dc in next 2 sc; rep from * across; ch 1, turn.

Row 14: Sc in dc, ch 1, sc in next dc; * sk next hdc, shell in next sc, sk next hdc, sc in next dc, ch 1, sc in next dc; rep from * across; end with last sc in top of turning ch-3; ch 3, turn.

Row 15: Dc in ch-1 sp, dc in next sc; * sk next dc, hdc in next dc, sc in dc, hdc in dc, sk dc, dc in sc, dc in ch-1 sp, dc in sc; rep from * across; ch 1, turn.

Row 16: 2 sc in first dc, sc in next dc, 2 sc in next dc; * sk hdc, shell in sc, sk hdc, 2 sc in dc, sc in dc, 2 sc in dc; rep from * across; end with 2 sc in top of turning ch-3; ch 3, turn.

Row 17: Sk 2 sc, dc in next sc, ch 1, dc in same sc; * sk next 3 sts, hdc in next dc, sc in dc, hdc in dc, sk next 3 sts, dc in center sc, ch 1, dc in same sc; rep from * across; end dc in last sc; ch 1, turn.

Row 18: Sc in first dc, sk next dc, 3 dc in ch-1 sp, sc in next dc; * sk hdc, 5 dc in sc, sk hdc, sc in next dc, 3 dc in ch-1 sp, sc in next dc; rep from * across; end with last sc in top of ch-3; ch 3, turn.

Row 19: Hdc in dc, sc in dc, hdc in dc, dc in sc; * sk dc, hdc in next dc, sc in dc, hdc in dc, sk dc, dc in sc, hdc in dc, sc in dc, hdc in dc, dc in sc; rep from * across; ch 1, turn.

Row 20: Rep Row 10.

Row 21: Rep Row 11.

Work 7 rows of sc over rem 45 sts; fasten off.

CUFF: (Make three jade cuffs and three pink cuffs for six ornaments.) With appropriate color, ch 48. Sc in second ch from hook, sc in next 46 ch; ch 1, turn.

Referring to previous stocking cuff instructions, make cuff, edging, and joining as for stocking. Sew seams as for stocking. Embroider hearts and trees as for stocking.

Stiffen cornucopia with fabric stiffener, shaping over a plastic-covered cone to dry. To make a hanging loop, ch a 3-inch strand of cream; form a loop and sew to open edge of cornucopia.

VICTORIAN STOCKING

Shown on page 172.

Stocking measures 20½ inches long.

MATERIALS

Patons Canadiana worsted-weight yarn (100-gram ball): 1 ball *each* ecru (No. 104), green (No. 46), and pink (No. 11)
Sizes G and H aluminum crochet hooks
Tapestry needle

Abbreviations: See page 186.
Gauge: 23 sts = 6 inches with Size H hook over sc.

INSTRUCTIONS

With Size H hook and green, ch 60. Sc in second ch from hook and in each ch across—59 sts; ch 1, turn.

Continue working evenly in sc with green until there are 22 total sc rows; fasten off green. Join ecru, ch 1 at end of last row; turn.

CLUSTER BAND: *Row 1:* With ecru, sc in each st across.

Row 2: Sc in first sc, * **in next sc (yo, draw up lp) 3 times, yo and draw through all lps—cluster (cl) made;** sc in next sc, rep from * across.

Row 3: Sc in each st across; fasten off ecru; join pink, ch 1 at end of last row; turn.

SINGLE-CROCHET BANDS: Work 6 rows sc with pink; fasten off pink; join ecru, ch 1 at end of last row, turn.

Work rows 1–3 of cluster band, changing to green after last st of third row; ch 1, turn.

continued

Work 6 rows sc with green; fasten off green; join ecru, ch 1 at end of last row, turn.

Work rows 1–3 of cluster band, fasten off ecru; join pink, ch 1 at end of last row, turn.

Work 6 rows of sc with pink; fasten off.

HEEL: *Row 1:* With right side facing and ecru, work sc in each of last 14 sts of last row, bring work around, and sc in first 14 sc to join sides and begin heel; ch 1, turn.

Row 2: Work sc in first 20 sc; ch 1, turn.

Row 3: Work 1 sc in first 12 sc; ch 1, turn.

Row 4: Sc back across 12 sc, work 1 sc in first st after turn (2 rows below); ch 1, turn.

Row 5: Sc back across 13 sc, work 1 sc in first st after turn (the next unworked st in row below); ch 1, turn.

Continuing in this manner, pick up 1 st in each row to turn heel until there are 26 sts across base of heel; fasten off.

FOOT: With right side facing, join ecru and work rows 1–3 of cluster band over unworked 31 sts at ankle; fasten off.

Beg at center back of heel, with right side facing and green, work across 13 heel sts, sc in all ankle sts, work across rem 13 heel sts— 57 sts.

Work 5 more rows of sc with green; fasten off.

Join ecru at end of last row, ch 1, turn.

Work rows 1–3 of cluster band; fasten off ecru; join pink, ch 1 at end of last row, turn.

Work 6 rows of sc with pink; fasten off pink; join ecru, ch 1 at end of last row, turn.

Work rows 1 and 2 of cluster band, ch 1, turn.

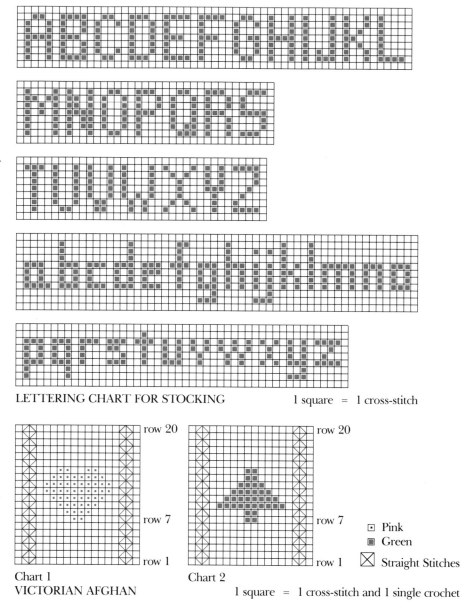

LETTERING CHART FOR STOCKING   1 square = 1 cross-stitch

Chart 1
VICTORIAN AFGHAN

Chart 2

row 20
row 7
row 1

☐ Pink
▣ Green
☒ Straight Stitches

1 square = 1 cross-stitch and 1 single crochet

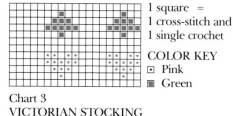

1 square =
1 cross-stitch and
1 single crochet

COLOR KEY
☐ Pink
▣ Green

Chart 3
VICTORIAN STOCKING
AND ORNAMENTS

3		5
4	6	
2	8	
1	7	

1 single
crochet

Chart 4
DETAIL OF STITCHING
SEQUENCE

TOE SHAPING: Sc in first 27 sts; **draw up lp in each of next 2 sc, yo and draw through 2 lps— sc-dec made**; join another ball of yarn in last dec st with ch 1, sc-dec over next 2 sts; sc across 27 sts.

Working both halves of row at same time, dec 1 st at *each end of every row* until 10 sts rem on each toe half; fasten off.

CROSS-STITCHING THE BANDS: Referring to Chart 3, *opposite*, cross-stitch pink hearts on green bands and green trees on pink bands, working 1 cross-stitch over 1 sc. Working on the bands *above the heel*, stitch six motifs equally spaced on each band with 8 sc between the bottom stitch of each motif. For these bands, begin stitching the bottom st of the first motif in the eighth sc from the edge. On the bands *below the heel*, begin stitching the bottom st of the first motif in the seventh sc from the edge.

ASSEMBLY: Sew back seams of stocking above and below heel. Sew the triangles at the heels shut. Sew toe stitches together.

CUFF: With Size H hook and pink, ch 62. Sc in second ch from hook and in each ch across—61 sts; fasten off pink.

Join ecru; work Row 2 of cluster band; work 11 rows even in sc; work Row 2 of cluster band; fasten off. Place cuff over stocking so top band of sock and cuff overlap. With Size G hook and pink yarn, sc top of sock and cuff together, working 2 sc in two of the sock sts to increase sock to match cuff—61 sts; change to ecru in last lp of this st, ch 1, turn.

CUFF EDGINGS: Sc in first st; * sk sc, 5 dc in next st, sk sc, sc in next st; rep from * across; fasten off. With wrong side of cuff facing and Size G hook, join ecru yarn along opposite edge of cuff, sc in first st; ** sk sc, 5 dc in next st, sk sc, sc in next st; rep from ** across; fasten off. Sew cuff seam closed.

With ecru and Size G hook, ch 10 to form a loop for hanging. Sew to top edge of cuff along seam edge.

CROSS-STITCHING THE CUFF: Cross-stitch name in pink, following the lettering chart, *opposite, top.* Backstitch the letters in green.

VICTORIAN AFGHAN

Shown on page 172.

Afghan measures approximately 48x60 inches.

MATERIALS

Patons Canadiana worsted-weight yarn (100-gram ball) in the following colors: 9 balls of ecru (No. 104); 8 balls *each* of green (No. 46) and pink (No. 11)
Sizes G and H aluminum crochet hooks
Tapestry needle

Abbreviations: See page 186.
Gauge: 23 sts = 6 inches with Size H hook over sc.

INSTRUCTIONS

With Size H hook and ecru, ch 232; sc in second ch from hook and in each ch across—231 sts across the length of the afghan; ch 1, turn.

Row 1 (wrong side): Work sc in first sc, * **in next sc (yo, draw up lp) 3 times, yo and draw through all lps—cluster (cl) made;** sc in next sc; rep from * across; ch 1, turn.

Row 2 (right side): Sc in each st across; ch 4, turn.

Row 3: Sk sc, dc in next sc, * ch 1, sk sc, dc in next sc; rep from * across; ch 1, turn.

Row 4: Sc in each dc and ch-1 sp across row—231 sts; ch 1, turn.

Rows 5–6: Rep rows 1 and 2; fasten off ecru.

** Join green yarn at right side of work. Work 18 rows sc—231 sts in each row; fasten off green; change to ecru; work 1 row sc.

Rep rows 1–6; fasten off ecru.

Join pink yarn at right side of work. Work 18 rows sc—231 st; fasten off pink; change to ecru; work 1 row sc.

Rep rows 1–6; fasten off ecru.

Rep from ** until there are 4 green panels and 4 pink panels. Rep rows 1–6 with ecru; fasten off.

TOP AND BOTTOM EDGING: With Size G hook and ecru, sc across one short side (top) of afghan; ch 1, turn. Rep rows 1 and 2 over these sts; fasten off.

Join ecru on opposite side (bottom) and work as for top of afghan; leave yarn attached after Row 2 is completed; ch 1, turn.

SHELL-STITCH EDGING: Sc in first st, * sk next st, work 5 dc in next st, sk next st, work sc in next st; rep from * around entire afghan; join with sl st to first sc; fasten off.

EMBROIDERY: On green panels, work pink heart cross-stitches over each single crochet following Chart 1, *opposite*. Begin stitches on Row 7 of panels; rep rows 7–20 to complete embroidery. Work the heart cross-stitches on the remaining three green panels. Stitch the border straight stitches over each sc at the sides of the panels following the stitching sequence in Chart 4, *opposite*.

On pink panels, work green tree cross-stitches following Chart 2, working the motifs in the same sequence as the hearts.

Abbreviations and Stitch Diagrams

Abbreviations

beg	begin(ning)
bet	between
bl(s)	block(s)
ch(s)	chain(s)
cl	cluster
cont	continue
dc	double crochet
dec	decrease
dtr	double treble crochet
grp	group
hdc	half double crochet
inc	increase
lp(s)	loop(s)
pat	pattern
pc	popcorn
rem	remaining
rep	repeat
rnd	round
sc	single crochet(s)
sk	skip
sl st	slip stitch
sp(s)	space(s)
st(s)	stitch(es)
tog	together
trc	treble crochet
ttr	triple treble crochet
yo	yarn over
*	repeat from * as indicated
**	repeat from ** as indicated or end last repeat at ** as indicated

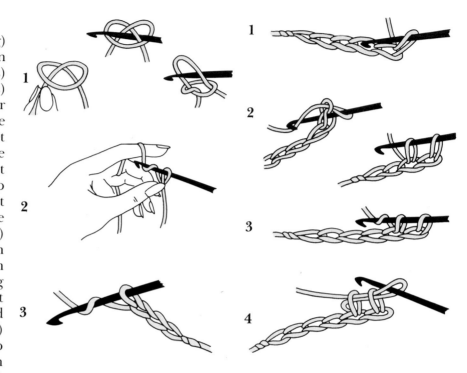

Chain Stitch

1 Start by making a slipknot on the hook about 6 inches from the yarn or thread end. Pull one end of the strand to tighten the knot.
2 Wrap yarn around the little finger of your left hand, and bring it up behind the next finger, under the middle finger, and back over the index finger. Hold the slipknot between your left thumb and middle finger. Hold the crochet hook between the right index finger and thumb, as you would hold a pencil.
3 Make a chain by wrapping the yarn over the hook and drawing it through the loop on the hook. Repeat Step 3 to make any number of chains.

Single Crochet

Chain 20.
1 Insert the crochet hook into the second chain from the hook, under the two upper strands of the stitch.
2 Wrap yarn over the hook and draw yarn through the chain—two loops are on the hook.
3 Wrap yarn over the hook.
4 Draw the yarn through the two loops on the hook—one single crochet made. Repeat steps 1–4 across the row of chains, working a single crochet in the *next* chain and in *each* chain across the row.

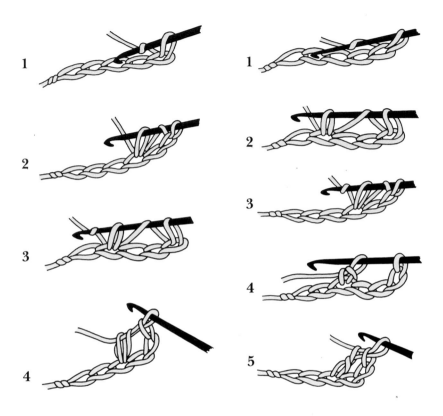

Slip Stitch

Chain 20.

1 Insert the hook under the two top strands of the second chain from the hook. Wrap yarn over the hook and, with a single motion, pull the yarn through the chain and the loop on the hook—slip stitch made. Insert the hook under the two top strands of the *next* chain; wrap yarn over the hook; draw the yarn through the chain and the loop on the hook.
2 Repeat Step 1, working a slip stitch in *each* chain across.

Half Double Crochet

Chain 20.

1 Wrap yarn over the hook, then insert hook into the third chain from the hook under the two upper strands of the stitch.
2 Wrap yarn over the hook and draw a loop through the chain—three loops are on the hook.
3 Wrap yarn over the hook.
4 Draw the yarn through the three loops on the hook—half double crochet made. Repeat steps 1–4 across the row, working a half double crochet in the *next* chain and in *each* chain across.

Double Crochet

Chain 20.

1 Wrap yarn over the hook, then insert the hook into the fourth chain from the hook, under the two upper strands of the chain.
2 Wrap yarn over the hook and draw a loop through the chain—three loops are on the hook.
3 Wrap yarn over the hook.
4 Draw yarn through the first two loops on the hook—two loops remain on the hook.
5 Wrap yarn over the hook; draw the yarn through the last two loops on the hook—double crochet made. Repeat steps 1–5 across the row, working a double crochet in the *next* chain and *each* chain across.

Treble Crochet

Chain 20.

1 Wrap yarn over hook *two* times; insert hook into the fifth chain from the hook, under two top strands of the chain.
2 Wrap yarn over hook and draw a loop through the chain—four loops are on the hook.
3 Wrap yarn over hook and draw the yarn through the first two loops on the hook—three loops are on the hook.
4 Wrap yarn over hook and draw the yarn through the next two loops on the hook—two loops remain on the hook.
5 Wrap yarn over hook and draw the yarn through two loops on the hook—treble crochet made. Repeat steps 1–5, working a treble crochet in *each* chain across.

Basic Afghan-Stitch Technique

Chain 20.

1 *Row 1* (first half): Insert the hook in the top loop of the second chain from the hook; wrap the yarn over the hook and draw the yarn just through the chain—two loops on hook. * Insert the hook in the top loop of the *next* chain, wrap the yarn over the hook, and draw the yarn through the chain, leaving this loop on the hook. Repeat this step from the * in *each* chain across—20 loops on the hook.

2 *Row 1* (second half): Working from left to right, wrap the yarn over the hook and draw the yarn through the *first* loop on the hook.

3 * Wrap the yarn over the hook and draw the yarn through the next two loops on the hook. Repeat this step from the * until one loop remains on the hook.

4 The drawing, *right,* shows the upright bars or loops that form the foundation for working the pattern in subsequent rows.

5 *Row 2* (first half): Skip the first upright bar; * insert the hook behind the *front* loop of the next upright bar, wrap the yarn over the hook, and draw the yarn through the bar, leaving the loop on the hook. Repeat this step from the * in each upright bar across.

Row 2 (second half): Repeat the second half of Row 1 (refer to steps 2 and 3, *above*). Repeat Row 2 for the desired length.

6 *Last row* (bind-off row): Working from the right edge, skip the first upright bar; * insert the hook in front of the next bar, wrap yarn over the hook, and draw the yarn through the bar *and* through the loop on the hook—slip stitch made and one loop on hook. Repeat this step from the * in each upright bar across. Fasten off the yarn at the end of this step.

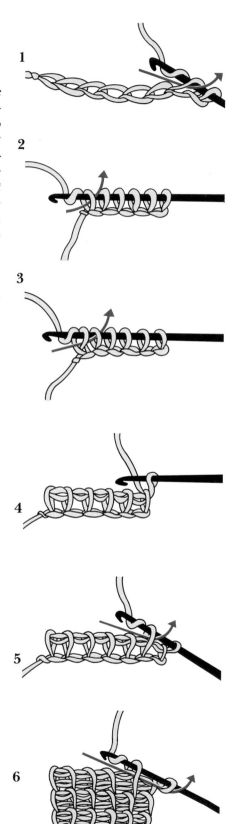

To make your crocheting as enjoyable as possible, use these helpful hints when working the projects in this book.

Kinds of crochet hooks

Crochet hooks are available in many different materials—plastic, aluminum, wood, and steel. They are sized to work with different thicknesses of yarn and thread. Keep several sizes of hooks available to easily adjust your gauge to conform to pattern instructions.

The smallest hooks, used primarily with fine threads, are steel. The sizes are numbered from 00, 0, and 1 through 14. The larger the number (Size 14, for example), the smaller the hook; the lower the number, the larger the hook.

Aluminum and plastic hooks are larger than steel hooks and are used for working with assorted yarn weights. These are sized by letters from C (the smallest) through K (the largest).

Afghan hooks resemble knitting needles, except they have a hook instead of a point on one end, and are used to work the afghan stitch. They are made of aluminum and are sized the same as regular aluminum and plastic hooks. They are available in 9-, 14-, and 22-inch lengths. For afghan-stitch projects, select a hook that is long enough to hold all the stitches in the first half of the row.

Working the gauge

Most patterns include a *gauge* notation. The gauge, or the number of stitches or rows per inch, is normally determined by the *hook,* not by the weight of the yarn.

Always work a gauge swatch to see if your tension equals the gauge cited in your instructions. If you have too many stitches per inch, you are working too tightly. You need to stitch with less tension or change to a *larger* hook.

If you have too few stitches per inch, you are working too loosely. You need to stitch with a tighter tension or change to a *smaller* hook.

Reading instructions

Following instructions may seem difficult when you begin. Pay attention to commas and semicolons; they set off the individual steps involved in the crocheting.

Crochet instructions are written in an abbreviated form. You'll want to familiarize yourself with these abbreviations (see page 186) before beginning a project.

Symbols are used to shorten directions and to indicate that a section of a pattern is repeated. Asterisks (*) indicate pattern repeats within a row or round. Asterisks are used in groups of two; when there is a beginning one, there also will be an ending one. Work the stitches *between* the asterisks, then *repeat* the pattern between the asterisks as many times as indicated. For example, if the pattern indicates you are to repeat between the asterisks two times more, you will actually work the stitches between the asterisks a total of three times.

Parentheses ( ) and brackets [ ] also indicate repetition. Repeat the instructions within the parentheses or brackets the total number of times indicated before beginning the next step in the instructions. Work the stitches within parentheses or brackets *only as many times as specified.*

Working in rows

As you finish each row of stitching, you must turn the work over to begin the next row. Note that you are then working on the *wrong* side of the stitches of the previous row. Also, notice the tiny holes at the tops of the stitches. Insert the hook into these holes so that you are working to the *left* of each stitch of the previous row. Keep this in mind as you work, especially when you work patterns that skip stitches.

At the end of each row, you will work a "turning chain" to begin the next row. Turning chains raise the level of your work along the edge to equal the height of the stitches of the next row. Work the required number of chains, then, without removing the hook, turn the work over to begin the next row.

With the exception of the single crochet, all turning chains count as the first stitch of the row. Following are guidelines for establishing the number of chains when working a straight-edged piece.

To begin a row of single crochets, chain 1, turn, and work the first single crochet in the first stitch of the row. For a row of half double crochets, chain 2, turn, and work the first half double in the second stitch of the row. To begin a row of double crochets, chain 3, turn, and work the first double in the second stitch of the row. For a row of treble crochets, chain 4, turn, and work the first treble in the second stitch of the row.

The last stitch of each row is worked in the top of the turning chain, except for the single crochet. Always work under two loops of the turning chain to avoid a hole in your work.

Working in rounds

Unlike patterns crocheted back and forth in rows, motifs such as circles, hexagons, some squares, and other medallion shapes are stitched in rounds that begin in the center. When you have stitched completely around the shape, you have completed one round. In most instances, you work with the right side facing you; the stitches are on the *right* side of the work. As you crochet each stitch, insert the hook into the hole to the *right* of the stitch in the round below (the opposite of when working in rows).

Increases are a part of the pattern, and instructions cite specifically the stitches required to keep the work lying flat. As the motif increases in size, so will the number of stitches in each round.

Most rounds are joined with a slip stitch in the top of the beginning chain. Work this slip stitch under two loops of the chain to avoid a hole in your work.

Keeping tension even

To keep stitches even and uniform in size, crochet over the *shank* of the hook. You will have better control over your stitching if you keep moving the thumb and middle finger of your left hand close to the area where you are stitching.

To avoid stitching too tightly when working with yarn, draw up the loop in the stitch you are making and allow this loop to be almost twice as large as the loop already on the hook. As a result, when you complete each stitch, the work will be soft and flexible rather than stiff.

When working with thread, it is better to keep the tension tighter than when working with yarn. Continue to work off the shank of the hook, but keep the stitches coming off the hook the same size as the hook.

Errors in your work

Correcting errors in crocheted work is easy. Simply remove the hook from the work and pull out the stitches until the error is removed. Establish where you are in your pattern and continue crocheting from that point.

Acknowledgments

We express our gratitude and appreciation to the many people who helped with this book.

Our heartfelt thanks to the following designers who contributed material that was especially developed for this book, to the photographers, whose creative talents added much to this book, to the companies who generously shared their products with us, and to all those who in some other way contributed to the production of this book.

Designers

Coats & Clark—67; 109, hooded sweater; 155; 168, doily
Gail Kinkead—50; 124–125, curtains; 152; 170–171
Magic List—6–7; 64; 127
Michele Maks—104–105; 109, sailor suit; 110–111; 148–149; 172–173
Jude Martin—107; 108; 110, bunny
Joyce Nordstrom—12–13, afghan; 153, lacy afghan
Joyce Nordstrom and Nancy Reames—146–147
Helene Rush—154
Sara Jane Treinen—11; 150–151; 153, pastel afghan; 168–169, star ornaments
Lee Valenti for DMC—106

For their technical skills, we thank:
Mary Kay Helt
Nancy Reames
Mary Vermie

Photographers

Scott Little—106; 171
Hopkins Associates—cover and all other photos

Acknowledgments

Bates Anchor, Inc.
212 Middlesex Ave.
Chester, CT 06412

Brunswick Yarns
P.O. Box 276
Pickens, SC 29671

Coats & Clark, Inc.
Dept. CS
P.O. Box 1010
Toccoa, GA 30577

DMC Corporation
197 Trumbull St.
Elizabeth, NJ 07206

Farm House Museum
Iowa State University
Ames, IA 50011

Paula Gins
Antique Linens
Littleton, CO 80123

Jabberwocky
203 E. Main
Fredericksburg, TX 78624

La Lune Furniture
930 E. Burleigh
Milwaukee, WI 53212

Althea Lord

Madison County Historical Society
Winterset, IA 50273

Magic List, Inc.
P.O. Box 375
Cold Spring, NY 10516

Paper White, Ltd.
P.O. Box 956
Fairfax, CA 94930

Raintree Designs
979 Third Ave.
New York, NY 10022

Margaret Sindelar

Betty Stanley

Clara Storm

Holly Swartzbaugh

Terrace Hill
2300 Grand Ave.
Des Moines, IA 50312

Phillip and Neoma Thomas

William Unger & Co., Inc.
P.O. Box 1621
2478 E. Main St.
Bridgeport, CT 06601

Waverly Fabrics
7 Hoosac St.
Adams, MA 01220

Patricia Wilens

Elaine Wilmarth

Linda Youngquist

Index

A–B

Abbreviations, 186
Afghans, **146–155,** 156–167
  with arrowhead border,
    155, 167
  granny-square
    with panels, **148,**
      159–160
    pastel, **153,** 164–165
    popcorn, **150,** 160–161
    with ruffles, **11, 24,** 26
  lacy-square, **151,** 161–162
  lacy white, **153,** 165–166
  Lily Pond, **12–13,** 28–29
  ripple, **149,** 158–159
  rosy-square, **130–131,**
    144–145
  Ruby Glow, **152,** 162–164
  shell-stitch, **154,** 166–167
  Victorian, **172,** 185
  violet bouquet, **146–147,**
    156–158
Afghan stitch, 188
Angel, **170,** 176–179
Angel ornament, **173,**
  181–183
Antimacassars
  pineapple, **126,** 134–137
  rose, **10,** 24
Arrowhead border, afghan
  with, **155,** 167
Baby items. **See** Children's
  items
Bear, teddy, **107,** 117
Bedspreads
  diamond popcorn, **49,**
    54–55
  with edgings, **30–31, 38,** 40
  five-panel filet, **52,** 60–61
  popcorn lattice, **46–47,** 54
  popcorn star, **48,** 55–57
  ribbons and lace, **130–131,**
    145
  rose filet, **80–81,** 89–90
  spiderweb popcorn, **51,**
    57–58
  Water Lily, **13,** 26–28
Bib, christening set with,
  106, 114–116

Bird and tree edging, **84–85,**
  97–98
Blanket sets, baby, **104–105,**
  110–111, 112–113,
  122–123
Bonnets, **104–105, 106,**
  110–111, 112–113,
  114–116, 122–123
Bootees, **106,** 114–116
Bunny, **110,** 121–122
Butterfly cloth edgings, **84,**
  98–99
  with poppies, **82,** 92

C–D

Caps. **See** Bonnets
Chain stitch, 186
Children's items
  blanket, cap, and sweater
    sets, **104–105, 110–111,**
    112–113, 122–123
  bunny, **110,** 121–122
  christening set, **106,**
    114–116
  dolls, **108,** 117–118
  hooded sweater, **109,**
    118–120
  sailor suit, **109,** 120–121
  teddy bear, **107,** 117
Christening set, **106,** 114–116
Christmas items
  afghan, **172,** 185
  angel, **170,** 176–179
  doily, **168,** 174–175
  ornaments
    snowflake, **171,** 179–180
    star, **168–169,** 175–176
    Victorian, **173,** 181–183
  stocking, **172,** 183–185
Clothing. **See** Children's
  items
Cluster doily pillow top,
  127, 137–139
Coasters, pineapple, **65,**
  72–73
Cornucopia ornament, **173,**
  181–183

Curtains, **124–125,** 132–134
Doilies
  dresser, **128,** 141–142
  heart runner, **64,** 74
  pineapple, **66,** 76–78
  scalloped, **129,** 142–144
  star, **168,** 174–175
  See also Pillows, doilies on
Dolls, **108,** 117–118
Double crochet, 187
Dust ruffles, edgings used
  for, **36,** 45, **52, 53,** 61,
  84–85, 97–98

E–O

Edgings, **30–37,** 38–45
  bedspread with, **30–31,**
    38, 40
  bird and tree, **84–85,**
    97–98
  curtain, **32,** 40–41
  dust ruffle, **36, 52, 53,**
    45, 61
  grape insert, **86,** 103
  hand-towel, **33,** 40
  picture-frame, **35,** 42
  pillow, **34,** 43
  pillowcase and sheet, **50,**
    58–60
    flower, **83,** 96–97
    rose filet, **36,** 44–45
    spiderweb, **37,** 43–44
  sachet pillow, **35,** 41–42
  tablecloth
    butterfly, **84,** 98–99
    butterfly and poppy,
      82, 92–95
    thistle, **87,** 100–102
Embroidery stitches, 39
  afghan with, **154,** 166–167
  bedspread with, **30–31,**
    38, 40
Filet crochet, **80–87,** 88–103
  antimacassar, rose, **10,** 24
  bedspreads
    five-panel, **52,** 60–61
    rose, **80–81,** 89–90
           continued

Filet crochet (continued)
  pillow, rose doily, **81,**
    90–91
  tablecloth, grape, **9,** 19–21
  table runners
    border of, **62–63,** 70–72
    heart, **64,** 74
    rose garden, **67,** 74–76
Flower pillowcase edging,
  83, 96–97
Frame edging, **35,** 42
Gauge, working, 188–189
Gown, christening, **106,**
  114–116
Grape filet tablecloth, **9,**
  19–21
Grape insert edging, **86,** 103
Guest-towel edging, **33,** 40
Half double crochet, 187
Hand-towel edging, **33,** 40
Hats. **See** Bonnets
Heart table runner, **64,** 74
Hooks, kinds of, 188
Infant items. **See** Children's
  items
Instructions, reading, 189
Lace, crocheted. **See** Filet
  crochet
Lacy curtains, **124–125,**
  132–134
Lacy-square afghan, **151,**
  161–162
Lacy white afghan, **153,**
  165–166
Lattice bedspread,
  popcorn, **46–47,** 54
Lily Pond afghan, **12–13,**
  28–29

P–R

Pillowcase edgings. **See**
  Edgings
Pillow edgings. **See** Edgings
Pillows, doilies on
  cluster, **127,** 137–139
  popcorn pineapple, **6,**
    17–19
  rose, **81,** 90–91
  star dahlia, **127,** 139–140
  star pineapple, **6,** 14–16
Pillow sham panel, grape,
  86, 103
Pineapple motif
  antimacassar set, **126,**
    134–137
  doilies, **66,** 76–78

Pineapple motif (continued)
  dresser, **128,** 141–142
  luncheon set, **65,** 72–73
  pillow, popcorn, **6,** 17–19
  pillow, star, **6,** 14–16
  snowflake, **171,** 179–180
  tablecloth, **69,** 78–79
Place mats
  breakfast, **124–125,** 132
  pineapple, **65,** 72–73
Poppy cloth edging, **82,**
  92–95
Rabbit, **110,** 121–122
Ribbons and lace bedspread,
  130–131, 145
Ripple afghan, **149,** 158–159
Rose antimacassar, **10,** 24
Rose doily pillow, **81,** 90–91
Rose filet bedspread, **80–81,**
  89–90
Rose garden table runner,
  67, 74–76
Rosy-square afghan,
  130–131, 144–145
Ruby Glow afghan, **152,**
  162–164
Runners, table
  arrow-pattern, **8,** 22–24
  heart, **64,** 74
  rose garden, **67,** 74–76
  star snowflake, **62–63,**
    70–72

S–Z

Sachet pillow edging, **35,**
  41–42
Sailor suit, **109,** 120–121
Sheet edgings, **50,** 58–60
  rose filet, **36,** 44–45
Shell-stitch afghan, **154,**
  166–167
Single crochet, 186
Slip stitch, 187
Snowflakes, medallion, **171,**
  179–180
Spiderweb pattern
  bedspread, popcorn, **51,**
    57–58
  in heart runner, **64,** 74
  insertion for dust ruffle,
    52, 53, 61
  pillowcase edging, **37,**
    43–44
Star bedspread, popcorn
  48, 55–57

Star dahlia pillow top, **127,**
  139–140
Star doily, **168,** 174–175
Star ornaments, **168–169,**
  175–176
Star pineapple pillow, **6,**
  14–16
Star snowflake table runner,
  62–63, 70–72
Stitch diagrams, 186–188
  embroidery, 39
Stocking, **172,** 183–185
Stocking ornament, **173,**
  181–182
Stuffed animals
  bunny, **110,** 121–122
  teddy bear, **107,** 117
Sweaters, baby, **105, 109,**
  110, 112, 118–120,
  122–123,
Tablecloth edgings. **See**
  Edgings, tablecloth
Tablecloths
  grape filet, **9,** 19–21
  pineapple-motif, **69,** 78–79
  wheel-motif, **68,** 78
Table runners. **See** Runners,
  table
Teddy bear, **107,** 117
Tension, keeping even, 189
Thistle cloth edgings, **87,**
  100–102
Throws. **See** Afghans
Towel edging, **33,** 40
Toys
  bunny, **110,** 121–122
  dolls, **108,** 117–118
  teddy bear, **107,** 117
Treble crochet, 187
Tree trims. **See** Ornaments
Violet bouquet afghan,
  146–147, 156–158
Water Lily spread, **13,** 26–28
Wheel-motif tablecloth, **68,**
  78